Pedagogies in English for Academic Purposes

New Perspectives for English for Academic Purposes

Series editors: Alex Ding, Ian Bruce and Melinda Whong

This series sets the agenda for studies in English for Academic Purposes (EAP) by opening up research and scholarship to new domains, ideas and perspectives as well as giving a platform to emerging and established practitioners and researchers in the field.

The volumes in this series are innovative in that they broaden the scope of theoretical and practical interests in EAP by focusing on neglected or new areas of interest, to provide the EAP community with a deeper understanding of some of the key issues in teaching EAP across the world and in diverse contexts.

Also available in this series
What is Good Academic Writing?: Insights into Discipline-Specific Student Writing, edited by Melinda Whong and Jeanne Godfrey

Pedagogies in English for Academic Purposes

Teaching and Learning in International Contexts

Edited by
Carole MacDiarmid and Jennifer J. MacDonald

BLOOMSBURY ACADEMIC
LONDON • NEW YORK • OXFORD • NEW DELHI • SYDNEY

BLOOMSBURY ACADEMIC
Bloomsbury Publishing Plc
50 Bedford Square, London, WC1B 3DP, UK
1385 Broadway, New York, NY 10018, USA
29 Earlsfort Terrace, Dublin 2, Ireland

BLOOMSBURY, BLOOMSBURY ACADEMIC and the Diana logo are trademarks
of Bloomsbury Publishing Plc

First published in Great Britain 2021
This paperback edition published in 2023

Copyright © Carole MacDiarmid, J. J. MacDonald and Contributors, 2021

Carole MacDiarmid, J. J. MacDonald and Contributors have asserted their right under the Copyright,
Designs and Patents Act, 1988, to be identified as Author of this work.

Series design by Charlotte James
Cover image © Tuomas Lehtinen, Getty Images

All rights reserved. No part of this publication may be reproduced or transmitted
in any form or by any means, electronic or mechanical, including photocopying,
recording, or any information storage or retrieval system, without prior
permission in writing from the publishers.

Bloomsbury Publishing Plc does not have any control over, or responsibility for, any
third-party websites referred to or in this book. All internet addresses given
in this book were correct at the time of going to press. The author and publisher
regret any inconvenience caused if addresses have changed or sites have
ceased to exist, but can accept no responsibility for any such changes.

A catalogue record for this book is available from the British Library.

Library of Congress Cataloging-in-Publication Data

Names: MacDiarmid, Carole, editor. | MacDonald, Jennifer J. editor.
Title: Pedagogies in English for Academic Purposes: teaching and learning
in international contexts / edited by Carole MacDiarmid and Jennifer J. MacDonald.
Description: London; New York: Bloomsbury Academic, [2021]. |
Series: New Perspectives for English for Academic Purposes |
Includes bibliographical references and index. |
Identifiers: LCCN 2021004536 (print) | LCCN 2021004537 (ebook) |
ISBN 9781350164802 (Hardback) | ISBN 9781350164819 (eBook) |
ISBN 9781350164826 (ePub)
Subjects: LCSH: English language--Study and teaching (Higher) | English
language–Study and teaching (Higher)–Foreign speakers. |
Academic writing–Study and teaching (Higher).
Classification: LCC PE1128.A2 P375 2021 (print) |
LCC PE1128.A2 (ebook) | DDC 428.0071/1–dc23
LC record available at https://lccn.loc.gov/2021004536
LC ebook record available at https://lccn.loc.gov/2021004537

ISBN: HB: 978-1-3501-6480-2
PB : 978-1-3502-5439-8
ePDF: 978-1-3501-6481-9
eBook: 978-1-3501-6482-6

Series: New Perspectives for English for Academic Purposes

Typeset by Deanta Global Publishing Services, Chennai, India

To find out more about our authors and books visit
www.bloomsbury.com and sign up for our newsletters.

Contents

List of Illustrations	vii
Notes on Contributors	viii
Series Editors' Foreword	xv
Foreword *Ursula Wingate*	xvii

Introduction		1
1	Embracing Critical Multicultural Education through Research-Informed Practice in EAP Teaching *John McGaughey and Heejin Song*	11
2	Addressing Literacy Brokering in the EAP Classroom *Nina Conrad*	27
3	Moving from Form to Function: Leveraging SFL Metalanguage to Illuminate Features and Functions of Texts in First-Year University EAP *Jennifer Walsh Marr*	43
4	EAP Pedagogies for Doctoral Students in Professional Fields *Kristin Solli and Tom Muir*	59
5	Using Developmental Teaching to Promote Critical EAP in an Academic Writing Course in English *Marília Mendes Ferreira*	75
6	Teaching English for Academic Purposes in Teacher Education: Examples from South Africa *Nhlanhla Mpofu and Mncedisi C. Maphalala*	91
7	Pedagogical Approaches in EGAP Coupled with CBI in an EMI Context *Tijen Aksit and Necmi Aksit*	107
8	Academic Teachers' Perceptions of Content and Language Integrated Learning (CLIL) Programme with EAP Teachers *Xiucai Lu and Bin Zou*	123
9	ESAP-in-EGAP: Implementing Sydney School Genre Pedagogy in Gulf Higher Education *Tony Myers, Jaime Buchanan, Jesse Balanyk and Timothy Nicoll*	137
10	EAP Teachers Working in, with and through the Creative Arts: An Exploration *Clare Carr, Clare Maxwell, Anna Rolinska and Jennifer Sizer*	153

11 Integrating a Signature Pedagogy into a Pre-sessional:
    Impact on Pedagogy in ESAP *Carole MacDiarmid,*
    Anneli Williams, Kat Irwin and Brían Doonan   169

Afterword   185
References   188
Index   215

Illustrations

Figures

4.1	Anna's community plot	64
4.2	Beatrice's community plot	64
7.1	Philosophical foundations of the PAS course	109
10.1	Our collaborative autoethnographic research process	156

Tables

3.1	Theme and Rheme	49
5.1	Texts and Questions Discussed	85
6.1	Summary of the Cases	100
7.1	Phases of PAS in a Nutshell	115
10.1	Practitioner Contexts	155

Contributors

Necmi Aksit is Assistant Professor at Bilkent University, Turkey. He is Director of the MA in Teaching English as a Foreign Language and MA in Teacher Education programmes. His research areas include language teacher education, international curricula, critical literacy and English for Academic Purposes (EAP). He is particularly interested in applying methods of qualitative synthesis to his research areas. He began his career as a teacher of English, and he has been teaching pre-service and in-service teacher education courses since 2002 at the Graduate School of Education in Bilkent University, Turkey.

Tijen Aksit is Assistant Professor at the Graduate School of Education and the Director of Faculty Academic English Program at Bilkent University, Turkey. She has contributed to the development of a quality assurance external review programme for the English language preparatory schools of higher education institutions in Turkey. She is the author of *Characteristics of Effective Schools* and co-editor of *Bridging Teaching, Learning and Assessment in the English Language Classroom* and *The Future of Teaching English for Academic Purposes*. She researches and publishes in the area of English-medium instruction (EMI), English-language teaching and quality assurance in English language programmes of higher education.

Jesse Balanyk was formerly the Curriculum Supervisor of the Academic Bridge Program at Zayed University in the United Arab Emirates and is now an eLearning Specialist with Algoma University in Sault Ste. Marie, Ontario, Canada. He is passionate about leveraging the affordances of educational technology to increase access to learning and employing gamification to increase learner engagement and motivation. Jesse also recently co-authored an EAP coursebook specifically designed for adult learners in Saudi Arabia.

Jaime Buchanan teaches EAP at Zayed University, United Arab Emirates. She has lived and worked in Abu Dhabi since 2008 and joined Zayed University in 2013. She is passionate about teaching and developing writing skills, both academic and practical. She has worked on several curricular projects, including the one outlined in this volume. Her main research interests include Sydney School genre pedagogy, feedback literacy and supporting EMI content delivery across the curriculum.

Clare C. Carr is Assistant Professor (Teaching) within Durham Centre for Academic Development at Durham University, UK. She has taught in a variety of contexts, working on pre-sessional and in-sessional programmes for over eleven years. Her current role involves nurturing collaborations with academic departments to help develop embedded EAP teaching for 'home' and 'international' students. A Cambridge University, UK, graduate in Music and Education Studies, her scholarship interests lie in teaching EAP to music undergraduates and postgraduates, working closely with music specialists within the Music Department at Durham University, UK.

Nina Conrad received her PhD in Second Language Acquisition and Teaching from the University of Arizona, USA. Her research focuses on literacy brokering among students in higher education, adopting an academic literacies approach to examine the role of social network composition and sociopolitical context in students' decisions to involve others in their academic writing practices. She has taught in the University of Arizona English Department and Writing Program and has previously taught K–12 social studies and worked as a professional editor.

Brían Doonan is Lecturer in EAP in English for Academic Study at the University of Glasgow, UK. He has been involved in EAP teaching, pre-sessional course directing and teacher education for thirteen years. Prior to this, he worked abroad in EFL and ran a language school in Yokohama, Japan, for a decade. At the University of Glasgow, UK, he has lectured on MSc and MEd TESOL programmes and currently convenes an undergraduate TESOL honours option. He is a qualified CELTA trainer and his scholarship interests include EAP pedagogies and systemic functional linguistics (SFL) analysis of written academic discourse, particularly in the field of Biomedical Sciences.

Marília Mendes Ferreira is Associate Professor at Universidade de São Paulo, Brazil. She has been working with academic literacy in English for over twelve years. She has created and run the Laboratory of Academic Literacy since 2012. She has extensive experience designing courses and materials, teaching EAP for different fields and investigating the challenges of Brazilian students learning academic discourse in English. Currently, her main interests are the challenges English teachers face when teaching EAP and their relationship with academic discourse.

Kat Irwin is EAP Lecturer at the University of Glasgow, UK. Kat has more than fifteen years of experience teaching English in both the UK and abroad. In her current role, she teaches on the year-round pre-sessional EAP course and courses offering in-sessional support to international postgraduate students. She is also involved in developing EAP courses and course materials and convenes a subject-specific pre-sessional course in Biomedical Sciences. Her research and scholarship interests include teaching and learning vocabulary, teaching English for Specific Academic Purposes (ESAP) and corpus linguistics.

Xiucai Lu is currently serving in the language school in Xi'an Jiaotong–Liverpool University, China. She received her MA in International Comparative Education from Stockholm University, Sweden, and holds the fellowship of UK Higher Education Academy and has been teaching EAP in EMI tertiary education for more than seven years. She is experienced in teaching academic skills in the university writing centre. She is also a practitioner of content and language integrated learning (CLIL) programme collaborating with various disciplinary departments. Her research interests lie in EAP pedagogy, foreign language acquisition with a focus on the role of mother tongue in learning process, assessment development and CLIL.

Carole MacDiarmid is Senior Lecturer and EAP Manager (Teacher Development) in English for Academic Study at the University of Glasgow, UK. Carole has been involved in EAP teaching, course design and teacher education for more than twenty five years. She currently co-leads the MSc and MEd TESOL programmes and convenes a Teaching English for Academic Purposes (TEAP) online postgraduate course. She has been an assessor for the BALEAP Accreditation Scheme and a mentor and assessor for the BALEAP TEAP Fellowship Scheme. Her research and scholarship interests include pedagogies in EAP, EAP teacher development and spoken academic discourse.

Jennifer J. MacDonald is Director of English Language Studies and University Access at Dalhousie University, Canada, where she is the academic lead on a variety of programs in EAP, and teacher and faculty professional development. She regularly researches, publishes and presents on topics at the intersection between critical applied linguistics, internationalization of higher education and EAP. Her most recent research tackles the challenges of language policies, politics and pedagogy in the linguistically diverse context of internationalized Canadian higher education.

Mncedisi Christian Maphalala is the Director of the Centre for Excellence in Learning and Teaching (CELT) at the Durban University of Technology, South Africa and a former Dean in the Faculty of Education at the University of Zululand, South Africa. He has edited two books, co-authored one book and published a number of book chapters and research articles in peerreviewed journals. He has conducted a number of large-scale commissioned research projects by external organizations such as the South African Institute of Distance Education (SAIDE), Human Sciences Research Council (HSRC), National Research Foundation (NRE) and Council on Higher Education. His research interests are teacher education, curriculum studies and assessment in education.

Jennifer Walsh Marr is an academic English lecturer in the Arts Faculty at the University of British Columbia–Vantage College, Canada. She holds a BA in Applied Linguistics and Japanese Studies, an MA in Curriculum and Instruction and has started doctoral studies in Language and Literacy Education. Her research work has looked at intersections of power, identity and language in the academy, particularly with regard to Indigenous and settler histories in Canada and incorporating linguistic research into pedagogy. For her classroom practice, she draws on critical pedagogy and discourse analysis to facilitate her students' familiarity with valued features of the disciplines.

Clare Maxwell is Lecturer in EAP within the Language Centre at the University of Leeds, UK. She is currently seconded to the School of Design, where she is responsible for the design and delivery of bespoke in-sessional courses for taught postgraduate students. She has taught and co-led modules on the International Foundation Year programme and content-based pre-sessional programmes. Having previously taught for many years in Italy, she is author of EFL coursebooks widely adopted in Italian state secondary schools. Her scholarship interests are in academic writing pedagogy, genre and disciplinary difference and specificity, with a particular interest in EAP in the Creative Arts.

John McGaughey is Lead Instructor at the International Foundation Program at the University of Toronto, Canada, where he teaches CLIL-based EAP classes. His recent teaching and research centres around the research-informed teaching of EAP reading and writing, antiracist approaches to teaching EAP and critical multicultural education. His research interests include Vygotskian sociocultural theory in understanding second language teaching/learning, teacher and learner identity and the first-year international English-language learner (ELL) student experience, teacher and learner translanguaging and language policy and planning.

Nhlanhla Mpofu is Associate Professor in Language-in-Education at Rhodes University, South Africa. She holds a PhD in Humanities Education (English Education) from the University of Pretoria, South Africa. Her research attempts to bridge theory and practice in ways that English is used as a second language in different disciplines in multilingual spaces. Her research also works to problematize our understanding of English as a language of instruction (ELI) in multilingual contexts, develop new language teaching methodologies that draw from culturally sustaining pedagogy and informed by disciplinary linguistic requirements and reorient second language education research in multilingual education systems.

Tom Muir is Associate Professor of EAP at OsloMet – Oslo Metropolitan University, Norway. He has a PhD in English from Sussex University, UK, and has previously taught at both Sussex University and Manchester Metropolitan University, UK.

Tony Myers is Assistant Professor at Zayed University, United Arab Emirates, teaching EAP in the College of Humanities and Social Sciences. His research interests include Sydney School genre pedagogy, legitimation code theory and feedback literacy. He has previously published books on essay writing, English literature and Slavoj Žižek.

Timothy Nicoll is Assistant Chair at Zayed University, United Arab Emirates. He has taught English in a range of contexts for over twenty years. In this time, in addition to moving to a specialization in EAP, he has gained expertise in educational leadership, curriculum development and assessment. His research interests include English as a medium of instruction, student motivation, genre pedagogy, student learning experience and educational technology. He is a qualified CELTA trainer, holds a DELTA and is a fellow of the HEA. He is currently completing a PhD in Educational Research at Lancaster University, UK.

Anna Rolinska is English Language Lecturer working with international students of Art and Design at the Glasgow School of Art, UK. She is responsible for designing and delivering EAP on the International Foundation Programme, as well as leading the bespoke Pre-sessional English Course for the Creative

Disciplines. Anna's research interests include academic literacies, formation and development of learner identity and agency meaningful use of educational technology, creativity in academia and the interplay between multimodality and academic discourse.

Jennifer Sizer is Lecturer in English for Academic Purposes in the International Study and Language Institute at the University of Reading where she teaches on English for Specific Academic Purposes and Pre-sessional courses. She is currently working on her Professional Doctorate in Education research project investigating the language of architecture at university. Her main research interests include linguistics and language teaching, EAP, ESAP, English for Specific Purposes (ESP) and academic literacies. Jennifer is also convener of the BALEAP Creative Disciplines Special Interest Group.

Kristin Solli works as Associate Professor in the Unit for Academic Language and Practice at the University Library, OsloMet – Oslo Metropolitan University, Norway. Her research interests span academic writing, multilingual writing and research practices, and country and western music. She is co-author of the book *Strategies for Writing a Thesis by Publication in the Social Sciences and Humanities* and she has published several articles and book chapters in the fields of American Studies, English for Academic Purposes and teacher education.

Heejin Song is Assistant Professor in the English as a second language programme at the Department of Languages, Literatures and Linguistics (DLLL), York University, Canada. Her teaching and research interests include EAP, ESL/EFL, action research, multiliteracies pedagogy and multicultural education for social justice. Her recent research focuses on the themes of culture and identity, equity and diversity and culturally relevant and multiliteracies-enhanced teaching in CLIL-based EAP classrooms.

Anneli Williams is Senior Lecturer and EAP Manager overseeing pre- and in-sessional EAP provision at the University of Glasgow, UK. She has been involved in EAP as a lecturer, course developer, course convenor and materials writer for twenty-five years. She has served on the BALEAP Executive Committee as ordinary member and currently holds the position of SIGs Officer, supporting the development of a range of special interest groups within EAP. Anneli has published a range of EAP-related study materials and has scholarship interests in ESAP and EAP pedagogies and assessment.

Bin Zou received his PhD in TESOL from the University of Bristol, UK. He has taught EAP for more than ten years at Xi'an Jiaotong–Liverpool University, China. He is the founding editor and co-editor-in-chief of the *International Journal of Computer-Assisted Language Learning and Teaching* and co-editor of the *International Journal of EAP: Research and Practice*. His research interests include CALL, EAP, CLIL and ELT. He has published more than forty papers and is co-editor for five books, including *Innovation in Language Learning and Teaching: The Case of China* and *Corpus Linguistics in Chinese Context*.

Series Editors' Foreword

It is entirely fitting that the second volume in this new book series is devoted to pedagogy. English for Academic Purposes (EAP) as a field is made up of two, sometimes intersecting, constituencies: EAP practitioners and EAP researchers. It is perhaps unsurprising that the focus of formal inquiry to date is largely one defined by the research constituency within EAP. Yet given how large the practitioner constituency is, the degree to which the agenda for scholarship in EAP is set by researchers is, arguably, overly skewed. This book series exemplifies what happens when it's the practitioners who ask the questions. In the first book of the series, *What Is Good Academic Writing?: Insights into Discipline-Specific Student Writing*, a set of practitioners in one institution collectively asked a question and explored it in their institutional context, each providing answers from different disciplines in order to articulate useful guidance for EAP.

This second book goes to the heart of the most important concern for EAP practitioners: pedagogy. And it does so in a way that captures the full context of EAP, with contributions evidencing the truly global reach of EAP. More specifically, the contributions in this volume come from Brazil, Canada, China, Norway, Turkey, South Africa, the United Kingdom, the United Arab Emirates and the United States. Pedagogy in this volume is explored within English-medium Instruction (EMI) institutions in both Anglophone and non-Anglophone contexts. The EAP programming considered in these chapters spans courses from first-year undergraduates to PhD students and includes both university and pre-service contexts. That some courses are credit-bearing while others are delivered either before or alongside degree awarding programmes adds to the richness of context which EAP pedagogy must take into account.

It seems a natural starting point to assert that it is EAP practitioners who are best placed to interrogate questions of pedagogy in EAP. Writing this foreword at a time when there is no clear end in sight from a pandemic that has had us all moving our teaching online in a very short span of time, I have been humbled by the impressive way in which EAP practitioners have led the way in our institutions, swiftly adapting their pedagogy as the educational landscape shifts, and doing so in a way that ensures quality of education with the needs of students of utmost priority. Yet perhaps we should not be surprised that highly qualified professionals who have been trained as teachers are well placed to be pedagogical leaders, especially in universities with a strong research orientation. Thus, this second volume devoted to pedagogy perfectly illustrates the logic behind the choice of preposition in the book series title, *New Perspectives for English for Academic Purposes*.

Melinda Whong, on behalf of the series editors
January 2021

Foreword

With the development of English as the international academic lingua franca, the field of English for Academic Purposes has over the last four decades witnessed enormous expansion in research and publications, as well as in student numbers, teaching contexts and pedagogical approaches. The growth of English-medium instruction universities and study programmes in many countries around the world has added diverse student populations to the original EAP target group, which were international non-native speaker of English students enrolled in Anglophone universities. This has brought new challenges to EAP pedagogy. In addition to improving students' English language proficiency, one of the traditional EAP practitioner's tasks was to acculturate students into the academic norms and conventions of the country and institution they had chosen. In EMI contexts, which are independent of the academic cultures of Anglophone countries, a stronger focus on the development of students' communicative competence within their disciplines is required. The need for EAP practitioners to engage with discipline-specific practices and discourses is not only imposed by EMI contexts, however, but also by the growing trend to offer academic literacy support to all students, instead of exclusively to non-native speakers of English. As diversity in contexts and student populations continues to move EAP work into new directions, many practitioners feel inspired by research-based examples of innovative EAP classroom practices from around the world.

This is what the present volume offers. It differs from most other books on EAP through its strong focus on the EAP classroom and its purpose to showcase the work of EAP practitioners. The widening EAP landscape is reflected in eleven case studies that represent a variety of geographical, disciplinary and level-of-study contexts as well as methodological approaches. The majority of geographical contexts are EMI, including Brazil, China, Norway and Turkey, while five case studies come from Anglophone countries, namely Canada, the United States and the United Kingdom. While some of the studies were conducted in general EAP courses, others report collaboration with subject experts in various disciplines in the creative arts and health sciences. The level of study ranges from undergraduate students, doctoral students, pre-service teachers to academics writing for publication. The book provides insights into the use of different teaching methodologies, such as the Sydney School approach and problem-based learning, as well as a range of theoretical frameworks, for instance, action research, systemic functional linguistics and activity theory. Thus, there is a broad offer of EAP practices from which potential readers, including EAP teachers, subject specialists and students in the field of EAP, can learn and gain new ideas and inspiration for their own practice. One of the most important messages from this book is that EAP has moved away from the one-size-fits-all approach of teaching generic academic English to cohorts of non-native speakers of English. By contrast, as the eleven case studies demonstrate, EAP is in the process of adapting to new contexts, identifying learner needs related to these contexts and developing innovative teaching approaches. Certainly, this book will encourage readers to work towards context- and discipline-specific pedagogies.

Ursula Wingate,
King's College London, UK

Introduction

Pedagogies *in* English for Academic Purposes (EAP)

This is a book about pedagogies, specifically in English for academic purposes (EAP). How we go about facilitating learning and the principles that underlie our practices are informed by the contexts we work in. In this book, we explore practices from the perspective of EAP practitioners in case studies and small-scale empirical research and scholarship projects. In this way, we provide an opportunity for practitioners to showcase their work, and in doing so, we aim to address recommendations and calls for a stronger link between research and practice (Ding & Bruce, 2017; see also Borg, 2010; Ellis, 2010), and thus give voice to some of the rich and varied work of EAP teachers around the globe.

EAP provision occurs in and is influenced by diverse geographical, cultural, political and educational contexts. Variation is also related to the level it is aimed at, from foundation through to postgraduate research students and academic faculty; whether it is offered before or during post-secondary study; to what degree it is English for general academic purposes (EGAP) or English for specific academic purposes (ESAP); and the extent to which EAP is integrated into academic programmes and courses. However, with a strong Anglo-centric bias to date, there is still a lack of visible insights into pedagogical scholarship and practices beyond certain horizons. Yet as EAP occurs around the world and in educational traditions with different affordances, constraints and sociopolitical influences, these impact on pedagogical practices. How these factors influence and shape EAP pedagogies are explored in this volume.

EAP practitioners will, we hope, find inspiration and insights into how EAP can be enacted and realized. Those engaged in scholarship and research may find areas worthy of exploration in their own contexts. We also note that although EAP is provided at the secondary level, the majority of provision reported on and researched is still in higher education settings (Riazi et al., 2020), and for practical reasons of space, the chapters concentrate on this setting. Finally, for better or worse, English is currently the predominant language for the dissemination of research. While this volume focuses on pedagogies in EAP, we acknowledge the importance of academic study, communication and dissemination in other languages. The insights provided in this volume may also, then, be useful and inspirational for those working and researching *any* language for academic purposes (see, for example, work on academic literacy in English, Portuguese, French and German (Ferreira & Stella, 2018); see also the *Journal of Languages for Specific Purposes*).

In this introduction, we first review the importance and rise of EAP in varied contexts and then provide a rationale for our focus on both EAP pedagogy and the practitioner-based presentation of practice.

The Development of English for Academic Purposes

EAP as a subject supports the development of academic language, skills and literacies of students and staff operating in academic contexts (Flowerdew, 2016; Hyland, 2016). This development has largely been in response to the increasingly global nature of academic endeavour and the internationalization agenda in higher education. Traditionally associated with students whose first language is not English (for ease here, users of English as an additional language, or EAL), EAP, with its focus on facilitating effective communication and engagement with academic study and practices, is now increasingly also available to all students, regardless of linguistic background. For practical reasons, however, this volume concentrates on provision to EAL speakers.

The internationalization of higher education and the resultant number of international students studying in majority English-speaking countries such as the UK, North America and Australia are well known (Kettle, 2017). This has led to an expansion and to an extent the increased visibility of EAP provision, now being augmented by a further expansion in the number of English-medium instruction (EMI)[1] higher education programmes in majority non-English-speaking contexts around the world (Dearden, 2014; Galloway et al., 2020; Macaro et al., 2018). As the contexts of EAP provision continue to develop geographically, the overall linguistic context within which the wider degree programmes and community operate also shapes the work of EAP practitioners. This evolution continues alongside developments in content and language integrated learning (CLIL), knowledge of genres and discourse in varied contexts

---

[1] Sometimes referred to as English-medium education (see Dafouz & Smit, 2020).

and the plurilingual turn in the wider field of English language teaching (ELT), all of which have potential implications for EAP pedagogy.

Contexts for EAP

What is the nature of these varied contexts? Study of English with an EAP focus may precede study on degree programmes: for example, it may be part of an English preparatory year, which may include more EAP as the year progresses, or may be provided as part of a foundation year completed between secondary and post-secondary contexts, aiming to bridge a gap with both language and content and prepare for the degree level content to follow. EAP is delivered alongside introductory foundation subject-knowledge courses in two ways: (1) in courses taken concurrently with those subject-knowledge courses or (2) EAP is integrated into those foundation courses. This is sometimes referred to as CLIL provision (Airey, 2016) or come under the umbrella of academic literacies (e.g. Wingate, 2015). EAP may alternatively take the form of intensive academic English pre-sessional courses typically offered in the months running up to a degree, particularly common in the UK.

Provision can be EGAP or English for more specific purposes, drawing more on academic disciplines and content (Hyland, 2016). This EGAP–ESAP trajectory and the extent to which discipline-specific content should be included in programmes are much debated in the literature (a range of issues are summarized in Hyland, 2016), although specificity is now being seen in more pre-sessional courses and foundation courses. In parallel to the discipline-specific question are the conditions for collaboration between EAP and subject departments and lecturers: is it consultatory in nature, are the two units entering into collaboration on equal footing or does EAP occupy a marginalized 'butler's stance' (Raimes, 1991) with regard to the subject unit? Finally, stand-alone, credit-bearing academic writing courses which would fall under the EAP umbrella, such as college composition or first-year writing, are commonplace in some university systems. EAP may also be delivered in the form of non-credit, extra-curricular workshops or courses, or drop-in one-on-one tutorials, on the fringes of an academic system where academic credit is currency (Ding & Bruce, 2017).

EAP provision may happen at a variety of levels, the level of student referring not only to the level of linguistic proficiency but also to the level of study. This may range from undergraduate to postgraduate taught or research students and more recently extending also to academics working in EMI contexts. Such diversity occurs not only in majority English-speaking contexts but, as we have noted, in many countries worldwide. This can mean, for example, that while a whole cohort is studying EAP in China or Brazil (or even the UK), the first language may be shared by all or the vast majority of students, and/or it may be that English is the lingua franca in the classroom but not in the wider community, as in EMI contexts. More homogenous groups may ostensibly bring cultural and educational expectations of higher education, but we may find very different groupings of learners, both from groups sharing the first L1 to those with different L1s, irrespective of context. What does this mean for pedagogy? The EAP practitioner frequently already has to work with students from a range of disciplinary, linguistic, educational and cultural backgrounds. These variations establish the need for a lens to be shone on the context in which EAP is realized and how they help shape and establish the pedagogy.

This Volume's Focus on Pedagogy

Pedagogy, or the 'interactions between teachers, students, and the learning environment and the learning tasks' (Murphy, 2008, p. 35), informs what the teacher does to 'transform' the content and enhance learning. It is axiomatic to say that what happens in the classroom then promotes and facilitates learning, but an exploration of pedagogies specific to EAP is particularly timely given not only the relative lack of focus and attention it has received but also, as we note, the rise in importance and recognition of EAP as a relatively new discipline and the increasing variation in contexts. Since the context and learner needs inform decision making and applications concerning what we do in the classroom, what, then, should we be looking at and for? What does pedagogy, and specifically a pedagogy for EAP, involve and include, and what does it need to take into consideration? What are the implications of these issues for EAP teacher education and development?

In order to facilitate learning, teachers need to draw on a range of 'knowledges'. These include not only knowledge of the subject area, i.e. 'the content', but pedagogical knowledge, i.e. of how to teach, and pedagogical content knowledge (PCK), i.e. how to most effectively teach a specific subject (Shulman, 1986). EAP practitioners can draw on a growing body of content knowledge relevant to EAP. Ferguson (1997) sets out a range of specialized knowledge for ESAP teachers, and the Competency Framework for Teachers of English for Academic Purposes (BALEAP, 2008) also provides a guide. There is now a significant amount of research explicating language use in academic settings along with disciplinary variation. This has been greatly assisted by studies of both written and spoken academic communication, using variations of, inter alia, systemic functional linguistics (SFL) (e.g. Gardner & Donohue, 2020; Halliday & Matthiessen, 2013), studies of genres (e.g. Hyland, 2007; Nesi & Gardner, 2012; Swales, 1990), tools from corpus linguistics to explore corpora of academic English registers and genres (e.g. Biber, 2006) and more recently Legitimation Code Theory (LCT) (Maton, 2011). Research is also increasingly demonstrating that distinct patterns of language use realized in academic communication reflect beliefs and discipline-specific approaches to teaching, as do 'signature pedagogies', those approaches to learning and teaching practices that characterize disciplines (Shulman, 2005, p. 52). Monbec (2018) makes a case for a greater focus on knowledge, and Bond (2020) calls for a much closer link between language and disciplinary content, EAP specialists and content lectures through collaboration and a language-embedded curriculum.

EAP practitioners are also not without general and language teaching-specific pedagogical knowledge sources. However, this aspect of teacher knowledge appears typically to draw on pedagogies for 'general' ELT. While not wanting to discount the basis of much of our work to date, there is still a limited amount of research and scholarship on the actual teaching of EAP specifically. In a review of empirical articles in the *Journal of English for Academic Purposes* (from inception to 2019), instruction was the focus of only 21 per cent of articles surveyed. While over 50 per cent included recommendations for developing EAP practice (Riazi et al., 2020, p. 15), exploration of pedagogy in itself does not appear a strong focus. Thus, while we are developing an increasingly sophisticated understanding of what to teach in relation to content knowledge, and can draw on general pedagogical knowledge, with the exception of approaches to writing (e.g. Hyland, 2007) and some exceptions noted further, we have limited information as to how this knowledge is transformed into curricula, syllabi, materials and teaching practices specifically for EAP: in other words, how this PCK is composed. This volume helps to expand on our understanding of what specific practices are found in EAP contexts: what makes up our content knowledge and how this is transformed via PCK.

A Focus on Practitioner Case Studies and Research into Practice

In addition to centring the practitioner via a focus on classroom-based research, this volume highlights research focused on practice to further target the practitioner. To date, the focus of much of the research in EAP has concentrated on the study of linguistic and rhetorical features of academic discourse or on student needs, rather than on pedagogical applications. In other words, it has focused on defining the 'E' or the 'A' or the 'AP' in EAP, rather than on how any or all of those elements may be taught. Of the chapters in *Routledge Handbook of English for Academic Purposes* (Hyland & Shaw, 2016), there is only one with a specifically named focus on pedagogy: Storch et al. (2016) write about EAP pedagogy in undergraduate contexts.

However, calls have been made for more focus on the pedagogies and practices in EAP (i.e. in Hyland & Wong, 2019; Riazi et al., 2020) and to some extent pedagogies are starting to become more prominent in EAP scholarship. In 2018, the *Journal of English for Academic Purposes* introduced its 'Research into Practice' series, a space within the journal devoted to articles specifically focused on EAP pedagogy, and the texts which are now appearing in this space add to the handful of academic journal articles published each year on EAP pedagogies. A few monographs published in recent years are concerned with the practice of EAP and envision the EAP practitioner as the audience (Blaj-Ward, 2014; Charles & Pecorari, 2015; Newton et al., 2018). Hanks (2017, 2019) includes some focus on practitioner research in EAP.

As well, two recent volumes focus on EAP pedagogies. Lillis et al. (2016) is a collection of case studies within the 'Perspectives on Writing' series, focused on EAP pedagogical practice within an academic literacies framework. These case studies showcase the pedagogies in a range of post-secondary academic writing contexts in the United States, United Kingdom, Ireland and Catalonia. Part three of Hyland and Wong (2019) focuses on the pedagogical practice of EAP, with four chapters that deal with data-driven learning in EAP in Hong Kong, feedback practices of subject and EAP lecturers on academic writing in the UK, teaching styles in academic writing tutorials in the UK and supervisor collaboration on research writing in English at a Chinese university. The current volume builds on the work of Lillis et al. (2016) and Hyland and Wong (2019), expanding the range of contexts, countries and underlying theoretical frameworks under examination.

Teaching is a pragmatic and generally ephemeral activity. In summary, the chapters here are firmly focused on pedagogical practice and centre on the EAP practitioner. This volume provides examples of classroom-based research and research-informed practice through case studies which explicate and make visible the pedagogy. These case studies also provide examples of activity worthy of further research and scholarship. In making the research visible, this volume aims to address the calls to bridge the gap between theory and practice. It also helps to further establish the EAP field and demonstrate the role of EAP practitioners in contributing to the dissemination of scholarship and through this obtaining 'cultural capital and ... academic identity' (Ding & Bruce, 2017, p. 166). Finally, a wider understanding of EAP approaches and the knowledge base required for these can contribute to the advancement of courses and programmes for EAP teachers themselves, an area also in need of further development (Ding & Bruce, 2017; Ding & Campion, 2016).

Contributions to This Volume

This volume covers a range of contexts including geographical, sociopolitical as well as pedagogical, and in so doing, it provides a variety of perspectives and approaches of how EAP is instantiated in policy, materials and classroom practice. Both design and delivery of EAP programming are examined, from the micro-scale instantiation of EAP pedagogies in an individual lesson, to meso-level course design considerations to the influence of macro-level government educational policy on EAP programme delivery. As mentioned earlier, an important contextual factor to how EAP is practised is the degree of interplay with the academic disciplines and collaboration between EAP and subject lecturers. The contributions to this volume deal with a conception of EAP as a stand-alone, general set of skills and practices –EGAP— – as well as a conception of EAP as a discipline-specific practice, or ESAP. This discipline specificity exists on a spectrum, from those contexts which might incorporate specific elements within an EGAP context to those deeply intertwined with a disciplinary pedagogy. The chapters in the volume have therefore been ordered to move from more general contexts of EAP to more discipline-specific contexts.

Chapter 1, by John McGaughey and Heejin Song, is a case study in critical multicultural education in a university EAP programme in Canada. Instructors guided students through engagement with institutional and government policy around equity, diversity and multiculturalism to raise cultural and intercultural awareness.

Chapter 2 addresses literacy brokering, or the involvement of people besides the authors in the production of texts, in the context of a university EAP classroom in the United States. Nina Conrad presents her unique pedagogical approach to teaching and awareness-raising around literacy brokerage in the coursework completion of undergraduate students.

Chapter 3 features SFL as the theoretical underpinning of the pedagogy taken by Jennifer Walsh Marr as she strategically deploys the metalanguage of SFL in first-year university EAP courses to illuminate the language features of successful texts.

How Kristin Solli and Tom Muir approach the pedagogies of EAP for Norwegian doctoral students in professional fields is the focus of Chapter 4. The authors discuss the efficacy of EAP approaches in meeting the academic writing needs and identity challenges of this distinct group of students.

Chapter 5, by Marília Mendes Ferreira, explores two critical approaches to the teaching of academic writing for publication purposes in the Brazilian context: Davydov's developmental teaching based on Vygotskian and activity theory principles and a Critical Pedagogy for academic literacy based on Canagarajah (2002).

The complex multilingual context of South Africa is the backdrop for Chapter 6, where Nhlanhla Mpofu and Mncedisi C. Maphalala discuss pedagogical approaches to training pre-service secondary school teachers to be EAP practitioners.

Chapter 7 centres on the pedagogies employed on a credit-bearing in-sessional EGAP course at a university in Turkey. Tijen Aksit and Necmi Aksit discuss the influences of EMI, content-based instruction (CBI) and educational technology that shape the pedagogy of EAP in that context.

In Chapter 8, Xiucai Lu and Bin Zou delve into the collaboration between EAP and subject-area teachers on a CLIL programme at a Chinese university. They explore teachers' perspectives of this collaboration and how to develop CLIL programmes to benefit students' academic learning.

Sydney School genre pedagogy is the focus of Chapter 9. Tony Myers, Jaime Buchanan, Jesse Balanyk and Timothy Nicoll detail how in-sessional teachers equip students with the academic English and genre awareness that will empower them to engage more fully with academic discourse communities in the changing educational landscape of higher education in the United Arab Emirates.

Chapter 10 explores the pedagogy of EAP teachers Jennifer Sizer, Anna Rolinska, Clare Carr and Clare Maxwell, who work in, with and through the creative arts disciplines such as art and design, music and architecture in a UK ESAP context. The chapter showcases pedagogic examples of collaborative teaching, use of student genres and working with students on reflective writing.

Carole MacDiarmid, Anneli Williams, Kat Irwin and Brían Doonan present a case study from a pre-sessional EAP programme in the UK. The impacts of integrating a signature pedagogy of medical school – problem-based learning – and in creating and delivering an ESAP course collaboratively with academic schools are explored in Chapter 11.

Lessons Learned in This Volume

The contributions which make up this volume underline the importance of context to EAP practice: EAP simply cannot be removed from its academic context and from the myriad of institutional, educational, historical, linguistic, sociopolitical factors at play within it. Context informs the content of EAP courses inasmuch as it influences the current and future linguistic and literacy needs of students to be successful in the academic environment. Institutional and sociopolitical factors also constrain course delivery, policies, staffing, materials and other aspects of EAP practice. Context also informs the constantly-evolving -terminology used to refer to aspects of EAP practice, and as such, a spectrum of terms such as English second language, foreign language or additional language, amongst others are used throughout the volume.

However, for all the diversity in contexts and pedagogies in these chapters, there are indeed certain elements of practice in common across contexts. A student-centredness can be seen in all the chapters of this volume: a pedagogy which centres the processes of learning and which is driven by student needs. This is at odds with the focus on text or academic discourse found in much published scholarship in EAP. The examples from this volume show EAP practitioners exercising their knowledge of how best to respond to students' needs in academic communication in a culturally and contextually appropriate way. The varied and multifaceted nature of EAP practice as showcased in this volume highlights the existence of and need for continued creativity and innovation in EAP pedagogies – one size certainly does not fit all.

We have learned a great deal about the pedagogical content knowledge of EAP through the variety of experiences described in the chapters of this volume. This gives us clearer insights into the classroom and what teachers are actually doing at the chalkface. From this, we gain a clearer idea of what their pedagogical content knowledge actually looks like: the nature of their teacher knowledge base, their know-how around the specifics of their context, past, present and future student needs and how those can be accommodated in the classroom and curricula tailored to it. Knowledge of student needs, as well as the future academic contexts they will be operating in and influential sociopolitical factors in that context, can inform localized and contextually informed developments in EAP teacher education.

EAP is a global endeavour and yet the pedagogies of EAP remain firmly on the margins of public knowledge and scrutiny. *This is EAP* – by furthering our understanding of the different contexts and practices as we do through these eleven chapters, this volume not only builds a more comprehensive picture of research-informed EAP practice, but it also enables us to develop a greater understanding of the needs and challenges EAP practitioners may face, which in turn can inform development, education or training of the EAP practitioners of tomorrow.

1

Embracing Critical Multicultural Education through Research-Informed Practice in EAP Teaching

John McGaughey and Heejin Song

As part of Canadian university and college internationalization efforts, the number of international students has shown a rapid increase with 498,735 students studying at post-secondary institutions in 2019 (Canadian Bureau of International Education, 2020). This increasing demographic has contributed to Canada's culturally and linguistically diverse higher education landscape and has led to concepts of multiculturalism and diversity being increasingly included in English for academic purposes (EAP) courses (see special issue on higher education in TESL Canada (Van Viegen et al., 2019)). Yet, this incorporation of multiculturalism and diversity is not without critique. Often the notion of multiculturalism as taught remains as tokenism and a symbolic construct, focusing on surface-level discussions of cultural diversity, for example, discussions centred around foods, holidays and celebrations (Apple, 2004; Bissoondath, 2002; Gérin-Lajoie, 2008; Kubota, 2015; McLaren, 2007; Nieto & Bode, 2011). In response to the critiques of teaching multiculturalism, and given the current social-political context seeing a resurgence of decolonizing social practices and social activism aimed at resisting systemic racism in Canada and around the world (e.g. Black Lives Matter; Idle No More; and Black, Indigenous, and People of Colour (BIPOC) movements), this chapter showcases how a two-cycle action research project led to the creation of materials and lessons embracing critical multicultural education (Kubota, 2015; Nieto & Bode, 2011) and contributing to students' development of critical intercultural communicative competence.

Theoretical Foundations

Byram's (1997) intercultural communicative competence (ICC) is adopted in recognition as one of the key essential skills for English language learners (Alptekin, 2002; Byram et al., 2002; Guo & Jamal, 2007; Song, 2013a, 2013b). Byram emphasizes learners' development of ICC in three dimensions: 'knowledge' of culture including surface culture (i.e. cultural symbols and products) and deep culture (i.e. beliefs and perspectives); skills of reflecting on, relating to and comparing other cultures; and attitudes towards other cultures (i.e. openness, inclusiveness). Despite the emphasis on reflexive skills and inclusive attitudes development, we contend that Byram's framework can be complemented with more critically oriented theoretical lenses such as critical multicultural education to equip EAP students with essential skills to reflect on global issues and resist unjust matters.

Pedagogues in critical multicultural education (Grant & Sleeter, 2010; Nieto & Bode, 2011) and critical race theory (Dei, 1999; Kubota, 2015) argue that a superficial understanding of multiculturalism can lead to silencing critical discussions of discrimination and prejudices surrounding race, ethnicity, gender, class and sexual orientation. Critical multicultural education (Grant & Sleeter, 2010; May, 1999; Nieto & Bode, 2011) calls for students' active participation in and practice of exercising democratic ideas and discussing topics of inequality and injustice. In this light, students are invited to examine the power relations in social reality and how structural discrimination is created and reproduced. Based on this critical approach to multicultural education, the discussion of issues of inequality and injustice should be actively incorporated in EAP curricula in a manner that unpacks and renders visible the unequal relations of power and the ideologies of diversity and difference.

Through the incorporation of these theoretical lenses, we focus on developing materials and pedagogical approaches that facilitate discussions of contested notions of power linked to diversity and systemic discrimination. We believe that such an approach will help develop students' critical intercultural communicative competence along with the capacity to actively participate in their globalized educational communities and beyond.

Methodology

Teaching Context: EAP Courses and Students

The teaching and research context for this study is an EAP programme at a university in a large Canadian city. The programme is for international students who have met the academic qualifications for entrance into their undergraduate programmes but do not have a high-enough English proficiency score for direct admission. As an alternative admission pathway, these students are offered admission into the two-semester programme, and upon successful completion of the programme, they are directly admitted into their undergraduate programme the following year. The three EAP courses that make up the programme are non-credit-bearing content and language integrated learning (CLIL) courses consisting of a reading and writing course, a cross-disciplinary skills course and a listening and speaking course. This chapter focuses on our teaching experiences in the cross-disciplinary skills course and the reading and writing course.

The students in the programme are high academic achievers on the basis of their high school grades; however, their English proficiency, based on IELTS, ranges between 5.0 and 6.5 overall. Within the programme, in our experience, student proficiency tends to vary both within and across course sections. The students enrolled in the programme reflect many different nationalities; however, the majority of students are Chinese.

We have observed that our students often hold a liberal view of Canadian multiculturalism, a view where Canada is a nation free of racism and discrimination. Furthermore, through focus groups and conversations with former students we have also learned that they often feel unwilling or unprepared to engage in discussions of systemic racism and discrimination with their classmates. Recognizing this gap and the need to develop students' ICC, we embarked on a two-year action research project.

Action Research

Our teaching practices were designed, analysed and reflected upon through the framework of educational action research advocated by Burns (2005, 2010) and Kemmis et al. (2014). Action research in education refers to research wherein educators examine their own practice in partnership with colleagues and/or learners to resolve tensions, improve teaching and make a positive change in their educational environment. Despite numerous types and variations of action research characterized by the purpose, context and social actors involved (see Burns, 2005; Kemmis et al., 2014; Song, 2019, for more information), the heart of action research is 'the process of its systemic planning, action and reflection in a spiral and cyclical progression and its goal, that is, change, transformation and improvement of practice, whether it is for short-term or long-term or infinite' (Song, 2019, p. 8).

The two-cycle action research project took place during two academic years. The first cycle took place during the 2017–2018 academic year while John and

Heejin were teaching different sections of the cross-disciplinary skills course. The second cycle, which built upon the first cycle, took place during the 2018–2019 academic year while John was teaching a section of the reading and writing course and Heejin was teaching a different section of the cross-disciplinary skills course.

In the following, for each action research cycle, we detail our theoretically informed instructional design. Then, through a reflective narrative approach, we discuss how our students engaged with the materials and lessons and provide our observations of students' outcomes on course assignments.

Action Research Cycle 1: The Canadian Culture and Identity Project

For the first action research cycle, our aim was to create and teach a unit on culture and identity where students would gain awareness of their culturally and linguistically diverse university community. As part of the unit, students engaged with two readings and a video to gain a theoretical understanding of culture and identity, understand why common Canadian stereotypes are inaccurate and learn why stereotyping creates a mistaken or incomplete picture of an individual or group from assigned resources (Adiche, 2009; Browne, 2008; Saunders, 2009). These materials were supplemented by in-class discussions and were intended to scaffold students' upcoming research project that culminated in a presentation on Canadian culture. We believed that the students would use what they had learned in class when researching and creating presentations and show a somewhat accurate understanding of Canadian culture and cross-cultural understanding. However, with rare exception, this was not to be the case.

The students' presentations had common themes mainly based on Canadian stereotypes such as Tim Hortons (a coffee shop franchise), maple syrup, hockey and igloos. Cultural diversity, if included, was based on Canada's white colonial settlers and European immigrants and omitted the presence of people of colour, and more recent immigration trends were notably absent. Moreover, the dominant pattern in students' presentations remained superficial by portraying Canada as a multicultural haven, exhibiting celebratory liberal multiculturalism and avoiding discussion of issues of unequal power relations between the culturally dominant and minoritized groups. This pattern reproduced a capitalist and neoliberal construction of the multicultural Canadian identity as a commodity, something that clients can consume, taste and experience through cultural products at prices ranging from two dollars (e.g. Tim Hortons' coffee and donuts) to thousands (e.g. winter sports and cultural excursions to the North).

At the end of the term, we met on several occasions to debrief the first action research cycle. We discussed how we were both surprised and disappointed that what we had taught in class and the discussions that the students had did not seem to scaffold their research projects. Rather, their presentations were reflections of the very stereotypes that we were trying to reject through our teaching. Our discussions led us to realize that simply teaching our students about the concept of culture and how stereotyping creates an incomplete picture of a culture was not enough if we wanted students leave the course with an inclusive understanding of Canadian culture beyond the dominant groups. We felt that going forward, we needed to take a much more critical and direct approach where students would not only learn about how Canada is culturally and linguistically diverse but also know that not all people in Canada are treated fairly and equally due to systemic racism and discrimination. These reflections in turn greatly influenced our practices the following year, part of which became the second action research cycle.

Action Research Cycle 2: Taking a Critical Approach to Canadian Multiculturalism

Based on our reflections on the first action research cycle, we modified the instructional design and our action research expanded to two different EAP courses in the following year, to the reading and writing course and the cross-disciplinary skills course. Here, we detail and reflect on what we did in our courses where we sought to better align with critical approaches to multicultural education including anti-racism education and multicultural education for social justice (Dei, 1999; Grant & Sleeter, 2010; Kubota, 2015; Nieto & Bode, 2011) with an aim to develop students' critical understanding of Canadian culture, diversity and equity.

John: Unpacking Canadian Multiculturalism in an EAP Reading and Writing Course

In the second year of the action research project, I began teaching in the reading and writing course. Based on our experiences in the first action research cycle, I embraced critical multicultural education as a theoretical lens when designing an overarching research project and when choosing academic readings in Fall term. I first provide an overview of the research project and the course readings and then discuss how they led to students developing a more critical understanding of Canadian multiculturalism.

Research Project Overview

The main assignment of the course was a multi-step scaffolded research project which began early in the Fall semester and culminated with a final paper in the Winter semester. The research paper was framed with the research question: 'What is the future of multiculturalism in Canada?' The different steps of the research project reflected the different academic genres that students would learn throughout the year:

1. Proposal
2. Annotated bibliography
3. Literature review
4. Argumentative essay (introduction and body section only)
5. Argumentative essay (final draft)

Each step of the research project was aimed to scaffold the following steps in the project. Students were also permitted to improve what they had written in one step and incorporate that writing in later steps. To complete the different steps of the research paper, the students were required to incorporate arguments from four requisite course readings and their own independent research.

Requisite Course Texts

In the Fall semester, students were required to intensively read four texts that reflected different genres and perspectives of multiculturalism and cultural diversity in Canada. Two texts, Marche (2016) and Winter (2015), were more theoretical and positively focused on multiculturalism. Marche argues that Canada is exceptional as it continues to embrace immigration and cultural and linguistic diversity in contrast to anti-immigrant, anti-diversity discourses through Donald Trump in the United States or underlying the Brexit in the United Kingdom. Winter's (2015) chapter is based on a discursive analysis of major newspapers in Canada, focusing on how multiculturalism became an important part of Canada's national identity. Of significance to the research project, she argues that Canadians began to positively view multiculturalism as part of their national identity as a result of the Quebecois' referendum on secession in 1995 where the deciding 'no' vote was attributed to the immigrant population in Quebec.

The other two texts, Go (2005) and Malone (2018), focus more on the practical lived realities of minority groups in Canada that are in essence overlooked in the dominant view of multiculturalism. Go (2005) highlights how Chinese-Canadians have suffered from systemic discrimination from the time of the construction of the Canadian Pacific Railroad and the subsequent Chinese Head Tax and the Chinese Exclusion Act. She further argues, in regard to political representation, that Chinese Canadians are limited to token appointments and they are not represented in positions of power. Malone's (2018) in-depth CBC news article focuses on First Nations in Kenora, a small Canadian city, in the broader context of reconciliation. Malone provides a historical background of some of the abuses faced by First Nations as part of Canada's, now defunct, residential schools. Through interviews, she shows how First Nations in Kenora continue to suffer from racism and discrimination in the community all of which impede or even prohibit the notion of reconciliation between the Canadian government and Indigenous peoples.

Intensive Academic Reading Method

The students intensively read the texts following Seburn's (2015) academic reading circle approach. In essence, students are placed into groups of five, and each student is assigned a reading circle role, for example, a student may be given the role of contextualizer. Then students independently read and seek to understand the text based on their role. As a contextualizer, students would research key contextual references in the text in preparation for an in-class discussion with their group. In class, in their group, the leader leads the discussion by going through each part of the text and asking comprehension and discussion questions. Individual students in turn share what they learned based on their roles. Class time is also spent clarifying difficult concepts and answering questions that students may have about the text. Through this in-depth reading of the texts, the students were expected to gain a solid understanding of the text and be able to apply what they had learned to complete the different steps of the research project.

Students' Critical Understanding of Canadian Multiculturalism

I found that my students varied in their understanding of the readings depending on the genre and content especially in the early steps of the research project. Students showed gaps in their understanding of the texts and often took an uncritical acceptance of the author's arguments. For example, some students argued, echoing Marche (2016) and Winter (2015), that the future of Canadian multiculturalism was overwhelmingly positive while ignoring the arguments of Go (2005) and Malone (2018). In other cases, students argued that for multiculturalism to succeed, echoing Go (2005), the Canadian government should apologize and make redress for the Chinese Head Tax. In other cases, students argued that the Canadian government should apologize and publicly admit to the historic abuses that Indigenous peoples experienced in residential schools.

The stepped nature of the research paper, however, allowed the space for students to make mistakes. Students received feedback on the necessity to address counterarguments in their writing. Thus, if they were to argue that the future of multiculturalism was overwhelmingly positive, they must include and rebut counterarguments, such as Go (2005) and Malone (2018). Relatedly, I was able to remind students to consider the timeliness of texts and the need to conduct additional research to triangulate the arguments of the assigned readings. This was especially true of Go (2005) given that the Canadian government did act and apologized for the Head Tax and Exclusion Act in the years after her paper was published. I was also able to share findings from the Truth and Reconciliation Commission of Canada (2015) and their 94 Calls to Action with my students, which emphasize that while the Canadian government has apologized to Indigenous peoples, this is only the beginning of a very long and complex path to reconciliation with Indigenous peoples in Canada.

The feedback that students received throughout the year led to more in-depth research on their topics and in turn accurate, at times critical, arguments in their final argumentative essays. For example, instead of students calling for apologies for the anti-Chinese taxes, some students argued that for multiculturalism to succeed, the Canadian government needed to dismantle systemic discrimination in employment for minoritized groups. In other cases, students argued for the rights of Indigenous peoples, calling for equity in health care and housing. While not all of the students' final papers took a social justice argument, overall, their understanding of Canadian multiculturalism became more critical, accurate and grounded in research.

Heejin: Critical EAP in a Unit on Equity and Diversity

As a response to our prior teaching of culture and identity and seeing the prevailing practice of students reproducing essentialist understandings of Canadian multiculturalism, in the beginning of the following year, I decided to include more socially and culturally sensitive materials and activities that were reflective of our students' educational reality and included a unit called equity and diversity. At the same time, to complement the lack of recognition of issues of power and ideology in students' work, I included teaching materials that were progressive and provocative to explicitly generate contested discussions and raise students' critical awareness of diversity and power. The intention was to scaffold our students' critical understanding of how the concept of diversity in education is politicized and how it is reflected in their educational context.

The lesson was designed first to familiarize students with the language and university policies around equity and diversity. It also aimed to help students critically reflect on and engage in contested issues related to equity and diversity that exist in their educational communities. The activities were based on a close examination of official university documents and institutional media texts with a long-term desire of students' generating tools to alter the unequal power distributions in inter- and intra-group social relations. The unit followed a three-component structure:

1. Understanding institutional discourses of diversity and equity through reading and viewing institutional texts
2. Comparing discourses of diversity and equity in practice
3. Analysing reality with the concepts of diversity and equity as follow-up activities

Understanding Institutional Discourse through Reading the Institution's Official Statements and Viewing a Video Clip of Racialized Students' Educational Experiences

Students were asked to read the university's official documents where the institutional perspectives towards equity and diversity are stated in formal and judicial language, namely the university's mission statement, the university's statement of equity, diversity and excellence and the university's statement of institutional purpose. The students then had a discussion including the following guiding questions: 'How are the concepts of equity and diversity defined in the official texts? What can be some examples of preserving those values?'

Through this first activity, the lesson attempted to help students engage with their close reading of the texts and uncover how the concept of equity and diversity is reflected in the language produced by the university. The institution's official statements include keywords like equal opportunity, equity and justice and diversity as our strength. Students were able to identify these keywords and point out the direct passages that highlight the university's promotion of equity and diversity. The following are the main messages:

1. Everyone's equal rights should be reserved for participating in academic activities and advancing scholarship.
2. The institution fosters diversity as a strength of the educational community.
3. Discrimination is never acceptable on the basis of race, gender, class, ability, origin of ancestry, sexual orientation for educational practices at all levels and in all sectors, and this is protected under the institutional jurisdiction of the academic integrity policy and the Human Rights Code of the province.

As a connected activity, students were asked to watch a video clip of racialized students' stories about their experiences related to equity and diversity at the university. They then had a discussion with guiding questions including:

1. What conflicts and problems did the university students experience?
2. What kind of discrimination/exclusion was told by these individuals?
3. Are the problems individuals' or society's?
4. Have you had any similar experiences?

After watching the video of the students who positioned themselves as racialized and minoritized, the students seemed to recognize that there is a group in the university student community feeling isolated at times and marginalized because of the exclusion of their culture and history and ignorance of the existence of people of colour, their prior knowledge and culture. Although students struggled to understand some of the language and concepts (e.g. marginalization, racialization, biased epistemology) which were then explained, it was clear that most students recognized that the issues addressed in the video were interrelated with the societal discrimination towards cultural minority groups. Also, based on their understanding of the university's official statements regarding equity and diversity, the students appeared cognizant that the institutional messages and perspectives of equity and diversity were not always consistently reflected in reality despite the university's well-intended statements.

Comparing Discourses of Diversity and Equity: Advanced Reading and Viewing Materials

Students in groups were invited to read three one-page texts illustrating discriminatory practices related to race, language and culture. They then discussed the social prejudice and discrimination issues that exist(ed) in various educational settings. The readings were:

1. *Summary of Lau v. Nichols*, 1974 (Beyond Brown, 2004)
2. Debate on prejudice and discrimination in a third-year sociology class (Egbo, 2009, p. 95)
3. A Canadian school teacher dealing with conflicts in a culturally diverse school (Egbo, 2009, p. 1)

After reading these texts, students then discussed which groups were discriminated, how they were discriminated and what the consequences of those exclusionary practices brought to the individuals' lives and society. Finally, I showed a short video clip on Canadian residential schools (Viceland, 2017) and had a whole-class discussion on the truth behind Canadian residential schools.

During this session, some students were confused with the concepts between equity and diversity. Some of the questions raised and discussed were why the *Lau* v. *Nicholas* case became an issue of equity in the first place and how the issue was justified and accommodated by the judicial decision as they had not heard any similar stories in their home contexts. Although some students had heard stories of Indigenous people in Canada, some questioned why it was still an issue since the government had issued an official public apology.

I then introduced the case of educational accommodation for English language learners through English language classes and multilingual resources in elementary and secondary education in Ontario, explaining that it is a way to provide an equal opportunity for learners to successfully participate in educational activities (Ontario Ministry of Education, 2008) by recognizing diversity as a resource, not a deficit (Cummins & Early, 2010). Furthermore, I elaborated on the complex issue related to Canada's conflicts surrounding the Indigenous peoples in that what is said officially is not always implemented in practice.

Analysing Reality: Decoding Semiotic Representations of Equity and Diversity and Intercultural Reflection

After teaching the unit, I assigned two follow-up activities. First, the students had to find and take a picture of something on campus that reflected the student's understanding of the concepts of equity and diversity. They then had to upload the image to the course website with a short explanation of the image. For the second activity, I had the students write a story related to discrimination in their home country. Students then uploaded their stories to the discussion board on the course website. They wrote about diversity in language, gender, sexual orientation, race and religion as reflected in student club posters, student service banners and signs and notes posted on the walls of campus buildings. Regarding students' reflection of discrimination in their home country, many students shared stories related to gender and racial discrimination that exist in employment or, linguistic and cultural discrimination against foreigners (i.e. xenophobia) and at times against people from different provinces (i.e. regional discrimination and linguicism).

At the end of the semester, we met on several occasions to debrief and reflect on our experiences in the second action research cycle. On these occasions we were much more satisfied with the impact of our respective curriculum and course units on our students' inclusive, and at times critical, understanding of Canadian culture, which we elaborate further below.

Discussion

In the context of decolonizing EAP teaching going beyond the denial of racism and race-blindness, the cyclical processes of action research served as a vehicle where we were able to not only achieve these aims but also improve upon the theoretical bases framing our pedagogy. In our case, the first action research cycle revealed a gap in Byram's ICC (1997). Considering the three components of ICC – knowledge, skills and attitudes – our students learned about different aspects of Canadian culture and developed skills to compare and contrast Canadian culture with their home cultures while also reflecting positive and open attitudes to Canadian culture. However, the culture that our students embraced and reflected on was the culture of the dominant colonial groups and our students, based on their presentations, showed little awareness of inequity between the dominant and minoritized groups. In essence, although it was not our aim, the project outcomes unexpectedly reflected the colonial discourses that we were attempting to resist.

Yet, through our reflection and discussions, the disappointments in the first action research cycle led to us adding the theoretical lenses of critical multicultural education (Kubota, 2015; May, 1999; Nieto & Bode, 2011) and critical race theory (Kubota, 2015) to Byram's (1997) ICC. This in turn complemented our pedagogical approach for the second action research cycle and positively impacted our two courses where the 'hidden curriculum' (Giroux,

1977) was rendered visible as a result. The courses brought forward the voices of racialized and minoritized groups from multiple levels including educational, institutional and national levels. The materials included various instantiations of the cultural, racial and linguistic discrimination. The subsequent discussions and assignments attempted to leave a message that the discrimination against and excluding certain groups from the mainstream social and educational practices is detrimental to society and is well documented historically in Canada (e.g. the issues related to Indigenous peoples still persist today). Moreover, not only did students gain critical awareness with these issues, they also gained competence in being able to discuss and at times advocate for racialized and minoritized groups, all of which we argue is a reflection of students developing a critical intercultural communicative competence.

Our experiences, however, do have limitations that should be taken into consideration. We were fortunate to be teaching at a university in a large multicultural Canadian city. There is an institutional position that courses and colleges need to do more to acknowledge and resist systemic racism at the institutional level and beyond. Thus, our critical approaches to EAP were consistently supported. This, however, may not be the case in all EAP contexts especially those where critical topics may be considered taboo or where a critique of the status quo of a state could lead to censure or be in violation of state laws and possibly lead to incarceration or harm. Lastly, our action research consisted mostly of Chinese students and these students intend to stay in Canada for their undergraduate education and perhaps longer. EAP educators teaching students reflecting different cultural groups may find that their students react differently to the course content. This is an area that could be explored in future action research projects.

Additionally, based on students' follow-up activities and research papers in the two different courses, despite the well acknowledged presence of the representations of diversity, we noticed a somewhat simplified understanding of the complex and intersecting aspects of discriminatory practices. The common understanding was that discrimination exists everywhere and that it was categorized in binary terms, the discriminator and the discriminated, the majority and the minority, with students positioning themselves as social minorities in Canada. This binary understanding does not show a complete picture of how the relations of power that exist among groups of different social categories (e.g. race, language, culture, gender, class, sexual orientation) operate in practice.

The majority of our students were Chinese, and they were associated with a linguistic and cultural minority in Canada. However, what is absent in this picture is that the majority of them were in fact from a socio-economically privileged group who could afford the costly university tuition. While some of them could be associated with subcultural groups with differing political, cultural and linguistic views, the majority positioned themselves and others from subcultural groups as representative of one homogenous culture of China. To this end, this intersectionality of diversity and power and the associated prejudice should be further developed and interrogated in our teaching.

Pedagogical Implications

We believe that our experiences and findings from research-informed practice have several implications for other teaching contexts. Our teaching practices in two EAP courses framed in action research that resulted in developing students' critical intercultural communicative competence show how we created and recreated the instructional design to equip students with essential academic literacies, and how we were able to engage students in reading, discussing, writing, sharing and presenting on topics of inequality and injustice through the lens of critical multicultural education. For educators working in a similar context with a similar demographic of students such as international students in an EAP programme, we feel that the approaches we have taken may be transferred to the design of a whole course syllabus or to a specific course module.

For a curricular implementation for a multiple unit, semester or a full-year academic reading and writing course, the inclusion of texts that directly address inequity and discrimination is a suitable starting point. We recommend the incorporation of texts that make clear the lived realities of minoritized and racialized groups in that community or nation. Moreover, students are likely to connect with readings that represent their demographic which may facilitate student engagement and understanding.

The primary implication from the reading and writing class is that students need to read what may be controversial or sensitive texts intensively such as through the academic reading circles approach (Seburn, 2015) and have multiple opportunities to engage with the arguments in the texts through discussions and assignments. The readings create opportunities for students to learn and discuss these issues while the research project builds upon students' growing awareness of the issues in the texts. One key aspect from the research project is that each step scaffolds the next. Students are given space to make mistakes and learn from them. Thus, students continue to improve their understanding and ability to engage with these complex issues and present more critical arguments as they develop their critical intercultural communicative competence.

For a unit/lesson level implementation, educators could follow an inquiry-provoking approach. For example, university or college educators could use their institutions' equity and diversity policy documents as a starting point. Students could first read and discuss their understanding of equity and diversity based on their prior knowledge and the institutional policy documents. Then, as a follow-up activity, students could go around their campus either in person, virtually, or both, and take photographs or screenshots reflecting their understanding of equity and diversity such as found on signs, posters and notices, and then post them on the course webpage. Then, as a follow-up discussion, online or in class, students could discuss in groups their experience finding semiotic representations of equity and diversity on campus with guiding questions such as:

1. Do you know any university services, clubs or student activities that expressly welcome cultural, linguistic and/or racial diversity? How do these places or events achieve this?
2. Do you feel your cultural, linguistic and racial values are respected on campus? Explain.
3. Have you ever felt excluded because of your cultural, linguistic and/or racial difference on campus? Explain.
4. If you feel excluded in educational practices due to racial, linguistic and cultural difference, how would you make a change?

This approach can lead to developing critical awareness of issues that impact minoritized and racialized groups on campus which, in the case of international students, they will to varying extents be a part of and in turn be impacted by similar issues. Students together with their peers have opportunities to think of ways to create a more inclusive educational space. Even if the ideas from the discussions may not bring an instant change or fix to reality, it is a way to move a step forward to social change as we believe that a recognition of the presence of social issues through a critical reflection is a prerequisite step to creating visions to social change.

Conclusion

This chapter manifests how our action research-informed practice led to the development of materials and lessons that embrace critical multicultural education and the creation of transformative opportunities for our students to develop critical intercultural communicative competence. The materials and lessons discussed in this chapter led to students interrogating issues of cultural diversity, discrimination and power, going beyond a liberal understanding of cultural diversity. Moving forward, we believe that our future EAP students will be better served if we continue to incorporate critical orientations in our pedagogical choices to teaching by developing materials and activities that question and challenge the status quo of the hierarchies of power (e.g. culture, race, ethnic origin, language, gender, sexual orientation, class) that operate in the social relations of their university communities and beyond.

2

Addressing Literacy Brokering in the EAP Classroom

Nina Conrad

It is common for students to receive writing support or feedback from others outside the instructional context. This practice is referred to as literacy brokering, defined as the involvement of people besides named authors in the production of texts (Lillis & Curry, 2010). Students' engagement in off-campus literacy brokering practices may raise discomfort for instructors, in part because of the difficulty of reaching consensus over what constitutes acceptable practice. Though some forms of literacy brokering seem innocent, others raise issues of ethics, equity and academic integrity for instructors and institutions of higher education. Factors such as the relationship between student and literacy broker, the literacy broker's qualifications and the exchange of payment further complicate things. For instance, an instructor who would allow a student to receive proofreading from an acquaintance might not feel comfortable allowing the same student to receive corrections from an online proofreading company for a fee. Yet social resources come into play as well: Would the scenario change if the student paid for proofreading because they did not have access to a friend or family who could correct their writing?

This chapter provides a brief overview of issues surrounding students' use of literacy brokering and outlines a lesson that could assist instructors in addressing this topic with their students. In the lesson, which was designed for use in a genre-based first-year writing course at a US university, students examine scenarios, analyse a ghostwriting provider's website for persuasive rhetoric and reflect on where they would draw the line regarding acceptable forms of literacy brokering. Excerpts from students' reflections serve to illustrate how this lesson helped them to recognize and articulate the differences between acceptable and unacceptable practices.

In line with previous research on literacy brokering, this chapter is based on an understanding that writing is a social practice. From this perspective, writing is rarely an individual pursuit; literacy practices always occur in a social context, and the production of texts is therefore mediated by other people, institutions and sociopolitical forces operating in these contexts (Barton & Hamilton, 2000; Lillis & Curry, 2010). It is the mediation of academic writing practices by individuals besides named authors of those texts that is the focus of this chapter.

Literature Review

Research has examined ways in which literacy brokers intervene in the production of texts and the outcomes of such interventions for texts and their authors. In a foundational study of literacy brokering among EAL career scholars in the context of academic publishing, Lillis and Curry (2010) distinguished two types of literacy brokers: *academic brokers* are colleagues in an author's discipline who can provide assistance with content, methodology and engagement with specific discourse communities, and *language brokers* are people with specialized English-language knowledge who can help authors with their use of English in particular. The latter can be further divided into two categories: professional language brokers are people with professional qualifications and expertise who receive payment for their work, including copy editors, translators and people employed to teach or provide support with English or writing. Informal language brokers are individuals with a personal relationship to the author who provide support with text production, such as friends and family members (Lillis & Curry, 2010).

Though most relevant research has focused on professionals writing for publication, students' use of specific forms of literacy brokering, such as proofreading services, has recently been gaining more attention. For the purposes of this discussion, literacy brokering is defined as third-party intervention in students' creation of academic texts (following Lillis & Curry, 2010). Such third-party involvement is understood to occur outside the classroom, and therefore instructors and classmates are not considered literacy brokers unless they provide support outside of planned class activities. While there are many potential sites for literacy brokering on university campuses, such as writing centres and individual tutoring services, their practices and pedagogical approach are well documented (e.g. Grimm, 2009) and unlikely to raise ethical issues. In contrast, types of literacy brokering that occur elsewhere are more problematic, not only because they occur without oversight from instructors or institutions but also because students do not have equal access to them. These include the involvement of friends, family, informal support networks and services that profit from serving the needs of student authors. The types of textual interventions offered by these groups occupy a grey area in institutional regulations and therefore deserve more focused attention in research and policy (e.g. Harwood, 2019). The remainder of this chapter explores these urgent questions of ethics and equity.

There are many potential reasons for students to engage in literacy brokering. They may be trying to please instructors, research supervisors or publishing gatekeepers (e.g. Conrad, 2020), who may have encouraged them to seek third-party writing support or correction (see Corcoran et al., 2018; Turner, 2012). They may hope the broker's intervention could help them achieve higher grades. They may feel that they are receiving ineffective or insufficient instruction in class and seek support in hopes of learning from a third party (see Newton, 2018). Access to writing support may factor into the decision as well: students may not be aware of services available on campus, such as office hours or writing centre tutoring, or may fear approaching the providers of those services (e.g. Angelova & Riazantseva, 1999). Or they may prefer to receive support from someone they know personally. Users of commercial services may take a transactional approach to writing support, and some may even feel entitled to services in exchange for money in the same way that they receive a degree in exchange for tuition fees (see Harwood et al., 2012; Starfield, 2016). When addressing literacy brokering, it is important to consider students' reasons for pursuing support outside of the classroom or beyond their existing academic relationships.

Types of Literacy Brokering in Academic Contexts

Literacy brokering practices can be placed along a spectrum from most to least involvement and influence in the production of academic texts. The most involvement a literacy broker can have is to complete academic work on behalf of a student, referred to as 'contract cheating' (Draper & Newton, 2017). Though contract cheating has traditionally been treated as a means of evading engagement in literacy practices (see Newton & Lang, 2016), some scholars are coming to view it as an extreme form of literacy brokering for students who succumb to persuasive marketing or see nowhere else to turn (e.g. Heng Hartse, 2019). Types of contract cheating include academic custom writing (ghostwriting) services, file-sharing sites, paid exam-takers and services that provide prewritten essays, termed *essay banks* or *essay mills* (Newton & Lang, 2016). In all types of contract cheating, the student claims authorship and takes credit for work performed by another person, which has led some to argue that contract cheating constitutes fraud and could be prosecuted as such (Draper et al., 2017). Most of the world lacks supporting legislation, however, and many institutions do not have clear policies in place to regulate students' use of contract cheating services (Draper & Newton, 2017).

Another contentious form of literacy brokering is proofreading, defined as third-party corrective interventions in academic writing (Conrad, 2020). Proofreading has been noted to occupy an 'ethical grey area' of literacy practice in institutions of higher education, in part because the level of intervention is often ambiguous. In the publishing industry, *proofreading* refers to the final quality check of a previously edited manuscript, whereas in academic contexts it functions as a catchall term for a variety of interventions (Scott & Turner, 2008), ranging from copy editing (word- and sentence-level corrections to spelling, grammar and punctuation) to substantive editing at the level of organization and content (see Matarese, 2016, for definitions).

In some disciplinary contexts, it is common practice for instructors and graduate supervisors to request that students seek proofreading for written work before submitting it for evaluation (e.g. Turner, 2012). For example, through interviews with ten professors at a UK university, Turner (2011) identified that proofreading was generally viewed as 'routine and broadly supportive of the learning process' (p. 429). However, some EAP instructors and writing specialists involved in the same study believed proofreading came into conflict with course learning objectives. When lexicogrammar is part of what is being assessed, any level of corrective intervention could interfere with assessment of students' learning, even though it might be acceptable in other contexts. Proofreading also raised ethical issues for EAP instructors: there were concerns about where to draw the line regarding the extent of third-party intervention and further concerns over students' access to qualified proofreaders. Commercially advertised proofreading in particular raised issues, as instructors feared that such services are not provided in the interest of students' learning 'and may indeed be exploitative of them' (Turner, 2012, p. 20).

At the other end of the spectrum are unobjectionable practices such as seeking feedback on one's writing from a friend or family member. Unless an instructor has expressly forbidden outside help (such as for a take-home examination), such interventions can be seen as a well-meaning form of social support. Innocuous as it may seem, however, support from friends and family members still constitutes a third-party intervention and thereby complicates the identification of acceptable forms of literacy brokering. In addition, though it may seem unproblematic in itself, receiving support from a peer or family member may obscure that a student is facing other inequities. For instance, students' pursuit of corrections or feedback from peers may indicate a lack of awareness of or lack of access to formal sources of academic support, such as feedback from instructors or campus writing support services. Students may also resist reaching out to formal supports out of fear of marginalization or a belief that such services cannot or will not help them. Numerous studies have documented cases of students who did not receive the types of corrections or feedback they desired from their instructors or research supervisors (e.g. Wang & Li, 2008) or from writing centres (Okuda & Anderson, 2018). In particular, students may experience frustration and rejection when seeking systematic correction of lexicogrammatical errors (e.g. Anderson, 2020), and peers may provide a more accessible and appealing form of support.

In a discussion of pedagogical responses to plagiarism, Mott-Smith et al. (2017) suggested that rather than viewing plagiarism through an ethical lens, it is advisable to distinguish between deceitful and non-deceitful behaviour. Deceitful behaviour, such as passing off another person's work as one's own, is never acceptable. 'Non-deceitful behaviour, which typically stems from a student not knowing that something is problematic or lacking the ability to avoid it, on the other hand, should be approached with a pedagogical response' (Mott-Smith et al., 2017, p. 3). In cases of both plagiarism and literacy brokering, teaching students to distinguish between problematic and unproblematic behaviours is key. There is no universally applicable dividing line, however. Rather, notions of 'acceptable' behaviour are context-dependent, requiring consideration of the course environment and objectives, the contextual forces that compel students to seek particular kinds of textual interventions and the social conditions that influence the types of literacy brokers they have access to. The following section presents a lesson in which case-based scenarios are used to help students navigate and reflect on these issues.

Context for the Lesson

The complexity of literacy brokering makes it an excellent topic to broach with students in EAP programmes, bridging programmes and first-year writing (FYW) courses, who are all just beginning to learn academic discourse expectations. The lesson presented here was developed for a genre-based FYW course at a large US research university where most students take two such courses in their first year. Though these courses are not explicitly intended to prepare students for disciplinary courses, they are designed to foster engagement with concepts such as rhetorical situation, genre awareness and discipline-specific writing conventions in hopes that developing awareness in these areas will facilitate transfer to other academic writing situations. These courses also place an emphasis on metacognitive development; students engage in ongoing reflection on their decisions and progress as writers, and each FYW course culminates in a reflective portfolio project. The courses are not designed specifically for English learners; however, the university, a federally designated Hispanic-Serving Institution, has a large population of heritage Spanish speakers, and the class for which this activity was designed included many multilingual students.

The lesson presented here was designed to complement an existing emphasis on writing as a social practice in the FYW course I taught. One of the stated learning outcomes for this course is to 'identify the collaborative and social aspects of writing processes', which is facilitated through group work and peer review among other activities. Yet while collaboration is actively fostered in FYW classrooms, the types of social interactions that may occur around writing outside the classroom setting are not typically addressed. This is partly because this university (like many others) lacks policy regarding students' engagement in literacy brokering practices, particularly the use of commercial proofreading and writing support services. Though the institution's Student Code of Conduct prohibits 'All forms of student academic dishonesty, including but not limited to cheating, fabrication, facilitating academic dishonesty, and plagiarism', it does not define those terms or specify how dishonesty is identified. Thus it is left to instructors to interpret the policy with regard to their own courses, explain their expectations to students and follow through with reporting procedures if they perceive a violation of the policy.

Unfortunately, it is often unclear how to proceed in cases of suspected violations related to literacy brokering. Numerous instructors and administrators have shared accounts of times when they were not sure how to respond when presented with student work that seemed suspiciously 'polished' or was inconsistent with writing that students had produced in class. Conversations with fellow instructors indicate that if a student claims sole authorship of a text when confronted, then the instructor is left with no avenue for recourse. In response to such conversations, I set out to develop a way of addressing literacy brokering within the greater FYW goal of exploring writing as a social and collaborative practice. Ideally, institutions would develop clear guidance on acceptable forms of intervention in students' writing, preferably with insight from instructors, and both students and literacy brokers would be held accountable for meeting them (Harwood, 2019). In the absence of institutional guidelines, however, it is up to departments and instructors to develop policies in line with their course objectives and suited for their instructional contexts (Conrad, 2019). In my classroom, this meant discussing literacy brokering in connection to related conversations about participation in academic discourses and development of genre and rhetorical awareness. In the next section, I describe a lesson in which students are presented with various literacy brokering scenarios alongside the Code of Academic Integrity and asked to consider where they would draw the line between acceptable and unacceptable practice.

The Lesson: An Exploration of Literacy Brokering and Ghostwriting

Prior to the day of the lesson, students are assigned to read a *New York Times* article titled 'Cheating, Inc.: How Writing Papers for American College Students Has Become a Lucrative Profession Overseas' (Stockman & Mureithi, 2019). Part exposé of contract cheating in North America and part profile of a Kenyan woman who makes a living writing essays for university students in the United States, Britain and Australia, this article complicates the ethical landscape of contract cheating by detailing the prevalence of internet-based contract cheating, persuasive tactics employed by essay providers and economic factors that make essay writing an attractive career for college graduates in developing countries with few other job prospects.

Class begins with a discussion of what students took from the reading, which allows them to grapple with ethical issues raised in the article. The following questions are examples of conversation starters:

- Who works in this industry and why?
- Who uses essay-writing services and why?
- What did you think of the statistic that up to 7 per cent of undergraduates have turned in papers written by someone else? Do you think it is accurate? Do you know anyone who has turned in another person's writing as their own?
- What did the director of the academic integrity office mean when she said, 'If we don't do anything about it, we will turn every accredited university into a diploma mill'?

Such questions can prompt students to think about the competing interests surrounding contract cheating and draw their attention to the nuances of the moral debate, illustrating that contract cheating is not a straightforward issue of right and wrong but occurs within a greater sociopolitical context that influences both students' and essay writers' decisions.

Next, students view an excerpt from the university's academic integrity policy (quoted earlier) and are asked to consider whether the institutional policy properly addresses the kind of contract cheating described in the article. When I have implemented this exercise in my class, students have generally expressed that the practice of purchasing an essay as described in the article is not permissible, but they tend to be unsure which part of the policy applies to ghostwriting: whether it constitutes 'cheating', 'plagiarism' or another type of infraction. They are then invited to read a section from the Student Code of Conduct that lists potential disciplinary sanctions for academic integrity violations, which include expulsion, suspension, degree revocation or other administrative action. The intention is not to scare students but to help them realize that it is necessary to understand the difference between acceptable and unacceptable practice, so as not to unwittingly commit actions that could expose them to such repercussions.

Next, students are presented with several scenarios and asked to apply the institutional academic integrity policy to the best of their ability. Case-based scenarios can facilitate problem analysis and active problem-solving (Kreber, 2001) and have been employed to teach and assess students' understanding of academic self-regulation strategies (Lee, 2007) and plagiarism (Newton, 2016). For this lesson, I developed scenarios (see Appendix) based on findings regarding students' reasons for engaging in literacy brokering or cheating behaviours (Conrad, 2020; Newton, 2018). Each of the scenarios introduces a university student who has engaged in some type of literacy brokering. After reading each scenario, the class is asked whether they think each student's action is acceptable or unacceptable. Volunteers are called on to explain their reasoning. Though students may easily reach a consensus on some scenarios, such as the case of a student whose father helps her revise an essay, other scenarios may raise uncertainty. In these cases, students can be encouraged to articulate which part of the scenario they are struggling with. If they changed one variable in the scenario, such as the student–broker relationship or the aspect of payment, would that make the student's behaviour more or less acceptable? This kind of question can encourage further reflection.

The next part of the lesson is optional, depending on the instructor's judgement and course aims. After the group discussion, students break into groups, each of which is assigned to analyse the website of a different ghostwriting provider. As students examine their assigned website, they complete two tasks. First, using a chart, they record their observations of the website in one column (including images, words, links and multimodal features) and their inferences about the features they have observed in another column. Then, each group conducts a brief rhetorical analysis, examining how the observed features serve to market the website's services and convince readers of the acceptability of hiring a ghostwriter. Students are also asked to speculate on which audiences the arguments are likely to appeal to and how convincing they find the arguments. This type of inductive exercise can help students to identify a genre's features and critically relate them to its context and purpose (Devitt, 2009) while reinforcing their genre awareness and rhetorical consciousness (Tardy, 2019). By analysing these texts as they have practised with other genres, students come to recognize each website as an instance of a genre and are invited to reflect on how the websites position their audiences and, critically, how uptake might reinforce that positioning (see Emmons, 2009). As Devitt (2009) pointed out, gaining consciousness of a genre and how it functions can help students resist the ideologies that genre engenders – in this case, the belief that writing is a product to consume rather than a process in which to engage.

When they finish their analysis, the groups share their findings with the rest of the class. At this point, students may notice similar use of imagery and persuasive features among the different websites, which can lead to a discussion of the intended audience for these websites and why certain features may be employed in marketing to that audience. In my experience, this activity facilitates critical awareness of persuasive devices, including graphics and visual design as well as language, and thus piques students' interest; they recognize themselves as the target audience for these websites and take pride in not being fooled by the sites' rhetorical appeals. Instructors should be wary of using this activity if they suspect some of their students might find the websites' arguments convincing, however.

In the final activity, students work individually to reflect in writing on where to draw the line between acceptable and unacceptable behaviour when it comes to students' involvement of other people in their writing practices (see prompt in Appendix). Depending on the instructor's judgement, it might also be fruitful to ask students how this lesson would inform their decision of whether or how to involve others in their writing in the future. Adding such a question would allow an instructor to assess how students would apply their learning from this lesson, and students' responses could provide a shared basis for negotiation if they were suspected of engaging in unacceptable practices after this lesson.

These lesson activities can be integrated over one class period or two, depending on the amount of time available, and the final reflection can be completed in class or as homework. Either way, it is worthwhile to provide time for students to share highlights from their reflections after they have finished writing. In this final discussion, the instructor can share their own expectations, making clear, for example, whether direct correction of a text by another person would interfere with their ability to assess students' learning. One limitation of the scenarios is that they do not mention the intended learning outcomes for each student's assignment, which might change the acceptability of certain types of support. At this point, it would be worthwhile to discuss with students why certain forms of literacy brokering might be acceptable in some contexts but not others. If in doubt, students could be encouraged to ask their instructors which types of writing support they would allow or recommend.

Students' Responses

In this section I share several excerpts from students' written reflections as examples of the sorts of nuanced discussions of academic integrity and the social dimensions of academic writing that can emerge from this lesson. The responses come from students enrolled in an English 101 course in Fall 2019. In March 2020, I contacted students individually and obtained permission to quote from their written reflections in this chapter. Their responses are quoted verbatim, with notes added in brackets when necessary to obscure identifying details. All students are represented by pseudonyms.

Strong Reactions to Ghostwriting

Students' responses fell into multiple categories. First, several students reacted strongly to the idea of ghostwriting in particular. In several reflections, students drew on their observations of the ghostwriting services' websites they had analysed to reject the rhetoric those sites employed to justify use of their services.

> These websites claim to be 100% plagiarism free but paying a site to write a paper for you and then turning in as your own is a form of plagiarism. (Sarah)

Some students viewed contract cheating as a practice that would not just disgrace the perpetrating student but also cast a stain on the institution, reflecting points raised in Stockman and Mureithi's (2019) article:

> Not only is cheating a disservice to the student's own education, but it discredits the entire academic community, institutions and takes away credibility of other students who have dedicated years and countless sleepless nights to achieve something they find worthwhile in their life. (Rob)

Both in class and in their written responses, students tended to view ghostwriting as a dishonest, immoral practice that would have negative consequences not just for students but for the value of education at their institution. No student considered ghostwriting an acceptable practice.

Using Their Own Words

Though all students agreed that contracting another person to write on one's behalf is unacceptable, through this lesson they discovered for themselves that there is no easily identifiable boundary between acceptable and unacceptable practice (see, for example, Harwood, 2018, 2019; Harwood et al., 2010). Many students suggested that an acceptable level of third-party involvement should be judged on the basis of a student's original contribution to a text, which they often expressed in terms of whether the student had used 'their own words'. In response to the scenario about a student who paid for proofreading, Jonah wrote, 'to me that's not plagiarizing because they did write their thesis in their own words and they only went to a website to fix their grammatical errors'. Marie commented:

> I think the line should be drawn when the student was literally not involved in the writing process. I think the universities should consider are [sic] how much of the paper the student wrote themselves or if the student was just getting help and corrections.

These students' responses suggest that the inclusion of ghostwriting in this discussion as an extreme form of literacy brokering may have helped them to view third-party interventions along a spectrum from 'no third-party intervention' to 'no student involvement'. Somewhere in between, they suggested, was a point where students would write in 'their own words' and merely receive assistance in the form of 'fixing errors' or 'getting help and corrections'. Implicit in these responses is a sense that students cannot honestly claim authorship for work that did not originate 'in their own words'.

Distinction between Direct and Indirect Interventions

Along similar lines, some students distinguished between literacy brokers who make direct changes to a student's writing and those who make suggestions without implementing any changes directly to the text. A point of commonality among such responses was that students learn from implementing feedback on their texts.

> I do believe that a student can look for outside help in the form of suggestions or pointing out grammatical errors, but when it becomes where the 'outside help' actually fixes the essay themselves. It robs the student of learning how to write or what they need to work on, and suggestions allow the student to do critical thinking about what to change or include that will help make their essay more understandable. (Elliott)

> A student should not have people changing their essay or writing their essays for them, and the person getting involved should only be allowed to critique and suggest some changes, not do it themselves as the writer learns nothing. (Mark)

To these students, just as it is important to write in one's own words, it is also important to make one's own edits. A key theme in such responses was that revising their own work allows students to learn from their mistakes, and therefore a literacy broker's direct intervention would rob them of a learning opportunity.

Literacy Brokering versus Peer Review

Though peer review is not discussed as part of this lesson, numerous students drew a comparison between peer review and forms of literacy brokering that occur outside the classroom. Peer review is an essential component of FYW courses at this university and others, and in genre pedagogy, it 'is a key element of the scaffolding provided by the teacher to build learner confidence and the literacy resources to participate in target communities' (Hyland & Hyland, 2006, p. 83). At the point in the semester when this lesson was delivered, students had already participated in peer review twice. Through this process, they had learned that the purpose of peer review is not to correct each other's work but to stand in for the writer's target audience and provide suggestions that would help each other make effective choices to meet (or critically resist) readers' expectations for the assigned genre (see, for example, Yu, 2020). They were also given the opportunity to reflect on their level of agreement with their peers' suggestions and plan how they would incorporate or reject peer feedback as they revised their work.

When considering the literacy brokering scenarios, many students used peer review as a point of comparison. In response to a scenario about a student whose father edited a printout of her paper, Daniel wrote, 'This can be thought of as a form of peer review; instead of having another student or a help centre worker review her work, she used her dad, who is more knowledgeable on the topic'. Drawing a comparison between peer review and contract cheating, Emilio wrote:

> I believe if the student intends to have another person review their work then it should not be considered cheating. In this class, we had our classmates give us feedback on our writing and some of us took their suggestions or simply ignored their comments. However, when a student does not do their work and uses another person's work or a website . . . then it would be considered dishonest.

Though none of the literacy brokering scenarios involved peer review, these students' reflections suggest that they nevertheless used peer review as a standard for acceptable practice. Emilio's characterization of peer review also reflects his understanding that student authors have a choice in how they respond to peer review feedback, the implication being that a literacy broker who writes or implements edits on behalf of a student subverts the process of making choices about one's writing. Experiences of peer review thus helped students appreciate the difference between receiving feedback as part of the writing process and avoiding engagement in that process. More broadly, the students' tendency to compare literacy brokering practices to peer review also indicates their developing awareness of the collaborative and social aspects of academic writing practices, one of the overarching objectives of this course.

What Can Be Done to Curb Unacceptable Practice

Many students concluded their reflections by discussing how instructors and universities could handle students' use of literacy brokering. Some, for example, offered suggestions for instructors on how to detect and respond to suspected literacy brokering:

> The easiest way for universities and instructors to consider whether a student's actions are in violation of the [university] Code of Academic Integrity is knowing the student and how they write. If something doesn't seem like that student's work a question should arise. (Allie)

> It's my assumption that most students don't turn to cheating out of desire or even laziness but necessity due to unreasonable expectations. So, I believe it's in the best interest of colleges to closely inspect the course work and grading in

their classes; adopting more flexibility in assignments and especially consider the typical student workload and importance of assignments. Perhaps word counts or grammatical errors should carry less weight in grading as opposed to the general thought processes or goal the student attempts, particularly if the assignment isn't intended for publication. (Rob)

Some students also suggested that if universities provided better or different kinds of writing support, then students would not need to seek third-party help. For instance, after discussing what she learned from analysing a ghostwriting provider's website, Sarah reflected, 'I think that universities should make it easier for students that need help with their writing so that they don't have to resort to sites like this one.'

Discussion

Students' engagement in certain types of literacy brokering practices, especially those involving for-profit services, raises concern for many EAP and writing instructors (Turner, 2012) but is difficult to address due to a lack of relevant policy at many institutions of higher education (e.g. Harwood, 2019), as well as inevitable variation in which practices are considered acceptable in relation to different courses and contexts. This lesson, which is partly modelled on the use of case-study scenarios in plagiarism education and research (Newton, 2016), invites students to consider multiple forms of literacy brokering in relation to their sociopolitical contexts, challenges them to draw the line between acceptable and unacceptable practice and raises their awareness of the consequences of crossing that line. The lesson also complements a genre approach to university-level writing instruction by incorporating critical analysis of contract-cheating marketing materials as a genre (Devitt, 2009). As the excerpts from students' written reflections show, all students recognized certain practices as acceptable (support from friends or family) and others as unacceptable (ghostwriting), and many seemed to conceptualize the practices along a continuum from least to most third-party involvement. In some cases, they seemed more comfortable with the idea of students receiving support from informal literacy brokers than from professional ones (see Lillis & Curry, 2010). Many students drew on experiences of peer review to justify the acceptability of certain types of third-party interventions, which suggests their growing awareness of social aspects of academic writing that occur beyond the classroom.

At many institutions, academic integrity policies fall short of addressing which types of third-party interventions in student academic writing are acceptable. As a result, students may unwittingly engage in practices that their instructors disapprove of or even commit academic integrity violations (Conrad, 2019, 2020). Therefore, where institutional policy is insufficient, it is incumbent upon instructors to develop classroom expectations in alignment with their own values, as well as institutional and disciplinary conventions, and to communicate those expectations clearly to students. The aim of the lesson presented here is to provide instructors with tools for helping students to understand the many considerations that go into developing such expectations.

Appendix

Literacy Brokering Scenarios and Reflection Prompt

1. Joey is a senior studying mechanical engineering. He is taking five classes in addition to working at [local restaurant], and he plans to graduate this semester. Joey is struggling to understand the readings in one of his courses and doesn't think he can write a final paper that will earn a passing grade, but he needs the credit to graduate. Looking online for help, he finds a website that will write an essay to his professor's specifications. Joey decides to buy a paper, reasoning that he can make a few changes to personalize the essay before submitting it, and his professor will never know. Is Joey's choice acceptable? Why or why not?

2. Amy is a first-year student from [city of institution] who lives on campus but goes home on weekends. Amy has a paper due in her history class next week. While she's home, she asks her dad, who is a high school teacher, to read her paper and correct it for her. Amy's dad prints a copy of Amy's paper and proofreads it with a red pen, pointing out errors and making word-choice suggestions. Then Amy edits her paper based on his feedback and hands it in. Is it acceptable for Amy to get her dad's help on her paper? Why or why not?

3. Natalia is an international student from Russia who has just finished writing her master's thesis. Natalia's research supervisor has told her that her thesis, which is 115 pages long, contains many grammatical errors, and he wants her to get it edited before she submits it. Natalia does not know anyone willing to edit her whole thesis, but she finds an online editing service that will correct the errors for her within three days for

about $1000. Is it acceptable for Natalia to pay this service to edit her thesis? Why or why not?

Overall reflection: Where should universities draw the line between acceptable and unacceptable behaviour when it comes to students involving other people in their writing practices? What are some of the factors instructors and universities should consider when deciding whether a student's behaviour is an academic integrity violation?

3

Moving from Form to Function

Leveraging SFL Metalanguage to Illuminate Features and Functions of Texts in First-Year University EAP

Jennifer Walsh Marr

Introduction

EAP instructors are key mediators in guiding international students through university. To be successful, EAP instructors need to incorporate sound pedagogy, disciplinary knowledge, relevant assessments and a deep understanding of language (BALEAP, 2008). That deep understanding of language can be significantly enhanced by systemic functional linguistics (SFL); this chapter shares how an experienced EAP instructor encountered SFL in a new teaching context, the realizations SFL afforded and some resulting teaching materials.

The discussion and examples that follow are from materials I developed in collaboration with colleagues for an arts-specific academic writing course at Vantage College, a programme within the University of British Columbia in Canada in which international students develop their academic literacy and English language skills concomitant with their first year of study. The students' linguistic development is supported by the Academic English Program (AEP), which adopted an SFL-informed genre-pedagogical approach from the outset (Ferreira & Zappa-Hollman, 2019). When I joined the nascent AEP faculty in 2014, few of us had any SFL knowledge, and there were few teaching materials to mentor us, particularly at the tertiary level. This chapter shares some of what I've learned, distilled and presented to students.

SFL is a multilayered, comprehensive description of language. It describes not only ideas (the field) but the relations between interactants and information (tenor), and the manner in which it is conveyed (the mode). These are realized by the experiential, interpersonal and textual metafunctions, respectively. SFL is described as 'a very useful descriptive and interpretive framework for viewing language as a strategic meaning-making resource' (Eggins, 2004, p. 2). Its major claims are that language use is functional in order to make meanings, and those meanings are both influenced by and influential upon the context (Eggins, 2004; Halliday & Matthiessen, 2004). While rich (if not 'extravagant' (Moore, 2007, p. 55)) in its theory, metalanguage and layers of detail, Halliday posits that essentially language is a semiotic meaning-making system that draws from a range of options to communicate, and that communication and context are dialogic.

This is a departure from my previous form-focused teaching contexts, where grammatical form was prioritized over purpose. A major shift is that form *follows* function: to assist students in their meaning-making with linguistic options available to achieve communication goals. Judicious deployment of SFL metalanguage with students has served as a lens through which to focus on what is happening in a text and how language makes it happen. A particularly helpful quote to ground this approach is from Derewianka's (2011) pedagogically focused, SFL grammar text for teachers:

> When introducing students to grammar from a functional perspective, it is not always a matter of whether something is 'right' or 'wrong' but whether students find the metalanguage useful for exploring the meaning of the text. (p. 14)

We use a curated selection of metalanguage to help define, recognize and refer to features while practising deconstructing exemplar texts and preparing our own. The snapshots shared here are in response to comments from disciplinary colleagues about student writing, either to me directly or in the margins of assignments brought to tutorials. As revision is an inevitable stage of writing, here I attempt to illuminate how some SFL theory and metalanguage can clarify what to do with frustrating feedback EAP students often encounter in their writing, and how SFL-informed EAP instruction can prepare students with a heightened awareness of contextualized language use.

'This Doesn't Sound Academic'

Students often say they need to develop 'professional' vocabulary, and teachers wrestle with the role of jargon, but realizing the phenomenon of nominalization is perhaps the biggest value-added SFL has brought to my EAP practice. Nominalization is a central feature of academic texts in which 'processes, and the qualities and properties both of process and things, are reconstructed as if they were things' (Kazemian et al., 2013, p. 151). This shift from verb to noun (nominalization) facilitates 'encapsulating' (p. 164) sometimes complicated actions or processes into nouns that can be held still and studied as concepts themselves. This can make all the difference whether writing sound 'academic' or not, helping achieve the first three characteristics Liardét (2018) describes:

> the language of academic discourse is characterised as abstract, having high lexical density, elaborated nominal groups, impersonal modality and objective evaluation that projects an authoritative stance to a non-interacting audience. (Halliday, 1993, Schleppegrell, 2001, 2004, in Liardét, 2018, p. 65)

Nominalization allows academic writers to 'pack up' ideas into more lexically dense, abstract concepts, representing more sophisticated vocabulary choices associated with academic success (Douglas, 2013). But beyond being a list of random academic words, we teach nominalization as a process and part of the larger phenomenon of grammatical metaphor (Halliday & Matthiessen, 2004).

Grammatical Metaphor

Instead of concepts being manipulated for the sake of imagery, as in literary metaphor, in grammatical metaphor the concept is kept consistent while its grammatical features and role shifts; for example a characteristic described by an adjective such as 'premature' might shift into a prepositional phrase 'before expected', maintaining its meaning while manifesting as another grammatical form. Nominalization is a specific type of grammatical metaphor, one that can also shift a concept from concrete to abstract. Across the disciplines, academic texts are likely to describe, study and discuss the implications of nominalized phenomena such as 'evaporation', 'consumerism' and 'citizenship' rather than just describe what individual actors *do*. Those phenomena are typically elaborated through pre- and post-modification within an expanded noun group that can function as a subject or object of a clause; functional grammar calls these participants, regardless of where they occur and are underlined in the following student-facing examples:

> Evaporation in food processing has enabled reductions in shipping and storage requirements.
> Mass consumerism in the modern era has led to increased environmental degradation.
> Scientists advocate for increased scientific literacy to improve democracy and citizenship.

Teaching Nominalization

My lectures acknowledge the challenging vocabulary prevalent in students' academic texts and break down the phenomenon of nominalization into related components. Where highly nominalized noun groups can seem abstract and removed from reality, the process of 'unpacking' the information they contain brings them closer to students' existing knowledge bases and help expand their linguistic repertoires.

We work through this step by step. First we identify the 'head noun' of a noun group: 'What's the central idea?' and 'If we replaced the noun group with the pronoun "it" or "they", what would it be referring to?' In the example '<u>An increasing food shortage in developing countries</u> threatens <u>economic stability</u>', the head noun of the first noun group (subject participant) is 'shortage'. To shift this head noun into a verb, we ask, 'What's happening?' or 'What does this mean?' Appropriate verbal groups include 'not have enough' or 'lack'. We note this shortage is 'increasing' or 'becoming more or larger'. Other characteristics include its type (it is a 'food shortage') and location (it is happening 'in developing countries'). We can represent the first noun group, unpacked, as '*Residents in developing countries do not have enough food, and the problem is getting worse.*' We check: which sounds more academic? That, or 'an increasing food shortage in developing countries'?

We also note that our unpacked, denominalized version has a new subject: 'residents'. When nominalizing, it is common to lose some information, sometimes through wilful omission. Writers don't always include who is doing what, reminding us of academic language's impersonal, objective features. When developing critical reading skills, however, looking for erased peoples or agents through the process of unpacking dense, abstract nominalizations gives students insight into who is included and/or erased from texts.

A focus on meaning, whether present, omitted or assumed, can extend from grand abstractions to small details; lessons on affixation focus on the underlying meaning, not just the grammatical category they represent. Noun suffixes useful in nominalization include '-tion' representing a process (*valuation* as the process of determining the value of something), '-ship' a relation or condition (*membership* is the condition of belonging or being a member of a group) and '-ism' a belief or practice such as *consumerism*.

Lessons on nominalization draw students' attention to it and give it a name. This helps novice scholars and language learners recognize this key feature of written academic discourse and build repertoires of key terms in their disciplines.

We also acknowledge that denser, more nominalized language choices are not always better; as with all language choices, context matters. Demonstrating gradual condensation of meaning and lexical density allows students to see some of the distinct shifts of grammatical metaphor. We also look for patterns, as texts that discuss a phenomenon might introduce it with a dense nominalization (perhaps in the topic sentence), unpack it and discuss distinct characteristics through the body of a paragraph, and then return to a denser nominalization when summarizing the concept and introducing a new piece of argument (Pessoa et al., 2017), perhaps in a closing sentence. The following examples show options moving from 'less academic' concrete representations to more metaphoric, nominalized versions:

> Agricultural activities need lots of land and water and this demand is increasing.
> The land and water demands of agricultural activities is increasing.
> Increasing agricultural demands for land and water . . .
> Agricultures' increasing water and land demands . . .

Depending on the context, it may be more or less important to sound a certain way, as writers need facility in 'shunting from everyday to technical or vice versa' (Irwin & Liu, 2019, p. 1). A practice task is to have students arrange excerpts from least to most metaphoric, identify the changes made from one form to another and then deploy those same shifts to another excerpt in the service of paraphrasing (Walsh Marr, 2019).

'This Text Doesn't Flow'

In talking about planning texts and connecting ideas, students receive two similar texts to compare:

Paragraph 1:

> Many consumers remain unaware of the consequences associated with their food purchasing habits. Cultural trends towards consumerism and high levels of disposable income cause overspending and overbuying. Buyers with a higher income can now afford to spend lots of money on food; they don't view wasted food as a significant personal loss. They can simply afford to replace it. The apparent abundance and availability of produce means these consumers can take food for granted. Consumers remain generally uninformed about the worries and concerns that the food supply industry faces. (Nance et al., 2017)

Paragraph 2:

> Many consumers remain unaware of the consequences associated with their food purchasing habits. Members of modern society are overspending and overbuying due to cultural trends towards consumerism and higher levels of disposable incomes. Buyers with a higher income can now afford to spend lots of money on food; they don't view wasted food as a significant personal loss as they can simply afford to replace it. These consumers often take the apparent abundance and availability of produce for granted. Consumers remain generally uninformed about the worries and concerns that the food supply industry faces. (Nance et al., 2017)

I ask which one is easier to follow, which one 'flows' better. (Most) students choose the second paragraph but aren't sure why.

The concept of 'Theme' or 'starting point' of a clause is the underlying concept and piece of metalanguage here. The information writers start their clauses with establishes the focus and direction of the text, and is developed through thematic choices in subsequent clauses. This starting information is typically known to the reader (because it's common knowledge or previously introduced) and can be developed through careful arrangements through a text. 'Theme' includes all the information up to the central verb (or, in SFL, the 'process') of the clause and is most commonly the subject/participant (Halliday & Matthiessen, 2004).

Separating out the Themes from the sentences in the first paragraph, I show students how they bump somewhat jarringly back and forth between concrete 'consumers' (and the pronoun 'they' to represent them) and more abstract, elaborated nominalizations of 'trends' and 'abundance and availability':

> Many consumers
> Cultural trends towards consumerism and high levels of disposable income
> Buyers with a higher income
> They
> They
> The apparent abundance and availability of produce
> Consumers

The second paragraph, however, maintains a more consistent focus on the consumer with a constant Theme pattern and various synonyms:

> Many consumers
> Members of modern society
> Buyers with a higher income
> They

These consumers
Consumers

We can see how in the following paragraph, while it, too, contains much of the same information, its focus is different through rearranging what information starts the clause:

Paragraph 3:

> The consequences associated with food purchasing habits are often unknown to consumers. However, overspending and overbuying are the result of cultural trends towards consumerism and higher levels of disposable incomes. Lots of money is spent on food by buyers with a higher income. Wasted food does not feel like a significant personal loss since it can be replaced by these buyers. The apparent abundance and availability of produce is often taken for granted, and the worries and concerns that the food supply industry faces is not generally understood. (Nance et al., 2017)

While simple, the second and third paragraphs flowed more smoothly than the first, serving to highlight the phenomenon and impact of Theme. We then expand our attention to the second section of the clause: the 'Rheme'. As Alexander (2019) succinctly states, 'Theme typically answers the question: what are we talking about. Rheme answers the question: what are we saying about it' (p. 3). As we push students to write more sophisticated texts, we move away from monotonous, constant Theme patterns (though useful in introductions) to 'sequential progression, in which sub-topics arise from previous Rhemes' (Alexander, 2019, p. 5) (Table 3.1).

Separating out the clauses as in Table 3.1 helps students see how information introduced in the Rheme shows up in the subsequent Theme, no longer 'new' information. The Theme of the first clause establishes the overall context of setting up community gardens and then the Rheme articulates that there are

Table 3.1 Theme and Rheme

Theme	Rheme
Those interested in starting community gardens	face certain hurdles.
One hurdle	is addressing soil-quality issues such soil compaction, contamination, and low fertility.
These soil issues	underscore the importance of site assessment protocols for areas that are to be turned into community gardens (UBC: The Centre for Sustainable Food Systems Teaching & Learning Team).

hurdles to doing so. 'Hurdles' is the Theme of the subsequent clause, which then specifies soil as a type of problem in its Rheme. The subsequent Theme summarizes the three types of soil problems introduced in the previous Rheme, ending with a Rheme that makes an argument for site assessment protocols to enable success in establishing community gardens. This is called a 'linear' Theme pattern, where information zigzags from the end of one sentence to the start of the next and develops the discussion in a more sophisticated manner.

In the following example from teaching materials, we see a more realistic combination of Theme patterns, both constant and linear, as well as derived, in which concepts introduced in a Rheme are dispersed and developed in separate Themes distributed through the text. Students are tasked with identifying where 'urban farms', 'community gardens' and 'health benefits' appear:

> Urban farms and community gardens provide many benefits to city-dwellers. Here, the term community garden is defined as a garden that has been developed on land to which communities have legally been granted access and have a governance system and a structure that has been decided and agreed upon by the community; urban farm refers to a food-growing commercial enterprise located within a city's limits. Community gardens and urban farms provide local sources of produce that has not traveled long distances using large amounts of fossil fuels; they also provide spaces that allow citizens to strengthen social interactions, encourage physical activity, beautify the neighborhoods, and much more (Alaimo, Reischl, & Allen, 2010). Community gardens and urban farms also provide opportunities for people to learn how to grow food. People who grow their own food not only have better access to fresh produce, but are also more likely to adopt a healthier diet (Alaimo, Packnett, Miles, & Kruger, 2008). These health benefits are further evidence that community gardens enhance life for urban residents not only socially and physically but nutritionally as well. (University of British Columbia: The Centre for Sustainable Food Systems Teaching & Learning Team, 2018)

The topic sentence introduces the major foci of the paragraph and makes the claim that 'community gardens' and 'urban farming' are benefits to people living in cities. Through constant Theme patterning, each term is first defined and then described with their benefits. A shift to linear (zigzag) Theme pattern happens with the third benefit (learning to grow food), as it reappears in the subsequent Theme with some causal effects of growing one's own food in the Rheme. The closing sentence summarizes the argument of the health benefits of urban farming and community gardens, derived from the Rheme of the topic sentence.

We connect our attention to Theme patterns to the purposes of texts and how more sophisticated genres deploy more complicated language choices. In the fourth paragraph on the benefits of urban agriculture, we see how simpler, background information (definition and description) is built through a constant Theme pattern, with a shift to linear as the clauses explain, and then a derived pattern as the text ends with argument.

Our teaching materials start with the excerpt comparison, interrogating which example 'flows' better, then introducing the concept of Theme. The process of separating out clauses, underlining and colour-coding the Themes (and any connected Rhemes) eases the exemplification of the concept and typical patterns.

More critical, attention-raising tasks include throwing in clauses with redundant or disconnected information into a complete paragraph and asking students to pick it out, as well as having students choose which version of a subsequent sentence best connects to the previous through alternatives in Theme patterns (Alexander, 2019).

Guided co-construction of texts offers the opportunity to brainstorm the content of a new text, to sort the information in broad strokes, then more carefully arrange information within the clauses through Theme and Rheme manipulation. Introductory information that is typically listed suits a constant Theme pattern. Critical questions such as 'how?', 'why?', 'where?' prompt Rheme expansion through causal expressions, non-finite clauses and prepositional phrases. We discuss the implications of taking a text in a new direction through those Rheme choices and also exemplify some of the mechanisms for 'fronting' information for Theme choice.

One of most common ways of summarizing a discussion to move an argument forward is through nominalization of a Theme (Pessoa et al., 2017), allowing the writer to encapsulate the key concept. We ask our students to look at thematized participants and determine if they are specific examples or summary terms of a category; we highlight how the starting point for claims are typically thematized abstractions as academic writers 'do not depart from our own experience, but from our considered generalizations about people, situations, causes' (Eggins, 2004, p. 323).

We saw this in the closing sentence of the fourth excerpt previously, where the Rhemes of having better access to fresh produce and adopting a healthier diet were represented by an abstract summary noun in the closing sentence's Theme: 'these health benefits . . .'. Putting such noun groups in the subject position can also use passive voice to swap the Theme and Rheme, as seen in the third paragraph. This paragraph shifts the focus from individual, concrete consumers (paragraph 2) to the more abstract 'consequences associated with food purchasing habits' by putting it into Theme position. We challenge the simplistic writing advice to avoid the passive voice, demonstrating how passive voice has a relevant role in prioritizing focus and determining direction of texts.

Introductory lessons use noun groups as Theme as these are most common and help maintain the focus of a text. However, we show how examples of 'marked' or unusual Themes can prioritize shifts in logic: starting with a prepositional phrase (i.e. 'in this case, . . .') narrows the focus, and fronted dependent clauses ('Because of consumer demand, . . .') are markers of academic writing, as they 'indicate[s] an amount of pre-planning that is less common in spoken than written language' (Eggins, 2004, p. 323). Other marked themes such as transitional terms can indicate attitude ('interestingly'), sequence ('thus far') and/or logic ('however'). In the following excerpt, 'however' shifts away from the previous constant Theme to take the text in a new direction:

> The consequences associated with food purchasing habits are often unknown to consumers. However, overspending and overbuying are the result of cultural trends towards consumerism and higher levels of disposable incomes.

We warn our students, however, that more explicit transitional phrases do not necessarily make for better writing. Careful thematic arrangement can make tedious 'first, second, finally' markers redundant, giving students an additional means of arranging participants' more nuanced relations to one another.

The lessons' metalanguage is fairly limited to Theme and Rheme and their role in organizing information within the textual metafunction. However, we can also see the overlap of metafunctions, where nominalized participants and logical connectors from the experiential metafunction are deployed to develop the 'texture' of a passage. We also see limited examples of the interpersonal positioning metafunction with attitudinal adjuncts ('surprisingly') as marked Themes, positioning the author in relation to the text and/or reader.

For students, the focus here is to showcase how the terms Theme and Rheme give insight into how information can be arranged within and between clauses to improve ease of reading and purposeful development of texts.

'You Need to Analyze, Not Just Regurgitate'

The student-facing examples shared thus far have highlighted nominalization and Theme patterns in academic writing; to save verbs until last here is almost heretical, as it is the verb that indicates what's happening. However, to most of us, verbs are verbs. They are actions, what happens. But by asking students 'What's happening?' in excerpts, we open up discussion of the different *process types* (SFL's term for verbs and verbal groups) that give important insight into a clause, text and representation of meaning.

The following excerpts have their processes bolded; the student task is to identify what type of activity each one represents, and what each excerpt does: describes and explains or makes an argument:

> Although global food crop production **is** sufficient to meet worldwide demand, the current distribution of resources **is** inequitable. Protective legislation **has restricted** farmers' access to fairly priced seeds and **encouraged** cash crops. Economists **argue** that intellectual property rights (IRPs) **are** a key barrier to food security. Inadequate access and protection **leave** countries without IRPs vulnerable to fluctuations in market conditions and weather. (Durnin-Vermette et al., 2016)

> Some places in the world **produce** excess food crops; however, there **are** still people in the world who go hungry. Because of various regulations and prices, there **is** an imbalance of production and need. Rich countries **have created** laws that protect certain crops and their seeds. Farmers **must pay** extra for protected seeds, but they **choose to grow** crops which will give them the largest profit. Bad weather and market conditions also **impact** farmers' profits. Farmers **claim** that the government **should pay for** research to develop new crops and **subsidise** operating expenses. (Durnin-Vermette et al., 2016)

Students recognize that the first excerpt represents deeper analysis and argumentation but not how or why. While there is a role for nominalization, it is the type of process at the centre of each clause that illuminates what is happening, whether it is an action, a thought, a definition, a statement, a relation or just an existence. Key is the relationship between processes and overall purposes of texts; if the assignment is to describe and explain, the second excerpt satisfies this. It summarizes what exists and what has happened. There is little evidence of authorial analysis, and in certain contexts, this detachment may be appreciated as being objective. In our arts courses, however, student texts such as these can be derided as 'regurgitation', essentially re-presenting information without analysis. The first excerpt synthesizes what exists and related causal factors into a claim in its first sentence: that 'the current distribution of [food] resources is inequitable'. Our lessons focus on the role verbs play and how can those seemingly simple 'be' verbs do so much heavy lifting towards satisfying analytical purpose.

It is essential for EAP lessons to discuss the prevalence and importance of what 'is' in academic writing; what types of processes verbs represent, and how types interact with one another to satisfy the purpose of the author and context. SFL terms this analysis of what's happening *transitivity*: who is doing what to whom under what circumstances (Butt et al., 2000, p. 46). Transitivity is more than just a verb type as listed in dictionaries; instead, SFL considers transitivity 'a system of describing the whole clause' (Thompson, 1996, p. 78) and representing 'realms of experience' (Moore, 2007, p. 53), be they actions manifest in the outside world, inner thoughts and reflections or states of being. The role (or process type) of an individual verb can shift depending on how it functions in context and can shed insight on the type of action underlying the clause. We share the following classic example from Butt et al. (2000, p. 52) that demonstrates the verb *feel* as different process types across different contexts:

> I felt the wood and decided it needed more sanding: an action manifest in the outside world
> I felt that I was at a crossroads in my life: an inner reflection
> I felt tired: a state of being

Admittedly, while we don't task our EAP students to write about sanding wood, we do use these examples to reinforce the importance of context, highlight some of the different types of processes that exist and serve as a springboard for investigating what's actually happening in the texts students read and are expected to generate.

Moving from 'Who's Doing What to Whom' to 'What Is It and What Does It Mean?'

Referring back to the excerpts earlier in this section, we show how subtle differences in two paragraphs have an impact on text purpose; the second excerpt relied on Material, Existential and Verbal processes that limited it to description. The verbal groups *produce, have created, must pay, choose to grow*,[1] *impact, should pay for* and *subsidise* all represent Material processes, actions (or results) that are observable in the outside world. This is the largest group that students associate with the simple definition of verbs as actions and is typically

---

[1] In this case, *grow* is what is happening; the aspect of *choice* (to grow) 'elaborates the unfolding of the Process' (Martin et al., 2010, p. 114) and can be considered as pre-modification of what's actually happening in the same way that modal verbs such as *should, might, will*, etc., do.

manifest in progressive tenses unless it is a habitual event (i.e. *the sun rises in the east*).

Claim is a Verbal process, communicating the inside world of thinking through language. *There is* and *there are* simply confirm the existence of something with an Existential process.

What this paragraph does is describe actions and what exists, mostly observable to all in the 'outside world'. While it is grammatically accurate, it is missing definitions, attributes and cognitive engagement with deeper meaning of what the actions and existence *mean:* that would represent analysis and better represent academic engagement where synthesis and interpretation of meaning is valued. Distinguishing and then making the connection between process types and their role in satisfying assignment expectations is the lesson.

We highlight how the first paragraph excerpt demonstrates synthesis and analysis in its first sentence, 'Although global food crop production **is** sufficient to meet worldwide demand, the current distribution of resources **is** inequitable.' It makes its claim with the 'be' verb functioning as an Attributive Relational Process; it establishes the attributes (or characteristics) of the two participants (food production = sufficient and distribution = inequitable) in direct relation to one another. We note how the author has used nominalization to synthesize meaning from what happens and positioned these participants through evaluation ('sufficient' yet 'inequitable'). The next move is similar to the descriptive paragraph, using the same Material processes (actions), explaining the impacts of protective legislation. However, because the topic sentence establishes a claim at the outset, the subsequent supporting sentences function as evidence for the claim, rather than merely additional descriptive information.

These Relational processes are prevalent yet easily overlooked in EAP instruction. How hard can the verb 'to be' actually be? Perhaps more important to consider is its meanings and prevalence. The previous paragraph hinted at the important relationship between grammatical metaphor, abstraction and process types. In the section on nominalization, we 'unpacked' the dense noun groups by asking 'what happened?'; this demonstrates the movement away from describing what happens in the 'here and now' (often represented by Material processes) to abstracted, internalized processes, representing synthesis and analysis of ideas in relation to one another. We revisit these features in a spiral curriculum to highlight their interaction and to reinforce the connection between lexicogrammatical features and meaning-making.

Our teaching materials make plain: Relational processes are not action verbs. Instead, they serve 'to signal the existence of the relationship' (Thompson,

1996, p. 86) of a participant and its characteristics. They are 'how we create links between bits of information', 'typically to describe, exemplify, classify or define' things (Derewianka, 2011, pp. 15–16). We distinguish between the two subcategories of Relational processes: Attributive and Identifying, both of which are 'different ways of referring to the same entity' (Thompson, 1996, p. 87). Attributive Relational Processes *describe* the attributes of an entity, often with an adjective as the second participant in the process ('global food crop production is **sufficient**', 'distribution of resources is **inequitable**'). When those adjectives are evaluative, they position the author's stance and help make their claim. Making this feature explicit to our students enables them to better satisfy tasks that expect synthesis and analysis, rather than regurgitation.

The second type of Relational process is more specialized; Identifying Relational Processes serves to identify the unique characteristics of a participant, distinguishing it from all others. This is very important in the context of definitions, establishing the parameters of academic discussions of terms and theories in the early stages of papers and prevalent in short answer questions on final exams. Identifying relational clauses can reverse the participants without changes in meaning:

> Food deserts are socially deprived areas within cities that have poor access to food retailers.
>
> Socially deprived areas within cities that have poor access to food retailers are known as food deserts. (Beaumont et al., 1995)

We consistently prioritize the function over the form – 'be' verbs describe as Attributive Relational Processes, or they define as Identifying Relational Processes; it depends on the usage. These relational processes may also take different forms beyond 'be' – in the previous example, the passive synonym 'be known as' achieves the same purpose. The major teaching point here is that in certain contexts, this level of detail is actually important to the success of a text; if a definition is required to articulate which concept is being discussed, a description that merely 'talks around' a term without actually defining it will impede its success (Walsh Marr et al., 2021). This highlights the relevance of asking if a clause is defining or describing and whether that satisfies the expectations of context.

In addition to Material processes (actions evident in the 'outside world'), Existential processes (what exists) and Relational processes (Attributive that describe and Identifying that define), we touch on the SFL process categories Verbal (for communicating or 'saying'), Mental (for thinking, feeling and desire) and Behavioural (acting on our inner thoughts). What is important to incorporate into EAP instruction is that these process types represent different types of actions, follow patterns of usage and are valued differently across contexts.

For example, in the methods section of a research report describing actions, we would expect to see mostly Material processes in the past tense to recount actions. In a narrative, Material processes are common until the complication stage (Humphrey et al., 2011), where the scene is often summarized and described with an Attributive Relational Process ('Everything was fine . . .') before taking a turn towards more actions ('. . . until the heavens opened'), including Verbal and Behavioural processes (Eggins, 2004). Reflective tasks rely on Mental processes to represent beliefs and understandings; reviews rely heavily on Verbal processes to report what others have written and said.

What we teach to our students is to appreciate that there are patterns of verb usage, in location, form and purpose, with some more valued in certain academic discourses than others. The guidance we give students is to interrogate what the overall purpose of a text is, and what stages and features help it achieve that purpose (Eggins, 2004). We encourage students to look at what happens in the texts they are reading and to confirm the types of processes that are used. For writing assignments, it is important to confirm what is expected: are they to describe, explain, argue or persuade, and then return to exemplar disciplinary texts to see how other authors accomplish this. Understanding what is happening in a text gives students insight into the valued processes of academic writing.

Discussion and Conclusion

The resources presented here were developed by an experienced EAP instructor previously unfamiliar with SFL. They represent a distillation of theoretical and pedagogical literature, collegial peer review and recontextualization for students' needs. They represent some 'hero moves' of functional grammar to supplement a previously form-focused EAP repertoire. There is much more to SFL beyond the scope of this chapter. The multiple, interconnected layers of SFL are both a testament to its rigour and an intimidating barrier.

It remains a barrier partly due to its unfamiliarity to many EAP instructors coming from traditional, form-focused educational contexts. There are few SFL-informed teaching materials for tertiary EAP contexts demonstrating how it has actually been employed in the classroom. To further confound access and engagement, the multiple layers of professional responsibilities EAP instructors inhabit, often in the tenuous margins of academia, manifest in a 'third space' precarity (Breshears, 2019; MacDonald, 2016) with little room for reconceptualizations of language off the sides of our desks.

The examples here are drawn from our student-facing materials that cite the research that informs them. They model academic referencing and rely on deconstructing exemplar texts, sometimes through comparison. Instead of the decontextualized presentation of a grammar feature, guiding questions interrogate the text's purpose, its success and its features. The deconstruction of texts draws from Martin and Rose's (2005) Teaching and Learning Cycle, incorporating Rothery and Stenglin's (1994) early work supporting literacy development. It is further enabled by Caplan's (2019) simplified revision of textual deconstruction questions to facilitate disciplinary faculty, EAP and ultimately students' 'control over and a critical orientation to how authors construct the genre' (Martin & Rose, 2005, p. 252).

These 'fine-grained analyses that highlight the use of linguistic features in particular social or disciplinary contexts' (Ding & Bruce, 2017, p. 69) represent the value-added of SFL for my EAP practice. The explicit connection between a text's purpose, context and lexicogrammatical features has helped me show students *how* texts achieve (or fail) their purpose. In trying to make our students' writing 'more successful', we need to have the language to make clear what that entails. While grammatical errors can be easier for highly proficient language users to catch, focusing on this superficial layer of language shouldn't prevent attention to deeper layers of meaning and choices.

These deeper realizations also serve a larger goal of academic literacy, propelling our students' success beyond accuracy and compliance to developing more varied linguistic resources to be deployed critically. With an enhanced awareness of the functions of language, particularly of the implications of some language choices, we can empower students' critical knowledge of language and language usage.

Acknowledgement

This work and my professional development have been significantly enhanced through collaboration with Sarah Lynch and Tanya Tervit.

4

EAP Pedagogies for Doctoral Students in Professional Fields

Kristin Solli and Tom Muir

Introduction

> After a while it's interesting with the theories and it's interesting with everything happening up here. And also I'm sitting here at OsloMet, so I'm in an environment that's . . . we're talking about lots of stuff . . . . so I was afraid that it would sort of tear me away from the [PhD topic's] origins. (Beatrice, PhD candidate)

Beatrice worked for ten years in a professional field – social work – before becoming a PhD candidate. She explains here the tension she feels between 'the theories' and 'everything happening up here' at the university and 'the origins', her professional field. This tension is typical of many of the PhD candidates we have met in our EAP work with doctoral students at our university, which has a profile in applied sciences and professions such as nursing, social work and teaching. Underlying this tension is the fact that no professional doctorate has been developed in Norway – there are no practitioner research-based PhD programmes, meaning that even a candidate who wants to conduct research on a field of practice is inducted into a very traditional academic PhD programme. There is, then, no automatic transmission route for the research back to the field and no way for the candidate to comfortably inhabit the roles of practitioner and researcher at the same time, which, we argue, complicates the 'identity work' of the PhD (Kamler & Thomson, 2014) and the pedagogies we might bring to that work as EAP practitioners.

The idea of identity change during doctoral candidature is well documented in the literature on doctoral writing. It has been figured as journeys (Barnacle & Mewburn, 2010; Wisker, 2016), transitions (Castelló et al., 2013), transformations (Lassig et al., 2013) and 'becoming' (Barnacle, 2005; Lee, 2010 and 2011). Some of the key pedagogical perspectives on doctoral writing similarly connect writing to changes in identity: from student to scholar, from novice to expert or from practitioner to researcher. Kamler and Thomson's (2014) articulation of the connection between 'identity work' and 'textual work' locates writing as the site where such transformations happen: 'When doctoral students write', Kamler and Thomson argue, 'they are producing themselves as a scholar' (2014, p. 17).

Much of current pedagogical literature on doctoral writing, then, presents approaches that support such production of a scholarly identity – clearing the path from 'the origins' to 'up here', to use Beatrice's words. We find the connections this literature makes between textual work and identity work and the emphasis on transformation very useful in our work with doctoral writers. And yet, with many of the doctoral students we met in our writing classes, this path seemed more winding and fraught. Like Beatrice, many of our students come from extensive careers in a professional field and their research focuses on professional practice. Their PhD programmes, however, prime them for traditional research, and most of them write a thesis by publication consisting of research articles that communicate with researchers. Many of our students seemed to share Beatrice's regret or worry about being detached from the work's origin, the professional field. This worry suggests the importance of some things to be preserved, as much as transformed, by doctoral work for this particular group of students.

Having recently conducted an interview-based study with PhD candidates in professional fields, this chapter finds us looking both back and forward. Our conversations with students like Beatrice have made us consider what our current pedagogies might be missing. More specifically, we have started to think about what pedagogical responses might be possible when there is a need for preservation as much as transformation? Our looking backward and forward has prompted us to look for ways to take these students' ambivalence about doctoral identity change seriously, rather than considering it something that must be overcome for successful doctoral transformation to happen.

In what follows, we begin with an overview of some of the central work on doctoral writing that informs our pedagogies. We continue by briefly summarizing the study we mentioned above as a way of getting a clearer sense of the writing experiences of the PhD students coming to doctoral education from professional fields in our own context. We then describe our semester-long academic writing course (AWC) where we meet the kind of doctoral students that participated in our study in the classroom. In this description, we use some of the findings from our study to pause at key moments in the course to wonder what was left untouched or ambivalent for these candidates. These pauses take the form of three questions, each emerging from an aspect of the course:

audience awareness, rhetorical positioning and imitation. We then suggest some possible paths forward, pedagogies that might – as we have said – make use of ambivalence and uncertainty as pedagogical resources rather than treating them as problems to be overcome. Thus, our project in this chapter is not to present a 'best practice' case or a model course; it is to reflect on a pedagogical challenge and start exploring what our pedagogies could become.

Doctoral Writing Pedagogies in the Changing Landscape of Doctoral Education

Over the last several decades, doctoral education worldwide has changed profoundly. Two of the most important changes are that PhD-holders increasingly work outside the academy and that sectors such as industry and commerce increasingly look towards academia for solutions to sector-specific challenges (Andres et al., 2015; Boud & Lee, 2009; Thomson & Walker, 2010). In many contexts – but, as we emphasized in the introduction earlier, not ours – various versions of work-based doctorates, professional doctorates, industry-PhDs and practice-based doctorates have emerged as alternatives to the traditional PhD (Boud & Lee, 2009; Thomson & Walker, 2010; Usher, 2002).

This diversification of different types and purposes of doctoral education has also prompted discussions about the form and purpose of the main form of doctoral assessment, the doctoral dissertation. Anthony Paré, for example, argues that 'changes in the past couple of decades have rendered the single-authored, paper-based, book-length dissertation obsolete' (2017, p. 408). Paltridge and Starfield (2020) trace the doctoral thesis genre over the last century and find evidence that the traditional monograph still dominates in some fields, but also find considerable diversity and innovation across fields and institutions. They also note several examples of recent doctoral dissertations that defy traditional conventions. However, scholars have also noted how the dissertation, conceived as a traditional monograph, appears resistant to change and advocate for doctoral dissertations that are open to texts written for diverse purposes and diverse audiences (Sharmini & Spronken-Smith, 2020).

In our Scandinavian context, the thesis by publication has, as previously mentioned, replaced the monograph as the most common format in most fields, except the humanities (Krumsvik, 2016). The kinds of publications that are included in such a thesis are peer-reviewed journal articles; however, some PhD programmes, but not all, permit chapters in edited volumes. Typically, then, doctoral students write three or four journal articles and a lengthy introductory text that demonstrates the coherence between the articles. The growing popularity of the thesis by publication in Scandinavia and elsewhere can be seen as part of a growing international emphasis on publishing for PhD students (Kwan, 2010; Lei & Hu, 2019; Nygaard & Solli, 2021).

This emphasis, in turn, has had significant implications for doctoral writing pedagogies, with calls for the development of explicit pedagogies for doctoral students writing for publication (Aitchison et al., 2010; Badenhorst & Guerin, 2016; Kamler, 2008; Kamler & Thomson, 2014; Lee & Kamler, 2008). Both Lee (2010) and Murray (2010) highlight the importance of 'becoming rhetorical' in such pedagogy. While in one sense all doctoral writing – whether for publication or not – is rhetorical, writing for publication and for a community of experts is perceived as different from writing for supervisors and doctoral committees. Paré (2010) sums up this difference succinctly in describing the purpose of what he calls 'school discourse' as 'display of knowledge' and in highlighting that such discourse often 'fail[s] to address an actual dialogue among working scholars' (p. 30).

In this sense, 'becoming rhetorical' can be understood as a term meant to indicate how doctoral students writing for publication need to move from 'school discourse' to 'scholarly discourse'. As such, becoming rhetorical entails developing an ability to orient the work to an audience of scholars, recognizing the (sometimes) granular differences between the discourse communities represented by scholarly journals, and recognizing and adapting one's work to the genre differences between coursework, conference presentations, articles and so on. To explain the term further, Lee (2010) draws on Bakhtin's concept of 'addressivity' (p. 17). To Lee, 'addressivity is at the heart of being rhetorical' (p. 18) and Lee uses this concept to highlight how the ability to imagine an intended audience is essentially how one becomes rhetorical. Successful rhetorical becoming, then, means that one in a sense becomes the intended audience. How might this process of becoming be experienced for candidates working on professional fields in Norway?

Student Experiences: Transformation, Preservation and Ambivalence

We conducted semi-structured in-depth individual interviews with five PhD candidates who entered PhD programmes at OsloMet following extensive careers in a professional field. The interviews focused on three areas: (1) the decision to pursue a PhD, (2) writing and publishing the first article of the thesis and (3) communities and groups that the participants deemed important to them in the writing process specifically and in the PhD process more broadly. Because we were also interested in the various forms of support available to them, we asked the participants to complete a 'communities plot' (Sala-Bubaré & Castelló, 2017). This plot permits interviewees to visualize their perceptions of networks of importance during the writing process and doctoral education more broadly. In the following, we draw on two candidates, Beatrice and Anna, to highlight some key findings.

This research showed that the tensions between 'up here' and 'the origins', the difference between the life before and the life afterwards, are pronounced for doctoral candidates in professional fields. The doctoral period becomes a pivot on which turns their ideas about their careers up to that point. This pivoting, however, can involve quite different dynamics, as illustrated when we compare Beatrice's experiences with those of Anna. The former sees the doctorate from the point of view of the practitioner, and the latter sees it from the point of view of the researcher. That is to say, for Beatrice, the PhD serves a purpose for a field to which she will return and for Anna, the PhD marks her embarkation on a new career (she is, she says, 'too curious' to go back to being a practitioner in her field. She doesn't miss it).

The respective journeys of Anna and Beatrice are suggested by the communities plots they drew.

As illustrated in Figures 4.1 and 4.2, Anna's field of practice is nowhere in her communities plot; Beatrice's is everywhere. A key finding from our study, then, is that the way the students perceive the role of their professional background in becoming a researcher (Anna perceives her professional background as something she needs to leave behind to become a researcher, Beatrice sees her professional background as integral to becoming a researcher) and how the students perceive research is configured in their professional field (Anna says her professional field is not interested in research to develop professional practice, Beatrice says her field is very much interested in research to develop professional practice). In other words, we were struck by (1) that the professional field figured in the students' doctoral trajectories in very different ways (2) and that the perceived dynamics between the professional field and research field made for very complex writerly positions. That is, the candidates expressed considerable ambivalence about both where they had been before entering the PhD and where they imagined themselves going after the PhD. These are the insights we use to frame our existing writing course and to consider some future pedagogies in the penultimate section.

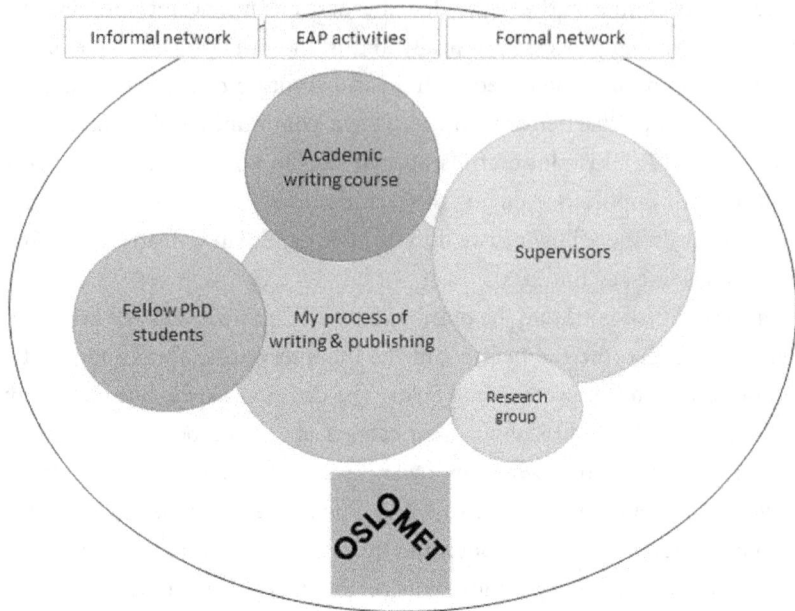

Figure 4.1 Anna's community plot.

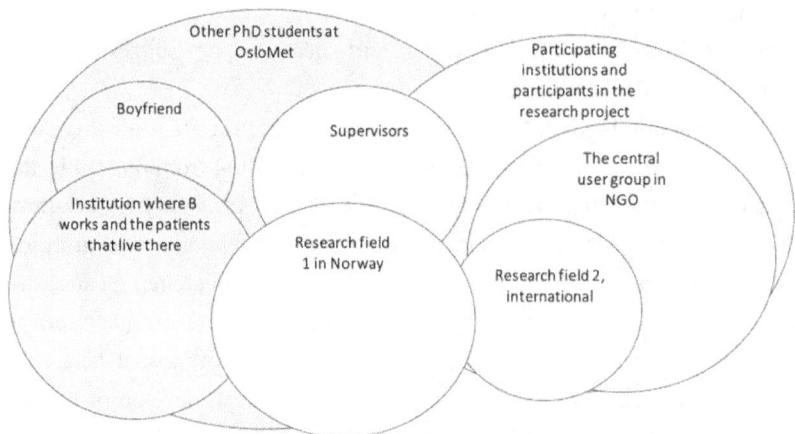

Figure 4.2 Beatrice's community plot.

The Academic Writing Centre at OsloMet: Key Aspects and Key Questions

We meet PhD candidates like Beatrice and Anna in our work in an EAP unit of a university that has gone through rapid institutional change. Our institution, OsloMet – Oslo Metropolitan University, started out as a merger of several separate professional schools and did not formally acquire university status until 2019. The various institutions that merged, and eventually became OsloMet, had remits for education in applied fields – health sciences, teacher education, social work and so on – and OsloMet preserves this remit, meaning that it is a natural destination for researchers interested in professional fields.

A significant number of doctoral students taking our writing courses, then, work with professional fields in the sense that they have worked, say, as nurses for a number of years, and then enter OsloMet's PhD programme in health sciences. In describing our main intervention – the semester-long AWC – here, we want to frame it with the contrasting communities plots from Anna and Beatrice. The contrasting stories of the plots prompt the questions that punctuate our sketch of the course's main aspects.

First aspect – Audience: AWC is a semester-long programme, aimed at PhD candidates, academic staff members and other researchers, with PhD candidates making up the majority of participants who sign up. A master's degree is the minimum entry requirement. Various versions of this course have been running at OsloMet for more than ten years now, and it remains guided by principles of genre pedagogy and academic literacies. Participants bring in a text-in-progress and work on this text for the duration of the course. The course always takes in multidisciplinary cohorts of no more than twelve students – part of the rationale being that exposure to the genres of other writers increases one's sensitivity to one's own genres (Swales & Feak, 2000). We also work with the principle that genre deconstruction tools are multivalent – if a writer can unpick the moves and conventions of one genre, they can do it for their own. Genre here tends to mean the research article – with the caveat that the genre features of research articles vary profoundly between disciplines – but the course has occasionally had candidates writing monograph chapters or sections of the extended introduction to a thesis by publication. Meetings are fortnightly across the semester, running for the better part of a day. At each session, two participants present their work in progress, followed by a discussion, so this is very much a learner-centred course. Following the presentations and discussions in each session, other elements of academic writing are introduced and discussed (and debated and queried – the academic literacies approach means that we work with the contingent nature of academic writing).

We start the semester by discussing audience – how one begins positioning one's work for an audience of scholars. One of the activities we use for this is Thomson and Kamler's (2013) Tiny Texts exercise. A Tiny Text is essentially a very condensed narrative version of an argument. Kamler and Thomson have developed four key moves of such a text (Locate, Focus, Report and Argue), and they offer helpful ways of understanding each move. Creating a Tiny Text requires the writer to have an overall command of the substance of their work and to tailor that substance for a specific audience. One cannot write the Tiny Text without a proper understanding of the research conversation the text participates in. Course participants begin by discussing the Tiny Text features and then finding examples of them in abstracts from their fields. The participant then creates a Tiny Text of their own, explaining the relationship between their research conversation and their approach.

First question: *Considerations of audience make real the ideas of addressivity, becoming rhetorical. On the one hand, this kind of immersion is essential for the becoming rhetorical that we have been describing; but on the other hand, we wonder if there must be times when participants – particularly participants like Beatrice – might bridle at such immersiveness. In other words, is it in such exercises that someone who feels their responsibilities to be elsewhere might start to feel dragged away from those responsibilities? Could one be captured by addressivity, could one become too rhetorical? If so, one could well end up feeling that some becomings are jeopardized by others.*

Second aspect – Rhetorical positioning: As a continuation of the discussion of audience, we begin working with the Creating a Research Space (CARS) model for writing introductions to research articles (Swales, 1990). Participants begin with the model and then observe the deployment – or lack thereof – of the model in their own fields. They can then begin building introductions for their own texts. We introduce CARS with a view to both explaining and questioning it, but it also serves a more general genre-pedagogical function because it affords participants opportunities to practice noticing textual features (Schmidt, 1990). In other words, when participants examine texts from their disciplines to see if or how the CARS model is employed, the process is metonymic of genre pedagogy as a whole – when you learn to notice what happens in introductions, you can notice what happens elsewhere.

At stake here is also the writer's ethos, which often concerns the move from master's-level work to the doctorate, which, when undertaking a thesis by publication, means writing for an audience of peers rather than for an examiner. Using the CARS model involves a sophisticated understanding of how an article deploys background knowledge and places the work amid an ongoing conversation. A hurdle many writers need to overcome is the urge to overexplain, to write many paragraphs of background before mentioning their own project. The process of noticing an article's genre features, then, means thinking of oneself as a different kind of writer and undergoing a different kind of becoming rhetorical – one must write as an expert whether or not one feels oneself to be an expert.

Even more so, though, our study indicates that for students in professional fields what an expert is, is not straightforward. Rather, ideas about expertise are shaped by the students' perceptions of how research is configured in their professional field. Anna, for example, explained how doing an MA was not necessarily valued by her colleagues in the profession. Anna felt that to her colleagues, her MA marked her off as an 'academic' in the sense of removing her from the practicalities of everyday professional life. Yet, when entering the PhD programme, and meeting researchers, she felt perceived as a practitioner and not academic enough. Anna's becoming rhetorical thus appears as a clear break, a further removal from her professional field.

Beatrice, on the other hand, describes having a professional background in her PhD programme as giving her 'capital'. Beatrice, then, perceives her professional experience as something that grants her legitimacy that other PhD students and researchers in her field without a professional background do not have. Beatrice sees her professional background as an asset, as something that gives her credibility in her research. Here then, the students display quite different ways to imagine how the research field perceives professional knowledge and expertise, and these different perceptions provide quite different starting points for writing.

For students like Anna, learning how to not sound like a practitioner is important. These students might be taking the course to learn 'the rules' so they can sound like the others than in developing a singular voice or wanting their writing to do something else than fitting in. Students like Beatrice, on the other hand, might be taking the course to insert herself, and to speak with a different voice, to capitalize on her professional experience in her writing.

Second question: *This question of ethos, the writer's relationship to the world, to their responsibilities, then, is conditioned by the students' professional backgrounds in quite different ways. Some students, such as Beatrice, perceive the role of their professional background as an asset. Others, such as Anna, perceive it as something that marks them as 'non-academic'. How do these differences shape the position from which they write? And how do these positions shape ideas about appropriate ways of expressing themselves as experts? How do we develop pedagogies that support different approaches to developing a suitable and purposeful voice?*

Third aspect – Imitation: The AWC is concerned with part genres (often the elements of the IMRAD article structure) and their linguistic features. This means that addressivity is baked into the course at the level of lexicogrammar as well. Various exercises across the semester enjoin participants to notice and take up the lexicogrammatical features of their fields. This may involve 'rhetorical consciousness raising' (Swales, 1990, p. 234), but also creating skeletal paragraphs, to perceive the otherwise invisible, conventional 'stuff' of academic discourse (Thomson & Kamler, 2013). One exercise requires participants to make a map of one or more articles, building up a comprehensive picture of their disciplinary discourses and observing how structures, moves and lexical choices map onto one another and cohere. Similarly, zooming in on certain sections of the map – Results, Discussions – and breaking those down into sentence skeletons can reveal the underlying structures of the sections; typical chunks of phraseology; academic language that participants can emulate. These structures and chunks can then be made available for candidates to experiment with as they write their own texts.

Third question: *What are the risks of imitation? Could the writer with a distinct sense of professional identity feel that this identity is encroached on by imitation? That they fail to find their own voice? That they speak about practices and realities of a field they know well in a language that feels removed, foreign, strange? And – looking at it from the other side – is there the risk here of an instrumental approach to teaching writing? When a writer is immersing themselves in new structures and lexis, to what degree might we or should we dwell on their potential ambivalences? And if so, with what aim? Does the EAP practitioner simply say 'My job is to help you publish, and there my responsibility ends'? Or does the EAP practitioner have a different kind of responsibility, one to the complexity of that moment and to its potential for teaching? Perhaps you will object – 'So the candidate has complex feelings about their career path? Well: don't we all; these are matters for the candidate's shrink.' But such an objection fails to take into account the becoming or being of becoming rhetorical, and the fact that it means, to no small degree, importing into oneself a species of new self: becoming the audience, becoming the other. So becoming rhetorical means that the writing is not easily parcelled off from the being of the candidate (if it ever was); becoming rhetorical insists that we think about the being within the writing, the writing within the being.*

The AWC Reconsidered: Pedagogical Initiatives for Doctoral Students in Professional Fields

Earlier, then, we have outlined three areas in which our conversations with students like Beatrice spoke back to our current pedagogical approaches and caused us to question them: audience, rhetorical positioning and imitation. How, in turn, might those questions help shape the kind of pedagogies we envision developing in the future? Learning more about the experiences of doctoral students in our courses prompted questions that in various ways deal with issues of ownership and voice in the process of becoming rhetorical. More specifically, these questions have inspired us to think about four concrete pieces of work that we would like to develop.

Using Legitimation Code Theory to Address Questions of Audience and Rhetorical Positioning

In terms of addressing the questions about audience and rhetorical positioning, we think including work inspired by Legitimation Code Theory (LCT) (Maton, 2014, 2016) will be helpful. Despite its name, LCT is not really a 'theory' but an analytical framework combining strands of sociology and strands of linguistics to form a complex set of analytical dimensions. LCT can seem forbidding, in part because of its ambitiousness: it provides a toolkit for understanding how knowledge is constructed out of field-specific processes of legitimization. But individual aspects of it are quite accessible, such as the Specialization dimension (Maton, 2014), which we propose using here. Specialization is typically used to create a description of the kind of 'knowing' that is privileged in a field of enquiry, whereby some fields privilege 'knower' codes (i.e. who I am, my distinct experience, is important to the construction of knowledge; examples would be disability studies or creative writing). Conversely, some fields privilege 'knowledge' codes, whereby the subject position of the researcher is expunged as much as possible, and knowledge is what can be observed and measured (in physics, for example).

Designing a set of tasks around exploring these codes might be a way for candidates such as Anna and Beatrice to map and process their journeys from practice to academia (and possibly back). For example, we can see Anna and Beatrice moving from fields defined by knower codes into fields defined by knowledge codes – that is to say, if one is a social worker, for example, a large part of one's personal legitimacy as a knower comes from experience (I have training, yes, but I have worked in the field for this many years and assisted service users with this many issues – my claims to effectiveness are embodied, experienced and, in many ways, unique to me). But to become a researcher – even in something like social work – often means moving into a field dominated by knowledge codes (my legitimacy as a researcher does not depend on my particular experience but on what I can observe and how precisely I can document it and theorize it). LCT, in other words, provides a pedagogically useful language to think about the transitions or transformations a candidate might undergo.

Here, we would be building on the work of others who have explored the pedagogical uses of LCT in writing and language-learning pedagogy (e.g. Kirk, 2017; Maton & Chen, 2020). In our case, the Specialization codes could be given to 'boundary crossers' (to use Prøitz and Wittek's (2019) term for candidates who work at the interface of different knowledge areas) as a tool to think through the relationship between practitioner-knowledge, research-knowledge and the space they occupy with those different knowledges. What this amounts to is a *de-individuating* – at least in part – of writerly ambivalence or uneasiness. It means seeing the 'I' who writes as made up of professional and disciplinary histories and that at any time in the writer's life these histories – these codes – may clash or match (Maton, 2014). De-individuation here means that the writer realizes that whatever uneasiness they experience is not only to do with the difficulty of 'writing' – it is because they are at a point where codes – and ethos – are in conflict.

This kind of more conceptual work would involve reading and discussing theory or pieces that are not necessarily about writing per se but about the configuration and codes of their field. The 'boundary crossers' we spoke to in our study possess a repertoire of codes and may have powerful feelings about the relationship of research to practice. An exercise might be to think about, or plan, an article that addresses a practice issue they have detailed knowledge of, and to metacognitively think about the codes they use when they think about it and the codes they would require as a researcher. It may be that as a code-aware 'boundary crosser' that a PhD candidate can see how to break open their 'research codes' to admit other perspectives. Such 'identity work' might be a way to address some of the questions our study raised for us in terms of audience considerations and rhetorical positioning. Armed with these insights, it might be easier to understand and, perhaps, accept one's ambivalences, rather than perceiving them as personal flaws. Such acceptance might in turn inspire less insecurity and self-doubt.

Glorious Failure: Becoming Unrhetorical and Moving beyond Imitation

Paré (2010) discusses the idea of a paper he calls a 'glorious failure'. This is a writing assignment for students to really let loose on – something that will be ambitious, overblown, magnificent and absurd. The aim is not to produce a text for publication – the aim is to take risks, to be 'unrhetorical', if you will. For those who teach writing in other contexts, it might seem bizarre that a text meant not for publication should make for a special kind of assignment. In many contexts, the papers not meant for publication is all there is. In our heavily publication-focused context, however, students have few opportunities to write anything else than texts for publication. Indeed, they might be warned against any other kinds of writing from supervisors and others, as it takes time away from the kind of writing that counts.

Some of the candidates we work with might themselves not see the point of writing such a text. However, for others, this kind of writing might be a way to use registers and try out ways of writing that might often be censored by the imagined internal readers that appear when writers become rhetorical. Such an exercise might in fact help students gain some confidence in themselves as writers. Hence, working in segments focusing on 'writing for non-publication' might allow writers to explore, get to know themselves or draw on previous experiences as writers in other ways than they are able to do when they primarily see the task of writing as the ability to identify and follow conventions. Such an assignment could serve as a contrast to writing as imitation, trying out what other forms of writing may achieve. Such a licence to fail might expand on the students' approaches to writing and language choices that might offer some students more confidence or perhaps a slightly different idea of what kind of writer they are or could be.

Experimental Writing and Life beyond IMRD

While the glorious failure assignment could quite easily be incorporated into our standard writing course, we have in fact already developed a separate course around the idea of moving away from conventional writing: Experimental Writing for Social Scientists. Although designed for social scientists more generally – those who would benefit from exploring life beyond IMRD – it would also be a home for students like Beatrice and others who would find discussions of voice, identity and innovation valuable. Unlike the AWC, this course does not start with the rules of the game. Rather, it begins with the question 'What do you want to do with the text'? A course like this is not for everyone, but it could respond to some of our interviewees' needs because of its emphasis on voice and text ownership, and – to borrow Swales's (2017) words – its emphasis on discontent with standardization.

The course takes the positive position that readers, reviewers and editors may sometimes enjoy departures from the norm and may even be happy and relieved when they encounter such texts. Participants are invited to consider a range of texts that are non-traditional in whole or part (e.g. Monastersky & Sousanis, 2015; Yerushalmi, 1991) and they are also asked to bring in examples from their own reading. At this time of writing, the first iteration of the course is still in progress. Participants have been doing work based around storytelling, voice and untypical introduction forms. Taking as a cue Bennett's (2007) fairy tale about the birth of English academic discourse, participants were asked to write a story of their own about some aspect of their research – not a fairy tale, necessarily, but a ghost story, a romance, a detective story, a comic strip. Subsequent sessions have considered unusual voice features (footnotes, anecdotes, lexical choices); different kinds of beginning (cf. Sword, 2012); and the emotions of the reader and the psychological development of the text (cf. Hayot, 2014).

Creating Metacognitive Space to Foster Text Ownership

As Anna and Beatrice's communities plots illustrate, doctoral writers in our writing course talk about writing with many different groups and individuals. They typically receive writing advice from a multitude of sources: peer reviewers, supervisors, co-authors, members of their research groups, fellow PhD students and sometimes from user groups or practitioners in professional fields. For some students, knowing what to do with all this advice is bewildering. Anna, for example, said she would accept the track changes the supervisors requested even if she didn't always understand why the supervisors felt these changes were necessary. We have met many students like Anna who follow advice, not because they see how it improves the text but because they do not feel they have the experience or skill to do anything else. In this way, some students end up distancing themselves from making writing and language choices, prompting feelings of distance from their own work and lack of ownership.

Another area for future work is thus to construct the writing course more deliberately as a metacognitive space. Such work would involve configuring the writing course as a space for PhD students to draw together, collate and think through all the disparate information and sometimes conflicting advice they receive about writing and writerly 'becoming'. In such a space, we would set aside time to discuss how writing is worked with, talked about and practised in the various communities that the students participate in. Putting these various discussions about writing in conversations might help students navigate the different voices that shape their own voices.

One specific activity to this end could be to ask students to draw a communities plot and use it to have them to reflect on how writing is figured and discussed in each of these spaces. Such reflection could, then, facilitate discussions that centre on understanding the advice of the different voices and why such advice might be offered. Such an understanding might allow the students to exercise greater ownership in the future.

Coda: Becoming Pedagogical

Earlier, then, we have outlined four pedagogical possibilities as a response to some of the particular challenges in the identity work of doctoral writers with professional backgrounds. What these initiatives have in common is that they offer course participants ways to understand themselves as writers by attempting to make use of ambivalence, hesitation and insecurity as pedagogical resources. Are Beatrice's concerns about drifting from her origins an appropriate topic to discuss in a writing course? Can Anna's understanding of herself as 'too curious' to remain in her professional field be relevant to discussions of how she imagines the purpose and audience of writing? Do discussions of the role of research in professional fields and the role of professional fields in research have a place in a writing for publication course? We believe the answers to all these questions are yes. And the four initiatives described previously are attempts at envisioning what kind of classroom work might support such discussions. The questions they emerge from are all versions of the question without which, perhaps, there is no teaching: 'What did I miss? What did I fail to see?'

The literary critic Barbara Johnson (1982), drawing on Freud and Coleridge, talks of teaching as a kind of repetition compulsion – teaching as the repetition of something we do not yet understand. There are many ways of understanding this cryptic – even mystical – statement, but one is perhaps that teaching is almost always repeating (an exercise, a question for discussion, a response), but the significance of it is always yet to be determined. I cannot grasp what I am saying because it passes away from me. And the teacher, too, finds herself within a constellation of addressivities – to her own future self, as much as anyone. I do not know the meaning of my words now because my future self has yet to be taught by them.

And I cannot be taught by those words, those repetitions – not without Anna, Beatrice and other students like them. The twin risks of becoming pedagogical: that whatever I say becomes mere dogma, the arena of self-parody; or that I, too, am transformed by these encounters. Addressivity must change me, too, always, making my teaching self perpetually hasty and provisional. Always stepping towards the teacher I can only try to become.

5

Using Developmental Teaching to Promote Critical EAP in an Academic Writing Course in English

Marília Mendes Ferreira

Introduction

In the context of Brazilian higher education, EAP teaching is generally provided by isolated disciplinary experts who, aware of the pressure to publish in international publications, venture to teach EAP courses for graduate students. Extra-curricular EAP courses may also be provided by university language centres; however, these are offered on a limited basis due to constraints in funding and a lack of institutional policy on academic literacy. Brazilian higher education needs to move from merely valuing publication in international publications to providing firm support and optimal conditions for those seeking to publish in such publications – for example, by providing proper EAP teacher education (Ferreira & MacDiarmid, 2019) and institution-wide academic literacy teaching and support.

This chapter reports an example of EAP practice at a Brazilian university which endeavours to draw connections with the wider context of knowledge production in the academy, and in doing so provides a model of what such support could look like. The Laboratory of Academic Literacy (LLAC) at the University of São Paulo offers academic writing courses in English for its different colleges. The course reported on here was offered to postgraduate students from the Interdisciplinary Institute on Energy following a combination of Vygotsky-based pedagogy, named Developmental Teaching, and Critical EAP. The result was a course in which *critical thinking* emerged out of the *theoretical thinking* promoted by Developmental Teaching, leading to the students' critical consciousness-raising and empowerment, as well as their accessing of the conventions of academic publishing.

First, I will discuss Developmental Teaching and Critical EAP. I then focus on the implementation of this EAP programme at the LLAC, which drew on both Developmental Teaching and Critical EAP. I then take a step back and include an autoethnographic account of this implementation to shed light on the practitioner's process of implementing Developmental Teaching and developing their own theoretical thinking, and examine the reasons behind pedagogical choices made on the spot. Finally, possible contributions of this experience to EAP pedagogy will be discussed. In summary, this chapter shares the unique challenges faced by EAP practitioners in a peripheral country like Brazil as we try to raise students' critical consciousness while also allowing students to have more agency via awareness of the types of knowledge (linguistic, generic and geopolitical) needed in the world of academic publishing.

Background Discussion

Davydov's teaching approach, known as Developmental Teaching (Chaiklin, 2002), is an activity-theory-based pedagogy which aims to create a zone of proximal development (ZDP[1]) in school subjects teaching. ZDP – although the word 'zone' can lead one to think of a place – refers to a zone where learning and development are intertwined (Newman & Holzman, 1993; Vygotsky, 1978). Through the learning actions to be described in the following, students develop cognitively: in this case, via the development of their capacity for *theoretical thinking*. Equipped with this mode of thinking students could better solve real-world problems, that is, transformation, or apply action upon the world to transform it (Davydov, 1999). A note on terminology: while empirical thinking provides sensory-based descriptions of phenomena and explanations based on causality, theoretical thinking seeks to identify an essential basic relationship that can explain an array of phenomena (Davydov, 1984). Development of the capacity for theoretical thinking is at the heart of Developmental Teaching.

Developmental Teaching consists of the following learning actions: (1) problem generation, (2) modelling, (3) modification of models, (4) application of models to solve a problem, (5) monitoring of learning, (6) evaluation of learning and (7) social interaction (Davydov, 1988a, 1988b, 1988c, 1988d; Lompscher,

---

[1] ZDP is defined here as a learning activity that aims to promote development. The ESL field often associates the term with pair or group work. However, this is a very limited view of the concept (Newman & Holzman, 1993). See Kinginger (2002) for a deeper discussion of the interpretation of the concept.

1984). It is important to clarify that actions 3 and 4 refer to theoretical thinking and are extremely intertwined. The modification of models can happen as they are applied to solve problems. Once students realize the model does not help (much), they can modify it.

Developmental Teaching has been applied to teach a variety of school subjects: math (Davydov, 1990), Russian as a first language (Aidarova, 1982; Markova, 1979), natural sciences (Lompscher, 1984) and an interdisciplinary project involving geography, biology and history (Hedegaard, 2002). This pedagogy has also been applied to EAP instruction in both American (Ferreira, 2005; Ferreira & Lantolf, 2008) and Brazilian universities (Ferreira, 2015).

Critical EAP is the manifestation of Critical Pedagogy in the field of EAP. Critical Pedagogy originates from Marxist influences in the Frankfurt School of critical theory and in Paulo Freire's work. It achieved great currency in North American universities and adopted the Freirean principles (Haque, 2007). The premise of Critical Pedagogy is that by revealing hidden ideologies (assumptions, beliefs, underlying messages) learners will undergo awareness-raising (*conscientização*) and, consequently, those learners who are oppressed will gain more agency. The transformation of the status quo will happen through discussion of topics related to social injustice in the classroom (Haque, 2007). For that to arise, both teachers and students should be engaged in this process of discussion (Haque, 2007).

The first phase of Critical Pedagogy applied to EAP is present in the work of Benesch during the 1990s. She takes the position that EAP courses should be linked to content courses and go beyond the traditional pragmatism of EAP. Classroom discussions should leave room for topics related to social injustice and power distribution and the problems students face in their lives. This class work should empower and, consequently, confer more agency to the students (Benesch, 1999, 2001).

The critical movement also reached second language writing and more specifically EAP writing. Canagarajah (2002) recommends that writing be seen as a situated construct, realized in material conditions that reveal issues of power; academic conventions can also be seen as resources for agency. To achieve this agency, he advocates for strategic resistance using non-canonical forms of discourse by students, who occupy positions of less power in academia.

In the next section I will illustrate and underline the contribution to research of the application of a combination of Developmental Teaching with Critical Pedagogy to course design and the teaching of academic writing in English in the context of a Brazilian university.

I will complement this illustration with an autoethnographic account of my implementation of this pedagogical programme. My position could be characterized as a critical pragmatist (Cherryholmes, 1988) in EAP teaching, which recognizes the challenges EAP professionals face in Brazil and, at the same time, pragmatically choosing to empower his/her students by providing access to the types of knowledge needed for international publication. By promoting awareness about knowledge production and its linguistic conventions, it was expected these novice researchers could have more opportunities to be included in international publication activity. Yet, from a Vygotskian tradition influenced by Developmental Teaching, my position would be of an educator who seeks awareness of her own teaching choices, which ultimately aim at fostering students' agency by promoting theoretical thinking about language functioning.

The Implementation of the EAP Course: Combining Developmental Teaching and Critical Pedagogy

Context and Course Aims

The English academic writing course in this study targeted graduate students from the School of Energy and Electrical Engineering from University of São Paulo. It had a credit load of fifty hours, taught as an extra-curricular intensive summer course. At the time, the Graduate Programme was very interested in improving students' writing in English in order to increase their number of international publications. Students had their proficiency in English for writing and speaking assessed through the First Certificate in English test; most were at B1 with a few at B2. All students spoke Portuguese as their first language (L1).

At the same time, the course aimed to teach three genres – the summary, the research article and the abstract of the research article – as preparation for future publications. The course also aimed to promote theoretical thinking about language functioning and, by extension, genre and writing. The first goal was clear to the students and the second one was promoted inductively by the instructor. The assumption adopted by the instructor is that it is crucial to have a theoretical thinking-based understanding of language functioning in order to achieve more agency, that is, apply action upon the world to transform it.

By means of theoretical thinking about language functioning, the course fostered critical thinking. Critical thinking implies the consideration of the influences of social factors (power, politics, injustice) on whatever we do and the adoption of a questioning position towards them. This questioning, which will lead to the unveiling of hidden assumptions, beliefs and ideologies, was carried out on the topics of language functioning and issues of power, as will be seen in the exercises to be described later. It is possible for an EAP teacher to promote critical thinking in classes without a commitment to theoretical thinking, in the way that Critical Pedagogy does; however, due to the common Marxist affiliations and origins of Developmental Teaching and Critical EAP, this combination is possible. Theoretical thinking enriches one's critical thinking, as it focuses on the essential relationship of language functioning: that which accounts for the social motivation behind linguistic conventions.

The Use of Visual Representations

Theoretical thinking is best captured by visual representations or models. These should be simple drawings which reveal essential connections among elements (Lompscher, 1999). A model based on Engeström (2015) and developed by the author demonstrating theoretical thinking used to understand language was used to guide the entire course, and parts of it were eventually shown to the students to help them develop their own models. The model illustrates the fact that language functions are based on two contradictory relationships, which constitute its essence: between rules and creativity (centripetal and centrifugal forces addressed by Bakhtin, 2002) and between this relationship and the social context, conceptualized as activity (Engeström, 2015).

This model was conceptualized in order to guide the course design, even before its use in the course to teach theoretical thinking. In other words, genres were taught (in this case, summary, research article and abstracts) by focusing not only on their structure and linguistic descriptions but also on the deeper reasons for such genre conventions in the first place. These reasons are to be found in the activities of knowledge production and publication. The emphasis on linguistic descriptions reveals empirical thinking, while the emphasis on the reasons for such conventions, theoretical thinking.

Three visual models were made use of in this course. A model illustrating the relationship between language and social context was shared with students, along with one detailing the relationship between language, rules and creativity. The rule and creativity component of the model was approached by focusing more on the rules, as academic discourse is highly conventional. However, there was a bit of discussion in class about the possibility of disobeying the rules or creating new rules and who would have more chances to do that and why in the discourse community. A model focusing on genre was drawn on only by the instructor; it was not shown to students. Instead, the instructor pushed them to draw their own model of genre.

The models were not just teaching tools but mediational tools for the instructor. The sequence of three models can be seen as an evolution, illustrating that the teacher's theoretical thinking development happens while the approach is applied, rather than just reading about it. For this reason, it is important to have mediational tools to assist him/her to use the pedagogy. This will be addressed further later in the chapter.

Lesson Plans and Activities for Implementation

The implementation will be reported in two parts: the description of the exercises given in the course that connects Developmental Teaching and Critical Pedagogy, followed by the rationale of my choices as stated in the lesson plans. The lesson plan had the following parts: (1) recent work, (2) organization, (3) rationale, (4) instructor's actions to teach, (5) homework, (6) assessment and (7) materials needed. It was a mediational tool to guide my own understanding and implementation of Davydov's pedagogy and to help me be aware of the choices made and its consequences along the way.

The following exercises are examples of problem-solving tasks, in which students had to use a model (of their own or of the instructor) to help them solve it. In other words, the exercises to be described are learning actions 3 and 4 noted earlier (modification/application of models). The problems created aimed at calling students' attention to the intrinsic relationship between language and social context, that is, the motivation for conventional use of language in academia. In this way, critical topics involved in the activity of knowledge production would be addressed.

Example 1 Summary Writing

Chapter 5 from Swales and Feak (2004)[2] was given to the students. The following two-part exercise was created with the goal of questioning the reason behind the conventions of this particular genre as stated by the manual. The students had to explain why the summaries had to have the following features: (1) a first sentence (source + reporting verb + the main idea of the text), (2) level of neutrality, (3) reporting verbs, (4) reminder phrases, (5) proper citation to avoid plagiarism

---

[2] Although there is a more recent edition, at the time this second was the only one available.

and (6) paraphrases. In the second part of the exercise, students had to identify the summaries in different genres and explain their role in them. The model to be used was the one drawn based on Swales and Feak (2004), chapter 5, and in the class it ended up being just a list of summary features (i.e. this was an example of students' application of empirical thinking).[3]

The texts given to the students were the introduction to a book, a book chapter, a literature review section, a book review, all from the broad field of energy. The task aimed (1) to make students compare the manual's recommendation on summary construction with its realization in other genres, (2) to develop theoretical thinking by motivating the explanation of phenomena and (3) to call students' attention to the reasons behind these conventions.

Academic discourse privileges paraphrasing over quoting, expects some form of citation and values clear distinctions between writer's and reported author's voices. These features described by the manual are motivated by knowledge production and publication activities. In other words, students were guided to question the conventions given by the manual in order to know their reasons and, as a result, be able to exercise more agency with language. This was done through group or class discussions based on rhetorical consciousness-raising exercises (Swales & Feak, 2012).

Proper citation – as the discursive community recommends – means giving credit to the author for its publication. This credit works as a form of academic currency that can be used to calculate citation indices. For example, impact factor is used to assess journals, scholars and institutions and highly influences promotions and research funding (Fernandez-Llimos, 2016; Moustafa, 2015). Summarizing and paraphrasing are in-demand skills from students which reinforce academia's stance against plagiarism. The discussion of these issues in class, motivated by this exercise, led students to reframe academic discourse features as part of these two broader social activities. By extension, issues of inclusion and power relations in discourse communities were addressed as well.

Regarding part two of the exercise (identifying summaries in different genres), the following questions were proposed by the teacher to stimulate students' theoretical and, consequently, critical thinking:

1. Why do introductions to books contain chapter summaries?
2. How do these summaries help promote the book in an increasing competitive environment in the publication field (for example, academic

---

[3] It happened because of my instructions which did not push them to represent the essential relations of the genre.

texts can be rented or purchased in different formats (e-books, physical copies))?
3. How does the purpose of different types of texts affect the writing of summaries based on them, for example, the level of neutrality or the amount and type of information reported?
4. How do the values of different discourse communities affect their way of writing?
5. Which values found the view of plagiarism as crime adopted by academia?
6. Why is the paraphrasing skill demanded by academia?
7. How does it relate with the activity of publication?

Example 2: Research Articles

In the following example, the goal was to show students how genres change over time and why. First the instructor and students discussed the following warm-up questions:

1. Why do researchers have to write research papers/articles (the role of the research article in the production and dissemination of knowledge)?
2. What kind of information do these texts have?
3. How are they structured?
4. What is the reason for such organization?
5. Who invented this organization?
6. Do you think the research article was always like this?

This discussion aimed at eliciting their knowledge about research articles and preparing students for the next problem-solving task, which was about the early experimental reports of the Royal Society of London. Here is the text given for them to read:

> The nitrous acid I have exhibited in the form of air [i.e., gas], though only, as it were, for a moment; since no fluid, that I am acquainted with, is capable of confining it. The more I consider the nitrous acid, the more wonderful and inexhaustible the subject appears. The kinds of air which it forms, according to its various combinations with phlogiston, are, I believe, more numerous than all the kinds that can be formed by the other acids. Many of the phaenomena which have lately occurred to my observation relating to it are, to me, altogether inexplicable; though I perceive certain analogies among some of them. (Priestley, 1775, as cited in Atkinson, 1999, p. 77)

The questions to be answered were as follows:

1. What kind of text is this?
2. What is the goal of this text?
3. Who is the audience?
4. What are the linguistic features/organization of the text?
5. This is the way 'researchers' (people interested in science) reported their experiments. What are the differences you notice between this text and the type of research article you read and write nowadays?
6. How do you explain these differences? Use your model of genre to help you.

   Afterwards they read another letter:

   Sir,

   It may seem, by the curious Remarks sent to you from Scotland, that we are yet to seek out the Causes and original Source, as well as the Principles and Nature, of Frosts, Heats, Winds, and Tempests. I know by experience, that the Situation of the place is considerable for some of these; but, after much diligence and believe, more numerous than all the kinds that can be formed by the other acids. Many of the phaenomena which have lately occurred to my observation relating to it are, to me, altogether inexplicable; though I perceive certain analogies among some of them. (Priestley, 1775, as cited in Atkinson, 1999, p. 76)

   And had to answer the following:

7. How do you explain the fact this letter does not describe how the study was conducted (methods section)?

The exercise addressed both empirical and theoretical features of the genre. The first four questions of the first letter focus on empirical features of the text while the last three approach the theoretical thinking perspective, as it addresses the social-based explanation of these features. In other words, it aimed to make students explain the diachronic changes of research articles by using the model genre they drew before. This model supposedly contained the essential relationship under focus in the course (language (rules ↔ creativity) ↔ social context). By doing the problem-solving exercise they could modify this model by adding or changing this relationship in the model.

The letters of the Royal Society of London strongly reflected the genteel and amateur scientific community of the time (Atkinson, 1999, p. 28). As this author explains, linguistic features such as the use of first person, adjectives, evaluation and the high level of politeness create an author-centred effect; its letter format is motivated by the social condition of knowledge production activity of the time: embryonic, amateur scientific doing. However, modern science is characterized by more advanced professionalization which affected the genres it produces. One example that can be given is the pursuit of objectivity not only via the methods but also via the text written (Bazerman, 1988).

To reinforce and promote theoretical thinking another task was given. The students in groups had to read an abridged version of chapter 3 from Bazerman (1988) and parts of chapter 6 from Atkinson (1999). The former text focuses on the evolution of the experimental report and the role of methods while the latter shows how the genteel way of life affected 'scientific' communication in its beginning. Based on these readings, students had to answer the following:

1. What is the evolution of the experimental report described by the text?
2. What does this evolution reveal about the relationship of humans and nature?
3. How can this evolution be explained using the scientific activity model (using the model based on Engeström [2015])?
4. Does the model language ↔ social context explain this evolution?
5. The basis for change is the change in the relationship between man and nature, but what caused this change?

Then students filled out a chart which aimed to find contextual explanations for the linguistic features of the letters.

As mentioned earlier, two activities[4] were under focus in the course – the activities of knowledge production and of publication – in order to take stock of the linguistic features of academic genres and English as a lingua franca, a tool of paramount importance in both activities. By revealing the social motivations of the linguistic features of academic genres, one inevitably is dealing with issues of power. By doing these exercises, awareness was being created. This was the focus of a further lesson.

The whole class discussed the following questions as a warm-up:

1. What is your opinion about English being the lingua franca of science and technology/publishing or perishing academic policy that has been incorporated by Brazilian universities?

---

[4] This work is further informed by Engeström's (2015) activity theory, but due to limitations of space, this concept is not elaborated upon here. See Engeström (2015).

2. What are the consequences of English being the lingua franca of sciences?
3. Should researchers have the option to publish in the language they want?
4. Should Brazilian journals in your area be published in English or Portuguese?
5. Does Brazil have international visibility in your area?
6. What are the other countries that have international visibility in your area?

Afterwards, the class was divided into three groups, which each had to read one of the three texts given, comment, discuss or react to one or two relevant excerpts for class discussion, discuss some given questions and draw a model of scientific activity (see Ferreira (2015) for this discussion). Then the students were regrouped to allow the sharing of their readings and discussion (see Table 5.1).

Table 5.1 Texts and Questions Discussed

Texts		Questions
Is There a Science beyond English? (Meneghini & Packer, 2007)	a)	Do you agree with the following statement from the text: 'any scientist must therefore master English to obtain international recognition and to access relevant publications', p. 112?
	b)	What suggestions do the authors offer for the language problem?
	c)	Does the energy field face the same difficulty to incorporate concepts in English into Portuguese?
Lost Science in the Third World (Gibbs, 1995)	a)	Do you think in your field there are also difficulties to have access to knowledge produced in the first world?
	b)	Did you know about the procedures involved to have a journal indexed by SCI?
	c)	Why has knowledge produced from the third world been neglected?
Excerpts from Canagarajah (2002), Chap. 6, pp. 190–2, 193–5, 196–7, 224–8	a)	Do you think what the text says applies to Brazil?
	b)	Do you think Brazil is more in the centre or in the periphery of knowledge production in general or in energy studies?
	c)	What about your university, your school? and in what aspects? What should be improved?

To conclude this class, students had to discuss the following questions:

1. Before reading these texts, did I know anything about the geopolitics in science?
2. Is this information relevant to achieve my goals of publication in English? Why (not)?
3. Why was this information given to me in this course?
4. How do I link this information with the models we have been using (models of the concept of genre, of the research article, of the abstract, of the scientific activity)?

Lessons Learned

The course was founded on three pillars: genre (Swales and Feak, 2004), linguistic analyses (Hyland, 2004, 2008) and a critical approach to this knowledge (Critical EAP). In other words, three types of knowledge were needed to write academically in English and to publish internationally: genre, linguistic and social context knowledge. The assumption adopted was that students should not be acculturated with cultural (in this case, Western) rhetorical patterns to academic writing but, instead, be exposed to them and their social conditions of production. With that information they would be able to make conscious decisions to acculturate, to resist or to use this knowledge to their service (Canagarajah, 2002). The texts chosen are often cited as references in the geopolitics of academic writing which offer a broader view of the academic activity in its centre–periphery characteristics (Canagarajah, 2002), politics of publication (Gibbs, 1995) and language issues concerning English as the lingua franca of sciences (Meneghini & Packer, 2007). These three texts approach the geopolitical and language issues concerning academic publication that can reveal the students the complexity of academic activity and, specially, the publishing one. The questions exposed earlier represented linguistic phenomena that needed explanation. This explanation would be mediated by the model of language functioning and genre. This way, theoretical thinking was nourished in the EAP classroom.

From a Critical Pedagogy perspective, the examples illustrate the questioning the instructor promoted about summary writing conventions, the change of conventions through time and awareness-raising on the geopolitical aspects of scientific activity. Thus, critical thinking emerges out of the theoretical thinking promoted by Developmental Teaching. The models and the problem-solving tasks are tools that can be used to promote critical thinking beyond class discussions that aim at unveiling ideologies. In this combination reported here, critical thinking is based on expounding connections between uses of language and social context that inevitably imply issues of power (in this case, geopolitical and economic powers, social struggle, etc. – very cherished topics for Critical Pedagogy). In addition, students with a theoretical thinking understanding of language functioning can have more agency and potential for transformation.

The goal was for graduate students to have more agency by being aware of the types of knowledge needed to publish (linguistic, generic and geopolitical). All three were addressed to prepare students to the rules of the game of knowledge production and publication activities. In the long run, it was expected that this approach could promote these novice Brazilian researchers' inclusion in international publications.

My Ethnographic Account on the Application

In this section, I step back and reflect on the approach from that of the instructor applying and developing their practice through this approach. Developmental Teaching pedagogy imposes several challenges on instructors. Firstly, as a non-mainstream pedagogical approach, there are no textbooks available on the market (an exception would be in Russia as this is one of the accredited pedagogies by the Ministry of Education[5]). Secondly, theoretical thinking is not common in the educational system. Also, Development Teaching's main goal of transformation (on both the individual and social levels) through development is demanding; teachers are educated to focus on learning (often times in the 'banking education' (Freire, 2002) mode), rather than on learning that leads to psychological development (Vygotsky, 1978). However, although this goal adds an extra burden on teachers' already loaded routines, it is still feasible by ensuring a balance between linguistic structures, genre and critical issues in the syllabus.

Annotated lesson plans and class notes were the tools used to do this autoethnography (Cadman, 2005). This qualitative research method allows the researcher to more freely reflect on his/her impressions without concerns to adhere to objectivity demands (validity, reliability, statistics, for example).

---

[5] International Colloquium Developmental Teaching and specific didactics sponsored by the Catholic University of Goiás, Brazil, in 2017.

This perspective acknowledges meaning-making of life experiences as valid knowledge. From a Vygotskian lens, these texts worked as mediational tools to construct my own ZDP. Performing simultaneously the teacher and the researcher roles, I had to develop my theoretical thinking about language and master the pedagogy not only by reading extensively about the theory but, fundamentally, by living it. It is important to remark that these annotations aimed primarily to assess my application of the pedagogy while teaching it; secondarily, to gain control of my own teaching actions in the course and finally to make sense of the whole experience.

Throughout my experience with Developmental Teaching in undergraduate studies (Ferreira, 2005; Ferreira & Lantolf, 2008) and graduate students (Ferreira, 2015), I have been using detailed lesson plans and class notes to mediate my implementation of the pedagogy. These plans detail the rationales of my task choices and predictions about students' difficulties and reactions to my tasks, and possible alternatives to the tasks.

For example, in the class about summary writing the following was written under the Rationale heading of the lesson plan:

Modelling chapter 5 will be a way to link Developmental Teaching with the information given in this textbook. Students should practice the features given by Swales & Feak (2004) with a previous summary (writing diagnosis). This will give them an opportunity to re-evaluate their writing. The next exercise is very important since it is an attempt to link the school summary to its realization in academic genres. Students should notice that changes occur in this process since what really will count are these summaries as part of these genres.

The rationale description was a form of externalization of my understanding of the theory and to what extent I was implementing it.

Regarding the anticipation of problems I wrote the following in the lesson plan about the history of research articles (see Example 2):

This is a problem-solving situation in which they have to use the germ cell model of genre to try to explain linguistic phenomena (the change of the research article across time). It is expected that students will miss things in their models and so this will put them in a situation to wish for more knowledge, to understand more about the social situation involving genres and the academic writing activity. The teacher should call attention to language ↔ context relationship. It is important to make clear to them that their model might not be suitable to explain this phenomenon and they might want to improve the model by making the relation between the problem and the basic relation real vivid. I don't expect students to explain everything here. I assume the task will be difficult for them and this will be a stimulus to nurture theoretical thinking.

The class notes written right after the classes registered my assessment of my teaching (*Today was the first time I think I used the word genre in the class. I associated it with types of text. Was that a good or bad thing?*), of students' performance (*The students do not know the concept of audience and writer-audience interaction and this hinders their performance in the writing task given [personal statement given as pre-test in the course]. Can there be a cultural element here? We [Brazilians] don't promote ourselves? Or we do but not through writing?*) and reactions to the pedagogy. (*This group did not expect formulas to write. I got astonished at this. Since the beginning of the course, I kept telling them there were no formulas; there are essential concepts that you will carry to any writing situation.*) Both tools were powerful to make meaning of my teaching experience with Developmental Teaching: Was the pedagogy worth the effort? Was I changing as a teacher and if so, how?

As I was both the instructor and the researcher, these two roles and their objectives often clashed: teaching versus doing/collecting data. My reflections in the notes and the lesson plan notes helped me be aware of this conflict and the reasons behind the choices made on the spot. A couple of times during classes, I had to prioritize students' goals to learn academic writing for future publications over my research interest, which was their theoretical thinking development. I was aware the second was my goal and not necessarily theirs. In addition, if I opted otherwise I would likely demotivate students to keep attending my course, with a risk of losing students/subjects. As a consequence, to achieve a balance between these two roles, I cancelled exercises devoted to theoretical thinking (*I could have given more exercises on theoretical thinking, why questions, applying models to the exercises*), discussed the example of language ↔ context relationship addressed by the exercise, instead of giving them to students or assign them as homework that would be more fruitfully carried out as group work in the classroom. Yet, to develop fully my research/teaching programme I completed all the units designed for the course, even though it meant a lot of work for them and for me considering the amount of time we had.

Transformation is a key concept in both Developmental Teaching and Critical Pedagogy. With the knowledge and experience provided by this course, it is expected students can be more active and critical towards the activities of knowledge production and publication. For example, our discussions and tasks could assist them to deal with institutional demands if they work in universities or with their own advisers and departments. Nevertheless, the transformation also affected the instructor. By the tools used earlier I myself expanded the conceptions of language and genre and developed a more critical stance towards academic discourse recommendations provided by manuals. Language was conceived as a psychological tool for theoretical thinking development rather than just as an instrument for communication or expression of thoughts. Linguistic conventions are not natural; they are socially motivated. Genres, rather than formulas to write, are instantiations of the essential relationship of language. The writing manual used, despite being based on extensive research on genre analysis, had an empirical view which prevented one from seeing the wider implications of academic discourse in the activity of publication. Thus, the development promoted by the pedagogy can affect both teachers and students.

Contributions of the Pedagogical Implementation

The experience reported here can reconfigure the EAP work in higher education: changing its traditional pragmatic focus to a transformative one and revealing the key role instructors have in this process. A critical pragmatist stance provided a good balance in the syllabus. EAP classes constitute a suitable – usually the only – venue to socialize novice researchers with critical issues regarding their work: writing, ethics, the motivation for the conventional and hierarchical nature of academic knowledge production, agency and the geopolitics involved in this production. Thus, a relevant task for the EAP teachers would be at least to sensitize their students to these critical issues, which can be neglected by other literacy brokers.

Moreover, the course illustrates ZDP construction out of the traditional pair/group work interaction interpretation (Newman & Holzman, 1993). The target shifts from learning only to learning that targets development, in this case, theoretical thinking, with transformative potential. EAP classes can foster transformation of both students by fostering their agency through awareness of linguistic resources at their disposal for this process (structures, genres, conventions) and of the activities they are willing to be part of (knowledge production and publication). For teachers, ZDP can be achieved through autoethnographic tools that assist them to make sense of their experimentation with the pedagogy, and as a result, to assess themselves in their professional development. This development has not been extensively researched (Basturkmen, 2019; Campion, 2016), despite EAP teachers' crucial role in internationalizing higher education (Hamp-Lyons, 2011). Developmental Teaching can contribute to EAP teacher education by engaging these instructors in learning actions that promote their engagement with the theories/pedagogical approaches and (re) interpretation of concepts needed or adopted in the enterprise.

6

Teaching English for Academic Purposes in Teacher Education
Examples from South Africa

Nhlanhla Mpofu and Mncedisi C. Maphalala

Introduction

This chapter presents an investigation into the models of instruction used at three South African universities to teach English for Academic Purposes (EAP) in teacher education programmes. In South Africa, most learners receive instruction in a language that is not their native tongue and most high schools use English as the language of learning and teaching (LoLT) (Klapwijk & Van der Walt, 2016). These South African second language learners are exposed to English as a subject at school and as the language for learning disciplinary knowledge across the curriculum. This means that the learners have to study English language and disciplinary knowledge concurrently for subjects such as Mathematics, Technology, Geography, Art and Accounting. This double learning burden has resulted in some university entrants being ill prepared for the level of academic language required at tertiary institutions. In its policy, the Minimum Requirements for Teacher Education Qualifications, the South African Department of Higher Education and Training (2015) highlights that to improve this bleak picture, every student-teacher should be helped to develop proficiency in the language of instruction they choose to work in. In South African high schools, the language of instruction may be either English or Afrikaans. Consequently, to support students' development, South African universities have developed EAP models, which incorporate academic language development and disciplinary knowledge in their teacher education programmes.

Background Discussion

Although the merits of EAP programmes in enhancing academic success at universities are no longer questioned, there is a paucity of pedagogical descriptions of the models such programmes are conceptualized with at universities (Lasagabaster, 2018). In situations where these descriptions are available, as Wingate (2015) points out, the language support offered has been at the grammatical and morphological level which differs from the discipline-specific epistemologies that university students require for academic success. In this chapter, we present an investigation into the models of instruction in three South African universities and highlight the instructional reasoning shaping their implementation in each context. South Africa recognizes eleven official languages, namely, Afrikaans, English, isiXhosa, isiZulu, Sepedi, Sesotho, Setswana, siSwati, Tshivenda, Xitsonga and isiNdebele. In 2018, the South African government also recognized South African Sign Language (SASL) in the education system. The government has also called for the development and promotion of other Indigenous languages such as the Khoi, San and Nam languages. Despite the eleven official languages, English is the dominant language in education and other critical areas of government, business and social interactions. In post-apartheid South Africa, marginalized groups gained entrance to educational institutions such as universities that had traditionally been reserved for a white minority. Twenty-six years after independence, South African high schools still exhibit the apartheid legacies as similar educational trends persist. For example, high school students who graduate from former model C schools (reserved for white students during the apartheid era) have better access to learning opportunities than their counterparts from resource-constrained schools attended mostly by Black students (Namakula & Prozesky, 2019).

English is used as a medium of instruction in all the universities in South Africa. However, university students bring with them various English language experiences with the majority requiring support to transition to the language level expected for academic and disciplinary communication (Dukhan et al., 2016). Different models of English as a medium of instruction (EMI) are simultaneously used as support structures and modelling the approach for student-teachers. EMI as applied in the South African context is aligned to Dearden's (2014, p. 2) description of 'the use of the English language to teach academic subjects in countries or jurisdictions where the first language (L1) of the majority of the population is not English'. In addition, Coyle et al. (2010) explain that the EMI is an approach in which language-supportive methodologies are used to integrate language and the content. South African universities have responded to this challenge by introducing EAP courses in the EMI programmes to support the students who, as a result of uneven language experiences, are unaccustomed to the tacit assumptions, discourse and culture of the disciplinary communication (Baker et al., 2019).

Thus, in this chapter, we present an investigation into the pedagogical models used in teaching EAP to non-native English speakers (NNES), namely student-teachers, at three South African universities.

English for Academic Purposes in the South African Context

The apartheid era left a lasting legacy in the South African education system (Namakula & Prozesky, 2019). During the apartheid period of South African history, universities had 'as [their] main purpose ... to maintain and reproduce, through legislative and other measures, apartheid's social order – a social order in which tertiary education was reserved for an elite few' (May, 2012, p. 138). In post-apartheid South Africa, this racial segregation has resulted in universities being classified as either historically white universities (HWUs) or historically Black universities (HBUs).

During the apartheid era, the HBUs were built to accommodate Black students who could not be admitted to whites-only universities (Ilorah, 2006). Poor funding characterized most HBUs, which have subsequently 'remain[ed] poorly funded and their incoming students comprise mostly those from financially disadvantaged and rural backgrounds. These students can hardly afford to buy textbooks and they lack the study habits necessary for university education' (Ilorah, 2006, p. 79). HBUs continue to attract underprepared students from impoverished communities that have a history of poor teaching and learning experiences (Sennett et al., 2003). By contrast, Bunting (2006) states that HWUs are universities that were funded to educate white students in pre-democratic South Africa. HWUs fall into two categories, depending on the medium of instruction that was used, that is, either Afrikaans or English (Bunting, 2006).

In terms of the language used as the medium of instruction, Wolpe (1995) explains that during the apartheid era language was an important determinant of the linkages that a university had with the government. For example, universities that had closer links with the apartheid project used Afrikaans as the medium of instruction and universities that were liberal used English (Wolpe, 1995), while rural Black universities used English as a medium of instruction. The imbalances left by the segregated apartheid education continued to shape the level of access and success among the Black, coloured, white and Indian students at universities (Soudien, 2008).

In post-apartheid South Africa, Afrikaans and English continue to dominate as the mediums of instruction. However, the Rhodes Must Fall movement agitated for the abolishment of Afrikaans as a medium of instruction and, thus, English dominance has intensified in universities (Hurst & Mona, 2017). This situation has led to universities urgently developing EAP programmes to enhance and support learning across the university curriculum. In teacher education, the Department of Higher Education and Training (2015) has indicated through its Minimum Requirements for Teacher Education Qualifications that all teachers who successfully complete an initial professional qualification should be proficient in the use of at least one official South African language as an LoLT. For the purpose of this study, we focused only on English.

In South African high schools, English is learnt at either the Home Language or the Additional Language level. English at the Home Language level is studied by learners who come to school able to speak and understand it, while English Additional Language is reserved for learners who do not necessarily have any knowledge of the language when they arrive at school. Hurst (2016) explains that the additional language espouses basic English language skills which fails to prepare high school learners for the transition to university. In fact, Hurst (2016, p. 223) highlights that 'although the learner . . . gets a good grade for "English", their proficiency is much more restricted than a learner who, for example, took English as a home language, and attended an English-medium school. This can have significant implications if a learner then transitions to an English-medium school at a higher schooling level, for example high school or tertiary levels'. Lending credence to this argument, Hurst and Mona (2017) note that the use of English as the medium of instruction disadvantages the majority of university NNES. In this chapter, therefore, we focus on the models that three universities use through their EAP programmes to prepare all student-teachers across the Bachelor of Education (BEd) curriculum to use English as the LoLT.

English for Academic Purposes Instruction at Universities

Alexander et al. (2008) present models of EAP instruction which include the adjunct, the stand-alone and the pathway models. The adjunct model is discipline-specific. According to Alexander et al. (2008), EAP and the disciplinary instructors work together to develop EAP content. In terms of this model, English language learning encompasses support in writing, reading and studying. The second model, the stand-alone model, covers English for General Academic Purpose (EGAP) that students require to be successful at university (Schmidt-Unterberger, 2018). Accordingly, English language instruction is not focused on a particular discipline and when this model is used, lectures draw students from across the university curriculum. Lastly, the pathway model is used by universities to allow NNES to enrol in their field of study while simultaneously completing their degree programmes. Importantly, the pathway model allows students to learn English in context. English language learning in this way is sometimes referred to as English for Specific Academic Purposes, which is an approach to teaching English as an additional language that focuses on developing communicative competence in a specific discipline (Schmidt-Unterberger, 2018).

Ultimately, universities determine the type of model used in EAP instruction by ascertaining the needs, goals and content required for students to navigate the academic culture successfully. Boughey and McKenna (2016) imply that in South African universities, the stand-alone model is commonly used. In commenting on the EAP models, Boughey and McKenna (2016) explain that South African universities have continued to use an autonomous model of literacy for EAP that is similar to Alexander et al.'s (2008) stand-alone model. This type of model views language as a set of generic skills that can be transferred to any discipline.

To investigate the EAP models used in the BEd programmes in South Africa, a qualitative case study design was applied with purposive sampling. Yin (2009, p. 1) states that a case study is conducted when a study provides answers to 'a "how" or "why" question asked on issues that researchers have limited control over'. Since our study sought to describe a phenomenon (EAP course) that was already in place in different universities without our influence, a case study design was considered appropriate for the exploration.

Case studies take either a single or a multiple format. Single case studies are ideal when exploring distinctive cases as a strategy to confirm or challenge a theory. Multiple case studies, on the other hand, are favoured for an in-depth analysis of complex and contextual interactions of events and human relationships in different cases (Nieuwenhuis, 2020). We conducted a qualitative multiple case study in an effort to provide a holistic portrayal of how the three universities in question approach the teaching and learning of EAP.

Document analysis was used to collect the data. Document analysis refers to the process of reviewing and analysing documents as a way of eliciting and constructing the participants' social reality in textual form (Bowen, 2009).

Qualitative researchers employ multiple data generation methods to ensure that corroborating evidence from different sources is used to shed light on a theme or perspective (Nieuwenhuis, 2020). Although document analysis was the only method used in this study, we were confident that the number of documents that we reviewed provided us with an account of rich, robust, comprehensive and well-developed data to attend to the triangulation requirement of qualitative explorations.

Specifically, we analysed and interpreted the three universities' Faculty of Education yearbooks (referred to as a 'handbook' at University C) and EAP course outlines that capture the aim, learning outcomes, learning activities and assessment criteria. Excerpts from the BEd programmes that referred to EAP learning were photocopied and analysed in terms of their purpose, learning activities and assessments. To capture the social context that shapes the language support model in each university, in the next section we describe each university's EAP focus as part of the general academic literacy programme. The EAP focus in all the universities forms part of the academic literacy programme for all students across the BEd curriculum.

University A EAP Course Aims and Content

University A is an HBU. At this university, the EAP programme forms part of two themes included in a course called academic and computer literacy. The course guides all first-year students in reading and writing for academic purposes while exposing them to different strategies for accessing and referencing library information (source: Excerpt 1 University A, Yearbook, 2019). The second aspect of the course is computer literacy. As an HBU, University A attracts students from lower socioeconomic education backgrounds who are assumed to possess limited knowledge of the use of technology in learning. The purpose of the EAP part of the academic and computer literacy programme at University A is to improve student knowledge, skills and awareness in the use of English as the university's medium of instruction.

The purpose of this academic literacy course is to enable students to apply the academic reading and writing skills acquired to their learning and use information technology to plan, administer and develop teaching resources and collect information (Excerpt 1 source: University A, Yearbook, 2019, p. 51). In their first year, all students, including the BEd majors, study different genres of academic writing, critical reading and comprehension, strategies for academic grammar and vocabulary development. The course also emphasizes skills such as study skills, note taking and general learning strategies for university. The learning activities in EAP include lectures, tests and assignments.

As an extension of the course, all student-teachers have sessions in the Writing Centre. The Writing Centre at University A on its website explains that it plays a supportive role as most of the students come from disadvantaged rural schools; there was therefore a need to provide guidance in academic literacy in order to enhance their academic performance. The Centre offers students an opportunity to enhance their graduate attributes; academic development; reading; writing and communication skills; presentation skills; cognitive development; and workplace preparation (University A, Writing Centre website). Formative (tests and assignments) and summative assessments are conducted to evaluate the extent to which each student was able to achieve the learning objectives.

University B EAP Course Aims and Content

University B is an HWU. The EAP programme at the university includes two EAP programmes spread over the first and second year of study. The first-year generic academic literacy course is offered by the Centre for Academic Practice. All first-year students, including those enrolled in the Faculty of Education, have to take the Test of Academic Literacy Levels (TALL). Their placement on the test determines the type of the academic literacy class they should enrol for. Thus, the purpose of the placement test is to identify the language needs of the students and place them in the appropriate EAP class. The students, including student-teachers, who do not perform well in the English proficiency test (below 75 per cent) are enrolled in a generic learning support course called Academic Literacy Development. In the first semester, this course supports the students' transition to the use of generic academic skills such as academic vocabulary usage, note taking, understanding academic skills, reading and academic writing. In this course students are taken through basic knowledge of learning strategies, academic vocabulary and register, as well as the reading and writing of academic texts in order to function effectively in the university space.

In the second semester, the Academic Literacy Development course, which forms part of the EAP programme at University B, is meant to support students to develop awareness of academic language usage using the four language skills in learning and accessing knowledge. In addition, students improve their usage of computers for learning. Students are also required to demonstrate the skills and ability to use the English language in oral and written mediums in academic communication. This course is conceptualized for generic academic literacy skills and not in relation to the different academic discipline-specific genres. On completion of this course the students should become part of the academic learning community and participate in this community as well as demonstrate a fundamental level of computer and information literacy (Excerpt 3 source: University B, Yearbook, 2019, p. 276). At the heart of the university's general academic literacy programme is the writing programme. In this programme, all first-year students focus on how to develop an argument, write a sentence, structure a paragraph and pay attention to genre, style, register and voice. The students are also introduced to library resources and referencing.

Also, in their second year, student-teachers read a course called Using English as a Medium of Instruction across the curriculum. The purpose of the course is specifically to support all student-teachers who will work in schools where English is the medium of instruction. English Across the Curriculum, on the other hand, is aimed at understanding the practice of using the English as the LoLT. The focus of this course is to expose student-teachers to the ideal of extending the learning of language skills, providing a context in which they can teach disciplinary concepts, skills and knowledge (Excerpt 4 source: University B, Yearbook, 2019, p. 297). That is, student-teachers are guided to an understanding of content and language learning by giving them strategies and skills for support.

University B uses a variety of instructional activities that encompass lectures, group work, presentations and lesson planning to develop student-teachers' knowledge of the four language skills as they are used in their discipline, as well as presentational skills and knowledge for integrating language skills and disciplinary learning. On completion of this course the students should be able to prepare lessons in different subjects, for example, History, Mathematics, integrating language into subject lessons and communicate complex information reliably and coherently using appropriate academic and professional language (Excerpt 4 source: University B, Yearbook, 2019, p. 297).

Another aim of the Using English as a Medium of Instruction course is to guide students in designing and teaching (through microteaching sessions) integrated language and content lessons in their different disciplines. The programme guides student-teachers to cultivate English language communication skills in teaching disciplinary concepts, skills and knowledge. Importantly, in the second year the student-teachers are provided with opportunities to practise the skills learnt and receive feedback and guidance from both the instructor and their peers. The learning opportunities in this course include lectures, group work, assignments, lesson planning, microteaching and reflective reports. At this university, these different configurations of support are embedded in the discipline-specific communication genres and strategies in English language as a medium of instruction and in the broader academic literacy required for use in the academic community.

University C EAP Course Aims and Content

University C is a new university that was built during the period following the demise of apartheid. In accordance with the South African Department of Education White Paper 3 (1997, p. 29), University C uses the academic literacy course as part of its EAP programme as a means of responding 'to the articulation gap between learners' school attainment and the intellectual demands of higher education programmes. It will be necessary to accelerate the provision of bridging and access programmes within further education'. All first-year students at University C enrol in a generic academic literacy course called the Core Curriculum Course, which is offered through the Centre for Teaching and Learning. As described in Excerpt 5, this course covers the following themes: transition into higher education, academic literacy and computer skills. The academic literacy aspect of the course includes information literacy (accessing the library, referencing and plagiarism) and academic writing (using different writing models and genres). Its aim is to 'introduce students to necessary skills that will enable them to function successfully in a higher institution environment. The course provides students with guidance in how to deal with the main listening, speaking, writing and reading tasks that are required of them in the academic context' (Excerpt 5 source: University C, Core Curriculum Course, 2019, p. 3).

In the fourth year of study, the students in the School of Education at University C read a course called English as Medium for Teaching and Learning. This course is studied only by student-teachers who are not enrolled in any language specializations. These are students who are studying Life Sciences, Physical Sciences, Mathematics, Technical Studies, Social Sciences, Business Studies and the like. As illustrated in Excerpt 6, the purpose of this course is to guide the student-teachers in integrating English language skills with disciplinary learning. The course develops the student-teachers' skills in designing lessons that create learning opportunities in language and content in an English-

Table 6.1 Summary of the Cases

	University A HBU	University B HWU	University C Post-apartheid
Placement Test for EAP	No placement test	Test of Academic Literacy Levels	No placement test is administered
English for General Academic Purpose	EGAP as part of academic literacy course for all first years across all disciplines **Location** Writing Centre **Instructors** Generic academic literacy lecturers and tutors **Learning activities** Lectures; group work; individual work; workshops; writing exercises **Assessment strategies** Assignments; tests and final examination	EGAP as part of academic literacy course for all first years across all disciplines **Location** Centre for Academic Practice **Instructors** Generic academic literacy lecturers and tutors **Learning activities** Speaking activities; reading and writing activities; computer exercises **Assessment strategies** Production of general oral and written mediums used in academic communication	EGAP as part of academic literacy course for all first years across all disciplines **Location** Centre for Teaching and Learning **Instructors** Generic academic literacy lecturers and tutors **Learning activities** Lectures; online learning; group work; individual work; computer exercises **Assessment strategies** Assignments: tests and presentations

English as a Medium of Instruction	No dedicated course for language development	A second-year course with the purpose of supporting all student teachers who will work in schools where English is the medium of instruction **Location** Teaching Practice Office **Instructors** Instructors are English as a Second Language specialists **Learning activities** Microteaching; teaching practice; lesson planning; reflective activities; tests **Assessment strategies** Portfolio of evidence; observations	This is a fourth-year course called English as Medium for Teaching and Learning that develops the student-teachers' skills in designing lessons that create learning opportunities in language and content in an English-medium educational environment **Location** Department of Language Education **Instructors** Instructors are English as a Second Language specialists **Learning activities** Lectures; group work; assignments; lesson planning; microteaching and reflective reports **Assessment strategies** Portfolio of evidence; observations

Source: Authors.

medium educational environment (Excerpt 6 source: University C, Handbook, 2019, p. 113). The course uses practical examples to guide the student-teachers in integrated language and disciplinary learning. The students are directed to an awareness of how English learning can take place across the high school curriculum. Using lesson planning and microteaching, the student-teachers practise and present lessons incorporating language and content learning both at the university and during teaching practicum.

Table 6.1 summarizes the similarities and differences among the three sampled universities in terms of students taking a placement test for EAP; aim of General English for Academic Purposes; aim of the English as a Medium of Instruction model; location; instructors; learning activities and assessment strategies.

Cross-Case Study Analysis

Similar to Benesch's (2001) view in the three universities, the EAP course is designed to respond to the student-teachers' academic history. In all three universities, EAP is seen as both a learning strategy and a pragmatic tool to prepare the student-teachers to be members of the general academic community. This assumption is what Lillis and Scott (2007, p. 7) call 'responding to deficit discourses in the context of an expanding higher education system'. The history of segregation in the South African higher education institutions produces university entrants with uneven English language experiences that the three universities through the EAP programmes sought to minimize. Boughey and McKenna (2016, p. 1) caution that this assumption has resulted in the 'decontextualized learner' whose success in higher education is predicated on the extent to which they have access to the English language. Such understanding of EAP as an instructional approach has resulted in what Boughey and McKenna (2016) describe as an autonomous model of literacy for EAP, which was prevalent in the three sampled universities.

The models at work in the three universities seem to articulate with the views that EAP courses involve two main areas: generic EAP literacy and the study of English as the medium of instruction (EMI) as a teaching and learning approach.

English for General Academic Purposes Focus

At all three universities, the year-long EAP focus in the first year serves as an introduction for students to develop the communication and critical thinking skills that are necessary for them to succeed at university. This introduction is based on the notion that students are apprentices who are being inducted into the broader university community and its conventions. This model of instruction for general EAP in the sampled universities focuses on providing what Gillet (2011) refers to as the language knowledge and practices that students require in order to undertake study at a university that uses English as a medium of learning and teaching.

This type of instruction is similar to Lea and Street's (1998) study skills model which was developed to remedy a deficit in student knowledge that requires attention in the first year of study. From the aims of all the sampled universities, this intervention supports students to fit into the new culture of the academy. The study aligns with Werther et al. (2014) who state that this orientation allows for the provision of generic language support that is located outside the discipline, for example the Writing Centre at University A, the Centre for Academic Literacy at University B and the Centre for Teaching and Learning at University C. All the universities orient a generic EAP course to what Boughey and McKenna (2016) refer to as an autonomous model of literacy, and Wingate (2015) refers to as a skills approach to literacy where the focus is on students becoming familiar with generic academic conventions and genres. Alexander et al. (2008) describe this study focus as a stand-alone model that focuses on students acquiring skills such as studying, reading and writing. This separation is problematic as it implies that there is no link between learning and studying successfully (Wingate 2018).

This generic academic literacy programme is centralized in all the universities. This means the student-teachers receive linguistic support that is broad as opposed to support that is responsive to their specific disciplinary needs. As a result, as noted by Wingate (2018), it is unlikely that student-teachers who are exposed to language skills in this manner will have epistemological knowledge of the conventions, practices and genres that regulate disciplinary interactions and communication. The arrangement of instruction in the generic EAP model in the three universities has an important implication in that it offers an acknowledgement that there is a need for student teachers to be exposed to courses that focus on language skills and conventions such as grammar, vocabulary, structure and syntax. These are meant to develop students' abilities to recognize and produce academic texts but also highlight the fragmentation of this process without a focus on disciplinary-specific language practices.

English as the Medium of Instruction Focus

The EMI approach in teacher education implies a paradigm shift in which content-subject teachers are responsible for learners' language development.

Unlike the findings from Dearden (2014) that student teachers hardly receive EMI preparation, some of the the participants in this study go through a generic EMI course that is not discipline-specific. The EMI focus is evident at Universities B and C but is absent from University A's curriculum. While in the literature, the main reason for the introduction of EMI in universities is to address the internationalization agenda (Dearden & Macaro, 2016), in South Africa, the intention is support of learning across the curriculum. In addition, in initial teacher education programmes, EMI courses serve a preparatory role as student-teachers use of this knowledge in their future high school classroom is critical. In the two universities where EMI courses were taught explicitly, all the BEd students who are not language majors study it as an instructional approach to content-subject learning and teaching. In this instance, as also shown in Wilkinson's (2013) work, the EMI courses prepare the student teachers to conduct their teaching in English as opposed to the study of the English language itself.

As a course of study, the student teachers explore current EMI research and practices to gain foundational knowledge on this worldview. At the same time, the instructors model EMI as an instructional approach. In this way, the student teachers are guided to strategies for teaching their subject matter in a way that is attentive to English as a language of mediating teaching and learning. In addition, the study of EMI as a teaching approach equips the student teachers with the strategies for facilitating and negotiating learning among culturally diverse learners who use English language as medium of instruction. However, across both the universities' curriculum, the student teachers' courses were taught in English as a communicative strategy for disciplinary delivery not as an instructional technique meant to improve language proficiency

In the context of the two universities, the EMI course is aligned to Macaro's (2018, p. 19) definition of the 'use of the English language to teach academic subjects (other than English itself) in countries or jurisdictions in which the majority of the population's first language is not English'. This EMI model is based on an understanding that the acquisition of language skills is more meaningful when located in how knowledge is shared, contested, presented and constructed in a discipline. The study situation is more specific, as many of the same areas of language skills introduced in general EAP are still taught but with particular attention being paid to the language used in the specific disciplinary context. It is critical that this study be located in the students' disciplinary and discursive communities to support their process of acquiring the epistemologies they require for socialization in disciplinary courses and practice (Wingate,

2018; Wingate & Tribble, 2012). Universities B and C presented the general EAP and the EMI courses on a continuum, where the former equipped the students with general language, information and literacy while the latter provided them with opportunities to apply these skills in the different disciplines.

In the EMI model, the universities used the adjunct model as the student teachers focused on integrating content and language skills. However, unlike the explanation provided by Alexander et al. (2008), this course is still generic in that the student teachers are taught by a non-discipline instructor in a class that includes all specializations such as Economics, Management and Accounting; Natural Sciences, Physical Sciences and Mathematics; and Social Sciences. Importantly, the course is used to develop student teachers' comprehensive understanding of language learning in schools that takes place across all subjects.

The study of teaching does not merely involve a simple transfer of knowledge from teacher to the learners. Pedagogical principles dictate that for student teachers to develop their knowledge in EMI, they need to practise this skill on a small scale (lesson planning and microteaching) and a large scale (teaching practice) using discipline-specific and embedded and contextualized opportunities to facilitate and influence the process of learning.

Formative assessment of the student teachers involves lesson planning, microteaching and teaching practice. In both universities (B and C), students are given the task of planning for a lesson applying their knowledge from the EMI course. The teaching practice and the portfolio of evidence are the summative assessment strategies used in both universities. Through the portfolio of evidence, the student teachers are given an opportunity to display their experiences, ideas, artefacts and achievements as developing EMI disciplinary specialists. The assessment for the portfolio of evidence is a reflection report where the student teachers provide the details of their own process of professional development in EMI. The student teachers obtain evidence of the learning by reflecting on their experiences with EMI instructors, mentor teachers during teaching practice and the study of theory in EMI.

The challenges that Macaro et al. (2018) highlight in the implementation of EMI instruction in higher education are also evident in two of the sampled universities. Although EMI development is included in the broad teacher curriculum, its assessment still takes a stand-alone approach, which Alexander et al. (2008) explain is divorced from disciplinary knowledge construction. For example, the microteaching, lesson plan and the teaching practice observation rubrics do not describe the student-teacher's ability to integrate EMI in the actual teaching practice. Secondly, in University C, the student teachers read the EMI course in their fourth year in their last semester. This means they have limited opportunities to practise and reflect on the skills that they have learnt in EMI in discipline-specific teaching practice.

Practical Implications and Relevance

There are important insights that can be gleaned from the different conceptualizations of the EAP courses in the three sampled universities in relation to language testing, curriculum design, learning activities and assessment. The courses here find meaning in the integrated principles for supporting and embedding language development for all student teachers. The EAP programme that results from the combined analysis of the three universities provides a structure that might underpin an EAP programme to support student teachers' language development in the context of disciplinary learning. This proposed EAP programme will have as its broad outcome the development of student teachers' academic vocabulary; use of different sentence structures; academic reading; academic writing; use of different academic genre; as well as critical and logical thinking. These programme themes are introduced through the generic EAP course and reinforced in disciplinary course material and activities (microteaching, lesson planning, etc.). Embedded in the course are pedagogical practices to guide student teachers in attending to the specific academic language demands of different disciplines when planning and delivering lessons, including the demands of English listening, speaking, reading and writing.

To sum up: firstly, EAP requires that student teachers have language skills that enable them to use and interpret different disciplinary genres across the high school curriculum. Student teachers, as future EAP practitioners, require preparation experiences that embed a strong foundation of a variety of language modes, as well as embody and document views and ideas of the academic culture and community. Secondly, student teachers benefit from EAP teaching that develops a sense of the way in which disciplinary knowledge is organized.

7

Pedagogical Approaches in EGAP Coupled with CBI in an EMI Context

Tijen Aksit and Necmi Aksit

Introduction

The number of universities implementing English-medium instruction (EMI) has been increasing rapidly (Macaro et al., 2016; Ozer, 2020; Selvi, 2014; Turhan & Kirkgoz, 2018), and Turkey as a non-Anglophone country has now many universities implementing EMI in their undergraduate programmes in various capacities. There are about 25 universities out of 206 implementing EMI in almost all undergraduate programmes. There are also tens of other universities with some undergraduate programmes taught in English. While some others teach all coursework totally in English, some do so for 30 per cent of their coursework (YOK, 2020). Although there could be more EMI in private than public education in Turkey, there are three private and two state universities among the top five applying EMI. The public ones, in particular, have adopted EMI since they were established, that is long before globalization or internationalization movements started – reasons ranging from attracting international student body and faculty to reaching out, and generating, knowledge in an internationally competitive environment.

The purpose of this chapter is to introduce the pedagogical foundations of an EAP course delivered in a higher education context which is reputable in many ways in Turkey including its approach to English language provision. To this end, first, some initial information about this EMI context will be given and then some background information about the bases of the philosophical foundations of one of its EAP courses, which will be called here *Productive Academic Skills (PAS) course*, will be presented. Next, detailed information regarding the pedagogical foundations, and the preparation and the implementation of the PAS course will be covered. The chapter will conclude with a four-quadrant pedagogical model embodied in this course.

Context

The EMI context explored in this chapter is a foundation university in Turkey's capital, Ankara. It has about 12,000 students, including international ones from seventy-three countries, in nine faculties, and two four-year applied schools. All degree programmes are fully EMI-based, except the Faculty of Law, where only 40 per cent of the courses are taught in English. There are about nine compulsory in-sessional courses offered by its EAP programme every semester. The courses offered range from English for General Academic Purposes (EGAP) to English for Specific Academic Purposes (ESAP) reaching out to more than 3,500 students every year.

To introduce salient characteristics of the pedagogical approaches used in the programme, this chapter focuses on a credit-bearing EGAP-based course: the PAS course. Teaching EGAP highlights the generic language and skills, and the general ability needed to function in academic activities of any given academic discipline, like listening to lectures, participating in classes, seminars and tutorials, carrying out practicums, reading textbooks, academic articles and other academic texts, writing essays, reports, theses, dissertations (Blue, 1988; Bruce, 2011; DeChazal, 2012; Dudley-Evans & St. John's "common core", 1998; Flowerdew & Peacock, 2012; Hyland, 2011). It is a seventy-hour compulsory course to cater for the academic needs of all freshman year students enrolled to the university degree programmes regardless of the discipline they study. To be eligible to start their freshman year, students are required to provide a minimum TOEFL iBT score of 87, a minimum IELTS score of 6.5 (with a minimum score of 5.5 in each section), or a minimum score of C from the university's in-house proficiency exam, which has been validated to be at the B2 level.

The pedagogical approaches in this course of the target context changed direction from late 1990s onwards after the university explicitly demanded the freshman English courses address both the *common academic needs* and varied *personal interests* of the students, while developing their *critical thinking skills*. This approach in time has evolved into a learning-management-system-enhanced, content-based EAP course with an emphasis on differentiation and critical thinking. The new approach demands fusing major curricular paradigms which are based on several educational philosophies.

Philosophical Foundations

The dominant curricular paradigms in higher education contexts are usually centred around understanding and developing academic disciplines and their way of thinking, while developing skillful, competent graduates for advancing the discipline or meeting the needs of the society. One of these paradigms is based on *perennialism*, which is subject-centred, relying heavily on 'defined disciplines or logically organized body of content' and 'develop[ing] the rational person and uncover[ing] universal truths by developing students' intellect' (Ornstein & Hunkins, 2018, p. 52). The second one is based on *essentialism*, which 'emphasizes mastering the skills, facts, and concepts' and aims 'to raise academic standards' (Ornstein & Hunkins, 2018, p. 54).

Focusing on developing the core essential EAP skills across all faculties, students' departments already provide a platform for enhancing academic and professional skills that these two educational philosophies and their accompanying curricular paradigms bring to the fore as depicted in Figure 7.1.

However, as demanded by the university concerned, the inclusion of the two additional variables, namely addressing *varied personal interests* and developing *critical thinking skills*, necessitated the inclusion of the characteristics of two other curricular paradigms. The former is based on *progressivism* and its

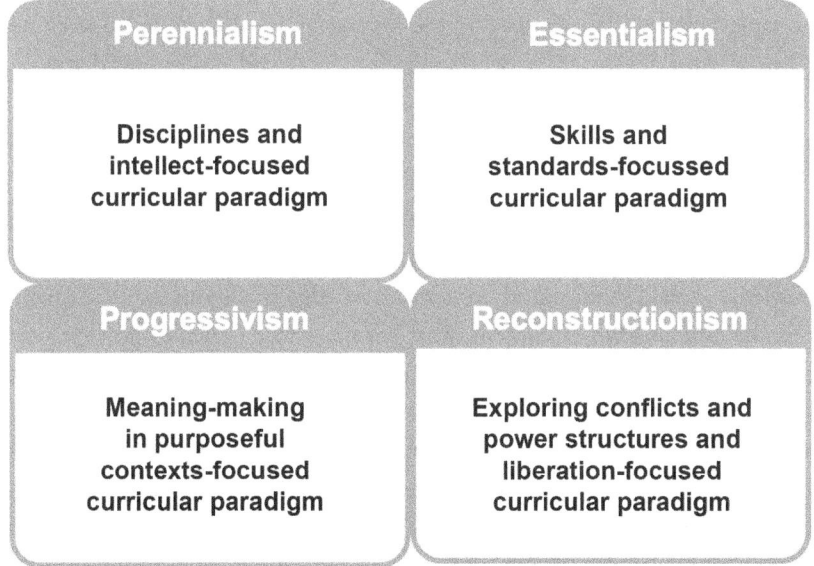

Figure 7.1 Philosophical foundations of the PAS course.

interdisciplinary and intradisciplinary nature, emphasizing both how to think rather than what to think and meaning-making processes (Ornstein & Hunkins, 2018). The latter, 'rooted in reconstructionist philosophy', draws attention to improving and reforming society (Ornstein & Hunkins, 2018, p. 63). One needs to be alert to all forms of status quo and conflicts in society and explore, interpret and question them as necessary. It is also concerned with power relations, oppression and marginalization in society, looking into ways of liberating individuals and societies (Freire, 1970; Giroux, 2010; Ornstein & Hunkins, 2018, p. 63). Both of these are reconceptualist in nature, allowing room for exploring how one's social context shapes views, individual growth, construction of meaning, and critical examination of present structures (Marsh & Willis, 2007; Pinar et al., 1995).

The PAS course embodies these traditional and contemporary educational philosophies and their accompanying curricular paradigms.

Pedagogical Foundations of PAS

To implement the PAS course as intended, one needs to be equipped with the ability to activate and use various pedagogical means concurrently and seamlessly, that is, technological pedagogical content knowledge, content-based instruction, differentiated instruction and critical literacy pedagogy.

Pedagogical Content Knowledge

The target context aims to develop the four language skills within the context of EGAP with a view to critical analysis of oral and written academic and non-academic texts, and identification and construction of well-reasoned and supported arguments. This suggests that to deliver a course as such one needs to be pedagogically competent in developing essential EGAP skills (Charles & Pecorari, 2016; Ding & Bruce, 2017; Hyland & Hamp-Lyons, 2002) and also one should be able to relate their pedagogical knowledge to their subject-matter knowledge, called pedagogical content knowledge by Shulman (1986), which 'embodies the aspects of content most germane to its teachability', including 'most regularly taught topics in one's subject area, the most powerful analogies, illustrations, examples, explanations, and demonstrations, . . . make[ing] it comprehensible to others' (p. 9). To function effectively in this context, EAP instructors are expected to be deeply knowledgeable in some academic and/or non-academic content areas.

Mishra and Koehler (2006) further developed Shulman's conception of pedagogical content knowledge and a conceptual framework for technology integration called technological pedagogical content knowledge (TPACK), which aimed to bring to the fore the need to educate and train technologically competent teachers. Technology has gradually been incorporated into instruction over the years and in time evolved into highly developed, responsive e-learning platforms offering lots of online tools for enhancing instruction. Earlier forms were first introduced in the 1990s without a common name. Current e-learning platforms are called learning management systems (LMS), and are mainly used for sharing documents, submitting and returning assignments, and communicating and collaborating online during and/or outside class time (Coll, 2015; Kim et al., 2014; Lonn & Teasley, 2009; Rubin et al., 2010). After the Covid-19 outbreak, they have been developed further, and many start-ups have emerged providing additional online means and a solution for difficulties (Dhawan, 2020); the *Zoom* platform has been an integral part of PAS.

Content-Based Instruction

Content-based instruction is defined as 'concurrent teaching of subject matter and second language skills' (Brinton et al., 1989, p. 2). There are at least eight approaches to content-based instruction, and one of them in particular is informed by EAP instruction at North American universities: in *sheltered instruction* and *adjunct instruction*, 'content is relatively predetermined', and in the case of *theme-based* instruction, 'content is selected by the language teacher (and/or students)'. To Stoller and Grabe (1997, p. 2), 'all CBI is fundamentally theme-based', which is 'a central curricular notion in the Six-T's Approach', and its design criteria are composed of themes, texts, topics, threads, tasks and transitions.

The empirical support for content-based instruction is strong. It is claimed that it enhances second language acquisition and language skills development through what is called comprehensible and meaningful input, leading to greater motivation and internalization of concepts and skills with the help of coherent and thematic presentation of content (Anderson, 1993; Curtain & Pesola, 1994; Glynn & Spenader, 2020; Stoller & Grabe 1997). To Richards and Rodgers (2001), language learning becomes more motivating when the focus is on ideas, issues and opinions rather than just language: 'People learn a second language more successfully when they use the language as a means of acquiring information, rather than as an end itself' (p. 209).

Differentiated Instruction

Tomlinson (2017) defines differentiated instruction (DI) as 'a systematic approach to planning curriculum and instruction for academically diverse learners', suggesting there are five classroom elements that teachers can differentiate, namely *content, process, product, affect* and *environment*, DI has been used in K-12 contexts for decades. Recently, there has also been interest in higher education contexts in the concept of DI for various purposes. Tulbure (2013) investigated, in experimental terms, and found significant improvement in academic achievement when learning-styles-based instruction, rather than uniform style instruction, is used. Motivated by 'accountability and attrition pressures', McCarty et al. (2016, p. 36) conducted a study focusing on how the use of DI in the form of 'renewing teaching practices' and 'integrating technology' enhanced student engagement. Driven by the need to meet 'diverse needs of individual students' in large classes in higher education, Turner et al. (2017) carried out a qualitative study, and the results indicate that it is challenging to implement DI in large classes at a research university, and instructors involved need 'a better understanding of differentiated instruction strategies'.

Critical Literacy Pedagogy

Critical literacy is a pedagogical practice stemming from Freire's (1970) concept of Critical Pedagogy. It questions 'power relations' in society, and 'challenges the status quo to discover alternative paths for self and social development', with a view to seeking liberation and emancipation, and inviting people into action (Shor, 1999, p. 2). To Freire (1970), 'critical reflection is also action' (p. 128). In educational contexts, it may start from critiquing existing structures. To Giroux (1992, p. 9), 'a critical pedagogy of literacy needs to erode rather than accommodate dominant disciplinary structures and discourses'.

The term *critical* within the context of language teaching suggested using higher order thinking skills (Luke, 2004, p. 21), and this has gradually evolved into second language educators' engagement with the critical, that is, power structures and relations, and language learners' becoming aware of cultural reproduction of the status quo (Ding & Bruce, 2017). As Benesch (2001, 2009) hoped before, there are now language classrooms that allow EAP teachers to choose areas of critical inquiry while having their learners become more and more critically cognizant through exposure to academic and non-academic texts.

PAS Preparation and Implementation

PAS course is offered to students from all faculties, from engineering to fine arts. Students take this first-year EGAP course with peers from diverse disciplines. In order to meet the 'common' academic needs of these students from various academic disciplines, the PAS course exposes students to varied content, depending on the instructors' interests and passions, but has common learning objectives and common learning outcomes which include, but are not limited to, critical analysis and evaluation of written and spoken authentic academic input, and construction and communication of well-reasoned and supported written and spoken arguments.

Every semester the PAS course is offered to about 1,000–1,500 students, taught by about fifty EAP instructors who are full-time employees of the university and on average have been affiliated with the university for more than ten years. Around 40 per cent of the instructors are native speakers of English and the rest are local Turkish instructors. All instructors have at least a master's degree in a relevant subject, and there are few PhD holders. The number of PAS sections offered each semester varies from forty-five to seventy-five, with about twenty to twenty-two students in each section.

Instructors offering the PAS course work in four academic units, each led by an academic supervisor, liaising with two curriculum and testing coordinators of the programme, and the EAP programme director. Unit meetings are held on an ongoing basis, providing information about all aspects of the course from planning to assessment before, during and after implementation. Outcomes of these processes are fed back into the current and next implementation cycle of the course.

Course Guidelines

Each instructor is required to prepare their own PAS course, following the programme's course design guidelines that reflect the characteristics of four curriculum paradigms and making various choices, including critical. The guidelines include specification of course goals, learning objectives related to each goal, and recommended process and product-based tasks and activities to facilitate critical analysis of course input materials and constructing reasoned arguments. The EAP instructors are given flexibility to change the order of the goals and/or objectives. They choose their own delivery method but are required to include one-to-one tutorials to provide individualized support. They also need to use a learning management system called *Moodle* to enhance instruction. Therefore, effective teaching of PAS necessitates the ability to amalgamate content, EAP pedagogy and technology (Mishra & Koehler, 2006). As a quick response to Covid-19, the instructors were able to integrate yet another technological component by delivering all classes via *Zoom* within a three days' period. To meet the Bologna Process (European Commission, 2020) expectations, the instructors are also provided with clear instructions regarding how to design their assessment tasks. The diagnostic common academic reading text and task are used at the beginning of the term to identify strengths and weakness of individual students in terms of their overall language and other EAP skills, and a common reading-into-writing final examination is administered at the end of the semester to assess student learning, compare performance and ensure standards across sections.

Course Themes

As far as content is concerned, to develop students' EAP skills, each PAS course instructor is expected to choose an overarching course theme and thematically arrange their course content around that theme in a meaningful way, ensuring that multiple perspectives and disciplines are included, and that they are conducive to argumentation. Given the number of instructors teaching the course, this suggests there are about fifty different themes, and tonnes of texts that are covered and focused on in this course. The first-year students are provided with information about these themes at the beginning of the semester and students are given the initial week for visiting various instructors' classes to explore, and choose from, the course themes that they would be interested in the most.

The theme selected by the instructor is expected to be conducive to making interdisciplinary, and intradisciplinary, connections, and it is usually, if not always, based on an area the instructor is already knowledgeable and passionate about, or an area the instructor is interested in and would like to explore and learn about further. This ensures that instructors have the content knowledge needed, and they are well-informed about various related concepts, ideas or theories, as well as practices and approaches leading to such knowledge (Shulman, 1986).

Implementation

Not only the content but also the process and product are differentiated throughout the PAS course (Tomlinson, 2017). Driven by a controversial central question, and some sub-questions, the PAS course is delivered following six phases (Table 7.1) during the course of a fourteen-week-long semester.

Phase 1

Students are exposed to *content and theme of the course* at hand in general, allowing them to get a sense of the course before they choose and formally get

Table 7.1 Phases of PAS in a Nutshell

Phases	Elements
Phase 1: Intro	Exposure to overall course theme and the central question
Phase 2: Diagnostic text and task	Diagnostic common reading and task
Phase 3: Process-based essay	Exposure to first sub-theme of the course and the sub-question
	Reading two to three texts
	Class and LMS discussions
	Critical reading and response
	Drafting the essay (around 800 words) after guided preparation
Phase 4: Product-based essay	Exposure to second sub-theme of the course and the sub-question
	Reading two to three texts
	Student-led class or LMS discussions
	Product-based essay (800–1000 words) after guided preparation
Phase 5: Product-based essay	Exposure to second sub-theme of the course and the sub-question
	Reading two to three texts
	Student-led class or LMS discussions
	Student presentations
	Product-based essay (800–1000 words) after guided preparation
Phase 6: Independent essay	Reading-into-writing essay (around 700 words) under exam conditions
	On a theme not covered during semester

registered. This normally takes about a week to ten days, constituting in total five to seven course hours (one course hour is fifty minutes).

Phase 2

A common unassessed *diagnostic reading text and task*, which is also used for discussion afterwards, is implemented in all sections across the programme to identify students' entry-level abilities in terms of reading, speaking, listening skills and language and vocabulary use. This phase normally lasts for another five to seven hours of the course.

Phase 3

This phase of the course takes about four weeks making up around twenty class hours. *Process-based essay writing* is the end product of this phase. One-to-one tutorials after the draft writing and the use of LMS ensure that more time is spent beyond available twenty class hours during this phase. In order to prepare students for their first essay writing experience in the course, at this phase students are exposed to the *first controversial sub-theme* of the course theme. Some of the prominent elements of this stage are as follows:

1. Students extensively and intensively read at least two or three, preferably multi-perspective, interdisciplinary, authentic texts from a variety of genres chosen bearing in mind Coxhead's (2000) academic word list and analyse the texts in terms of content, style and language use.
2. Instructor-led discussions are carried out in class not only to facilitate students' in-depth understanding of 'what text means', as in a standard approach, but also to make them question 'what text does' (Bazerman & Prior, 2004, p. 3) to identify the social impact of the text.
3. Students are asked to critically read course texts and write a response in 300–500 words. The purpose is to develop note-taking skills, and to identify, summarize and critically evaluate arguments in a text. Answers are uploaded onto the *Moodle* and *Turnitin* similarity reports are generated automatically.
4. Students produce their essay drafts in class, getting support from their peers and instructors as necessary within three class hours. They are a minimum of 800-word argument-led process-based essays where clear expression of a stance is expected. The support and evidence for student arguments are based on course readings. Students cite sources using a referencing style selected by the course instructor.
5. Students are first given written feedback on argumentation and organization of ideas in their drafts, and one-on-one tutorial time of about at least fifteen minutes is allocated to encourage students to both come with questions about written feedback given in critical terms, and to pose and defend their line of argument orally. The whole process is completed using outside class time. An action plan is prepared out of this student–instructor interaction and is expected to be incorporated into the final version of the essay. It is important to note that tutorials are not compulsory and not graded, but there is very high attendance rate.
6. The final version of the essay is uploaded onto the *Moodle* for grading, and a *Turnitin* similarity report is generated automatically. Students have access to this report, and the instructor may use some reports during instruction for giving good examples or showing some problematic cases.

Phase 4

This phase takes another four weeks of the course, making up around twenty class hours and additional non-class hours for tutorials and the *Moodle* activities. During this phase, students are exposed to the *second controversial sub-theme* and its sub-question through three or more further course-reading texts, which have the same qualities as the ones read in Phase 3. The following are some common elements of this phase:

1. Student-led discussions are carried out as explained above under Phase 3.
2. The essay of around 800 to 1,000 words produced in this phase and the preparation and stages followed before and after the production of the essay are of exactly the same nature as the one written in Phase 2.
3. One major difference of this phase compared to Phase 3 is that after weeks of guided preparation in and outside class time, students produce their essays in class, getting support from their peers and instructors as necessary within three class hours.

Phase 5

During this phase, students are exposed to the *third controversial sub-theme* and its sub-question through three or more further course reading texts, which have the same qualities as the ones read in Phases 3 and 4. The final product of this phase is the writing of the second *product-based essay* of the semester during a period of three class hours. This phase encompasses similar elements of the previous essay-producing phases. One additional element at this stage is as follows:

1. Students make individual presentations to demonstrate their in-depth understanding of an oral (e.g. TED Talk) or written text. To do so, students are expected to understand, analyse and evaluate arguments in the text, making links with course content. Each presentation takes about eight to ten minutes, followed by a three to five minutes question-and-answer session.

Phase 6

This phase constitutes the writing of an *independent academic essay* under exam conditions of three hours. During the exam students are provided with one or two academic reading texts (each 1,200–1,800 words) on a controversial issue exposing students to multiple perspectives around the issue on a topic not covered in any of the sections in that semester. Students are expected to read the texts provided and produce an argument-led academic essay of around 700 words applying the same strategies practised all through the semester.

Discussion

The PAS course is different in many ways from such courses offered by many other EMI universities in Turkey. To begin with, it is a compulsory course with many strict requirements including 90 per cent attendance, and it has the capacity to offer many sections of the same course, each with a different set of themes and sub-themes.

The course is found to be challenging and demanding for both its students and instructors. Based on student evaluation of the course, although the workload is considered to be heavy, the course has students read, and research about, controversial texts, which they would normally never read about. It gives the message that when they know or have background about a topic, they would write more successfully. The course is also found to be instrumental in how to write an academic essay and improve academic skills, language skills and analytical and critical thinking skills. To most students, the skills gained throughout the course are considered to be transferable to other courses. Students also acknowledge that the course also helps them to listen to others' point of view in a critical sense and at the same time helps with how to express oneself in difficult, controversial situations. They also express that they benefit a lot from one-on-one tutorials. Therefore, the feedback from students always notes that the course is totally appealing and rewarding. One student says,

> The expectations of the course are very high and the readings are very advanced. The course really pushes the students but once you get used to, you see how much you have improved.

Another one notes,

> The course and the topics at hand were both interesting and quite controversial. Thus, it is possible to say that learning English while finding the chance to talk about such topics may be a very rare and beneficial opportunity.

Another student summarizes the perspective of many of their peers by saying,

> The course improved my skills about writing essays and doing presentations. How to summarise ideas most important to other people to support my own

ideas to create a new strong argument. I had a chance to learn how to express myself in difficult controversial issues and a chance to hear other people's point of view. Had a better understanding of planning things and figuring out which ideas will work for presenting, writing or speaking.

The EAP instructors teaching the course find it extremely motivating to be able to design a course around a theme of their own choice. To them, their courses are built around stimulating themes that are intellectually and emotionally engaging. It also gives an opportunity for professional and personal development. They feel they are more committed when they plan their own course content. The theme-based approach gives flexibility in terms of changing sub-themes and texts. They believe they pass on their enthusiasm to their students. The most common feedback from instructors denotes how *'intellectually stimulating'*, *'challenging'* and *'rewarding'* it is to be an instructor of PAS. One instructor puts their experience of how they design their course simply as follows:

> As I prepare my courses, I always start with coming up with a number of topics that I am interested in. Then, I look for some challenging texts from a variety of disciplines and prepare tasks and student-centered activities.

Feedback coming from the students' departments highlights the fact that the course is 'academically supportive', 'enhancing students' ability to express themselves effectively in written and oral forms'.

The PAS course is firmly constructed with clear means and ends but it is also responsive and adaptive, which means there is room for modification based on the results of the diagnostic assessment tool administered at the beginning of the course to look into how else to provide more support to the diverse student levels and needs in the group (Tomlinson, 2017), and which also means that there is also room for including more, or different, texts and activities that would engage students cognitively, emotionally and critically, depending on their level of questions and level of interest. It, therefore, evolves and thus is co-created with the students. If for any reason students do not feel motivated enough by the end of the first week of instruction, they are allowed to choose another section of the course with a totally new set of themes and sub-themes.

In addition, the course includes many tasks which are made gradually more demanding, but it is flexible enough to provide personalized support through individual tutorials, constant feedback including peer, concept questions and plans of action. Students are gradually and increasingly given more control and expected to demonstrate the extent to which they are able to transfer the skills they have developed over the course of the semester.

Furthermore, the PAS course also promotes students taking responsibility of their own learning. During each essay-writing phase, both instructors and students are required to follow explicitly stated tutorial guidelines, which expect and encourage students to engage in the critical reading of texts, develop and defend their lines of arguments, and write a plan of action in terms of what to do and what not to do in their future essay writing. Individual tutorials are offered as a support mechanism, and student participation rate is found to be considerably high in all cases. Students are also asked to take responsibility of their learning by having them reflect on their own progress in relation to academic writing skills by specifically addressing a number of guided questions and providing evidence in relation to the extent to which they meet task requirements (Glynn & Spenader, 2020).

The last but not least, the course is based on solid philosophical foundations, and by the same token, the course is based on well-founded pedagogical approaches guiding design and implementation processes magnificently.

As discussed, to design their PAS course, the EAP instructors tend to choose a theme they are already knowledgeable or passionate about and therefore they are well-informed about various related concepts, ideas or theories, as well as practices and approaches leading to such knowledge. They are also expected to incorporate LMS into instruction. The course has been delivered with the help of a *Turnitin*-integrated LMS system since 2007, which has been helpful in many ways. For example, it has increased course exposure time, eased the process of collecting assignments and giving feedback, and facilitated online group discussions through forums.

while there are very detailed course design guidelines, the EAP instructors in the programme, and the newly recruited ones in particular, are given support throughout. Anybody new to the programme goes through a thorough induction process, liaising with their academic supervisors on a regular basis to understand, and fine-tune if necessary, what the course design and implementation expectations are. Then, they start designing, and re-designing, their course, they follow detailed course design guidelines and get consistent feedback. Finally, they design and propose a course ready for implementation. To increase the impact of PAS course, the EAP instructors are offered an in-house training programme, which is compulsory for newly recruited instructors. It is composed of three modules, which include a minimum of 250 hours of reading, research and assignments. One of the modules is action research-oriented, requiring instructors to be involved in teacher action research stemming from their teaching-learning process. Upon successful completion of the training programme, participants are given a certificate, which underlines the institutions' support given to teaching English for academic purposes. Finally, through classroom observations, and yearly reviews, the instructors are given feedback on their performance, based on EAP teacher competency framework adopted from the Competency Framework for Teachers of English for Academic Purposes (BALEAP, 2008).

The PAS course embraces the principles of DI. As far as *content* is concerned, each EAP instructor chooses his or her own theme and sub-themes, topics and sub-topics, central questions and sub-questions conducive to argumentation. The course instructors also choose their own texts and use them as a means to an end, the end being the development of EGAP skills. As regards *process*, the course is composed of several phases, and each phase has a different focus with different sets of activities and tasks, offering different modes of learning through LMS and one-on-one tutorials, encouraging peer support and extending access outside class time. With regard to *product*, at the end of each phase, there is a clear outcome, which is usually assessed.

Within the light of critical literacy pedagogy, the PAS course instructors select their own themes which are meant to engage and challenge students critically and which encourage the exploration of conflicts and related multiple perspectives. The course instructors are expected to arrange their pedagogical means to involve students in decoding meaning and meaning-making processes, deconstructing academic and non-academic texts, constructing reasoned stances and arguments, questioning positions and critically analysing, and responding to, written and spoken input both discrete and in intertextual terms.

It is also important to note the university's position regarding the EAP programme. The university administration is always accessible and approachable, giving utmost importance to effective academic language provision and providing any support to increase its impact. The university made a policy decision decades ago to move towards the direction of a content-based EAP instruction and let the policy evolve gradually. The administration made two of the EAP programme courses (first-year EGAP courses) compulsory, increasing the minimum passing grade of one of them, and encouraged other faculties to include additional ESAP courses in their curricula to ensure continuity. There are now many other courses meeting the needs of various students in technical, professional, philosophical and creative terms. Also, five of the EAP instructors in the programme have a PhD degree, and all other instructors, except two, have a relevant master's degree. They are not required to conduct academic research but if they do, the university recognizes any academic efforts by means of its merit system. The high status given by the university helps develop academic identity and agency in the programme.

Conclusion

This chapter focuses on the case of an EAP programme in an EMI context at a non-Anglophone higher education institution. It outlines how a credit-bearing in-sessional EGAP course, in particular, offered in this context operates within the framework of pedagogical principles and practices. What makes this context unique is that its pedagogy is multifaceted, blending the four pedagogical approaches in an in-sessional EAP context: *technological pedagogical content knowledge, content-based instruction, differentiated instruction* and *critical literacy pedagogy*, which we would like to call the four-quadrant pedagogical model of EGAP.

The Four-Quadrant Pedagogical Model of EGAP

The vision of the university necessitated a multifaceted four-quadrant pedagogical model (Figure 7.1) based on four educational philosophies and their accompanying curricular paradigms for in-sessional EAP provision on campus:

To design, develop and implement an EGAP course towards these ends demands successful amalgamation and interplay of the following dimensions and their accompanying pedagogies:

1. Utilizing technology-enhanced pedagogical academic or non-academic content knowledge and developing higher order thinking skills: technology-enhanced pedagogical content knowledge
2. Identifying and developing target EAP skills that need to be developed across departments: EGAP
3. Using varied content, generating interest, and providing platform for constructing meaning and using language in purposeful situations: differentiated academic and/or non-academic content-based instruction
4. Identifying and exploring the concepts of conflict, power and emancipation in academic and non-academic texts: critical literacy pedagogy

The *four-quadrant pedagogical model to EGAP* intends to spark interest, cultivate intellect, develop language and EAP skills, sustain curiosity and inspire critical engagement, using academic and non-academic texts in discrete and intertextual terms.

8

Academic Teachers' Perceptions of Content and Language Integrated Learning (CLIL) Programme with EAP Teachers

Xiucai Lu and Bin Zou

Introduction

The of CLIL Scene

English for Academic Purposes (EAP) teaches students to write for a wide range of disciplines such as science, mathematics and economics (Jordan, 1997; Scarcella, 2003). Tasks in EAP class include reading abstracts, writing critiques, summaries, annotated bibliographies, reports and research projects (Swales, 1990). EAP can help learners for academic study and research and contribute to the success of all students in long-term academic learning (Hyland & Hamp-Lyons, 2002; Hyland, 2006; Scarcella, 2003).

Grown out of Europe in the 1990s, content and language-integrated learning has experienced rapid development in secondary education sectors ever since. It is 'an educational approach where curricular content of subjects is taught to students through a language that is neither their first language nor the dominant medium of instruction in the respective education system' (Dalton-Puffer & Nikula, 2014, p. 117). Due to its fundamental feature of 'integration', CLIL is open to interpretation where it is also referred to as bilingual education, immersion education, interdisciplinary learning and so on. The principle of CLIL is that 'foreign language development is facilitated in subject classes, and content knowledge development is supported by content-based language learning strategies in language classes' (Denman et al., 2013, p. 287). In recent years, CLIL has also been identified as an important integration in helping university students to enhance their learning in academic disciplines. For example, in the university context, CLIL provides academic literacy instruction including academic reading, presenting, evaluating and communicating in subject community, understanding subject content and writing (Wingate, 2015). Thus, it can be seen that CLIL is related to EAP and can be integrated into EAP lessons. CLIL programmes can be co-delivered by EAP teachers and subject teachers to further enhance students' academic study in higher education (Jordan & Ford, 2016). Furthermore, CLIL has expanded rapidly in the past decades and into a wider range of contexts such as outside of Europe (e.g. Japan, China) and in tertiary education sectors as well. In China, this approach still stays fresh except in Hong Kong, where English-medium instruction (EMI) has its prominent status in educational and social sectors due to its colonial history. In mainland China, CLIL is gaining popularity in English language programme classroom teaching in public universities and colleges. However, the focus remains solely on language improvement using content-based materials. As Swain (2006) pointed out, conceptual internalization through foreign language is a crucial part of the learning process. The emphasis of CLIL shifts to the principles and conditions to promote collaborative knowledge construction and deeper learning across languages. Stimulated by the theoretical support, some EMI universities have adopted this approach to promote academic learning. Thus, it is important to explore CLIL in tertiary education in mainland China.

CLIL Research Context

This study aims to investigate the CLIL programme in an EMI university in mainland China. The CLIL programme was established in this EMI university in 2013. Ninety per cent of the undergraduates in this EMI university are local Chinese who need to complete their degree study in English. In this monolingual social environment where Chinese is the only daily communication language, students' English proficiency was not evaluated in the university entry exam. Many have never spoken with a non-English-speaking foreigner. Meanwhile, subject teachers in this university are from more than ten nationalities. Despite being provided sixteen timetabled hours of EAP lessons per week, undergraduates are faced with many linguistic challenges of specific requirements from disciplines. Hence, the CLIL programme was established in 2013 with the purpose of developing students' academic literacy and meeting the specific disciplinary needs. Meanwhile, it also aims to reinforce communication between EAP teachers and subject teachers (Jordan & Ford, 2016) and ideally to promote pedagogies for both sides. What deserves mentioning is that CLIL at this university is more than the traditional integration of content and language where the content is taught in a foreign language by one teacher. There is a distinct feature of collaboration between content instructors and EAP instructors. In this CLIL programme, an EAP teacher and a subject teacher collaboratively teach a subject module both in and outside of classrooms. Nearly all faculties have CLIL modules for both undergraduate and graduate programmes. There are two major types of CLIL in this programme. One type is that the lecturers and language teachers have separate scheduled teaching hours for the module. Lecturers disseminate the subject content in the lecture and the language teachers usually observe and take notes, aiming to better understand the academic content so as to provide effective and relevant support to students in the subsequent seminar. In the seminar, the language teachers engage students with various linguistic activities to consolidate students with the concept and help them reproduce the knowledge with language assistance. The other type is integrative CLIL where the language teacher will be given time in the lecture to participate in teaching and facilitate activities. The collaboration is flexible and CLIL teachers in one module will meet a few times in a semester to discuss plans and make adjustments. Supplementary to general EAP courses, CLIL was meant to provide more timely and specific language support for students. The reflective survey conducted by Jordan and Ford in 2016 suggested that activities such as providing pre-class glossary, note-taking exercises, providing pre-reading materials and facilitating discussions in/after class are very helpful from the language tutors' perspective. However, how subject teachers perceive this collaboration was missing in this survey.

Dalton-Puffer (2013) pointed out that seeking convergences in the curricular goals of foreign language education and subject education and understanding how classroom learning and teaching can work together towards those goals helps integration. One issue in these scenarios is that subject teachers usually lack qualifications of teaching academic literacy and the EAP teachers usually lack the background of the content. Therefore, the collaboration between language specialists and subject teachers is meant to be a solution. To evaluate this implementation, qualitative research was conducted to investigate the CLIL programme in an EMI university where language and subject specialists co-teach content modules. This study aims to explore the academic staff's perceptions of this type of integrated learning in improving students' learning experience and performance. It also intends to identify what EAP activities are considered helpful for students who learn in various disciplines. The research may also propose potential improvements for more effective collaboration to operate. The research questions are:

1. From content lecturers' view, what are the benefits of co-teaching with language tutors?
2. How can CLIL bridge the gap for EAP and disciplinary teaching and promote deep learning?

Literature Review

Much research about CLIL in relation to EAP has been conducted since the 1990s. Most of the literature has focused on the benefits of CLIL to students' language development. The CLIL groups outperform non-CLIL groups on cloze and receptive tests (Jimenez Catalan & Ruiz de Zarobe, 2009). A case study in a Chinese university conducted by Gao and Cao (2015) proves that CLIL motivates doctoral students to acquire deeper understanding of strategies and purposes in learning EAP. More attention these years has been shifted to CLIL's non-linguistic benefits. Some research investigated the effectiveness of language content instructor collaboration based on the level of engagement. Insights have been gained about the role of academic literacy and language-focused instruction in content learning. Jacobs (2007) discovered that collaborations were less successful when the discourse of language is considered as only a tool for communication or supplementary. Zappa-Hollman (2018) conducted qualitative research about the collaboration of EAP and content instructors. She has found that EAP instruction in the adjunct-CLIL courses was a 'fundamental complement to the disciplinary course' (Zappa-Hollman, 2018, p. 600) and therefore enriches students' learning experiences. Grandinetti and Langellotti (2013) agreed that CLIL enhances subject content learning if learning materials are appropriately designed. Jappinen (2005, p. 163) also pointed out that CLIL 'supports thinking and content learning, in particular, in situations where the learners have to compare different concepts and meaning schemes'. Coyle (2018, p. 167) pointed out that the emphasis of CLIL as a pedagogy has shifted from initially promoting EFL learning to the promotion of 'collaborative knowledge construction and deeper learning across languages'.

Many CLIL programmes show the inclination to use academic content as a setting to learn the English language. For instance, it has been found to motivate foreign language learning (Lasagabaster, 2011; Ruiz de Zarobe, 2013). In addition, CLIL benefits language lesson planning and teaching as Coyle (2005) addressed that CLIL approach always sets the content as the starting point before lesson planning, and students are instructed to 'use the language to learn' which is different from the traditional way of 'learn to use the language'. The Language Triptych (Coyle et al., 2010) raised students' language development in three stages of content learning: language *of* learning, language *for* learning, language *through* learning. In the first stage, students are scaffolded with needed language to conceptualize the content. In the second stage, students are encouraged to operate using their language experiences and explore new knowledge. In the final stage, new language emerges in the progression of learning. This triptych can serve as a very helpful tool for lesson planning on the EAP teachers' side. Teachers need to define objectives and design talks, discussions, debates and other types of activities in the CLIL setting to achieve the learning purpose and the development of language in the learning progression.

Swain (2006, p. 98) defined deep learning as 'successful internalizing conceptual content knowledge and shaping knowledge and experience through knowledge'. It is well accepted that students' academic success relies considerably on them being able to use academic language to help them understand and attain the learning goals of content subjects. Namely, students need to be equipped with academic literacy skills such as academic reading, writing, presenting, evaluating and note taking in that specific subject community. Language development in this setting is not constrained to grammar and lexical words or even to subject-specific vocabulary and phrases. Students should also learn the purpose of the language, the genre and style of that particular disciplinary subject. This is one significant feature of language learning in CLIL compared with EAP.

The significance of disciplinary literacy is also emphasized by education policy makers:

> If all students are to learn effectively, they must become literate to learn in different areas of the curriculum across the phases of learning. . . . If these literacy demands are left implicit and not taught explicitly they provide barriers to learning. (Queensland Government, Department of Education and Arts, n.d., p. 4)

Considering the significance of language (disciplinary literacy) in the process of deep learning, EAP teachers need to collaborate with content teachers to define the target content and learning outcomes. EAP teachers also need to scaffold students with needed language and design tasks and activities for learners to use the accessible language to activate deep learning. For the integration between language and content truly to be fulfilled, materials and activities need to be 'cognitively demanding' and 'linguistically accessible' (Coyle, 2005).

Llinares et al. (2012) has identified that the research on pedagogy, integrative planning and assessment that accounts for both content and language concerns as urgent research needs. Dalton-Puffer and Nikula (2014) called on research to involve subject specialists to fill in the research gap. In the meantime, some researchers have concerns about the benefits of CLIL programme to content learning. The major ones are the lack of qualified CLIL teachers (Luo, 2006; Prasongporn, 2009), and that there is no hard evidence and empirical research to show the effectiveness of CLIL programme on content learning. One of the very few research projects of this kind was conducted by Yang (2014). He attempted to examine the correlation of CLIL programme in a tertiary education sector in Taiwan with the learners' content achievement. He noted that the entry level of language proficiency could positively enhance content performance at the initial stage. However, the effect is not sustained after the first semester. This is because students' language proficiency continues to improve, and evaluating content performance involves many other non-academic concerns.

Following the previous studies discussed earlier, the subject specialists' perspective can be an integral part of the multifaceted picture of CLIL research.

Methodology

Participants in this research included eleven subject teachers from a variety of departments such as Architecture, Civil Engineering, Urban Planning and Design, Chemistry, Biology, Business, China Studies, English and Media. All thirteen subject teachers had been co-teaching with EAP teachers for one to three years. They volunteered to participate in this study. The number of undergraduates taking each CLIL module is roughly 30 to 200 and modules for postgraduates have around fourteen to twenty-three students. All the CLIL modules are credit-bearing degree courses.

The research instrument was the individual, semi-structured interview. Questions prompted the subject teachers to describe their experiences in CLIL teaching and reflect on the collaboration with EAP teachers. For example, the interviewees were asked about what linguistic skills students need to learn more effectively in the content module, how critical thinking is taught in the module, why language teachers' help is needed in the subject teaching, what practices of material and assessment development were helpful in the collaboration, how effective collaboration is to enhance students' learning in the content module, etc.

All interviews were individual and each lasted at least thirty minutes. The purpose of the interviews was stated clearly to the interviewees when the request was sent and oral consent had been received before the interviews took place. All interviews were recorded by a digital recorder and transcribed into the computer. Data analysis was followed by research questions. Participating teachers were coded as T1, T2, T3, etc.

Thematic analysis was used in this research. The analysis for RQ1 included participants' perception of aspects of helpfulness, enjoyment and pedagogical development in co-teaching. The analysis for RQ2 included the importance and effectiveness of communication between the subject teachers and EAP teachers, as well as language support promoting content knowledge for deep learning.

Findings and Discussions

Research Question 1: What Are the Benefits of Co-teaching with Language Tutors in the CLIL Programme?

All eleven participating academic teachers provided positive comments on co-teaching with language teachers in the CLIL classes. They perceived that the CLIL programme is significantly helpful and they were quite happy with support from EAP teachers and enjoyed co-teaching. They contended that the CLIL course was extremely successful:

> T1 (China Studies): 'The language center instructor did a great job. Students think it very useful; co-teaching is still important.'
>
> T3 (Urban Planning and Design): 'I mean we worked together very well. I mean for in the past two years, I was lucky working with this language teacher. Extremely helpful.'
>
> T7 (Year 1&3 Biological Science): 'I personally did enjoy working with someone coming from a different field. It's a nice thing I learned well when I work in this framework. I mean that would be the best programme I did.'

Their answers to the follow-up questions showed that co-teaching benefits disciplinary teaching in many ways. The subject teachers are usually well aware of how the English language impedes their students' performance in classroom activities and assessments. However, subject teachers are not language experts and are unclear about how to improve students' language skills and academic literacy. As

T9 (Civil Engineering) commented, 'without this help, I end up having to try to do all this which is a lot of extra work. I am not trained as a language tutor. What kinds of problems students are having feels like another sort of expertise and I don't have a big interest in it'. For postgraduate CLIL modules, students' language abilities may strikingly differ in the same class. Subject teachers may not have a good strategy to deal with the differences in teaching. In addition, subject teachers are not very familiar with how to engage students to participate in group discussions and, as such, group discussions in seminars need language teachers' support. Apparently the language support improves the efficiency of disciplinary teaching and enables a kind of labour division when dealing with students' learning problems.

The research also found out that among all the involvements of language tutors, participants have identified some most helpful activities, for example, providing feedback in tutorials and consultations on assessments, post-class exercises, small summaries after reading, engaging students in group discussions in class and creating glossaries or listening quizzes on ICE – an internal online system which provides a number of resources and exercises for students to access in and after class. Teachers highly praised the EAP teacher's involvement. As T2 (Architecture) stated: 'Many students are shy to speak in discussions in Year One. The language teachers encourage/facilitate them to talk and they are good at encouraging students.' The Final Year project lecturer from English department (T8) gave evidence of the EAP support being recognized by students. He commented that the consultations where the EAP teacher instructed students on dissertation organization, critical thinking and referencing were very popular among students because they were always fully booked. The chemistry lecturer (T6) also found it effective to involve language teachers when giving feedback. The students received feedback on content from him and feedback on language from the EAP teacher for the formative assessments in the same time slot. Another two teachers gave more details to elaborate language teacher's contributions:

> *Since the text is also challenging to the language teacher, so he becomes a kind of generator of some of those questions about what is this text? What is this that all trying to say what is this whole debate and it brings? He can articulate those questions maybe better at this stage than many of the students can do. So it helps them a lot. (T4)*
>
> *The student told me that uh, because of the seminars she attended, she can then she can use that time to get familiar with the lecture . . . The students may feel lazy, they don't really prepare for the lecture. But because there is a seminar a few days in advance, they are forced to read the textbook and our pre lecture. (T9 Year 1 Business)*

In addition to the benefits in disciplinary teaching and learning, CLIL also shows positive signs in promoting innovative teaching. For example, quizzes were recognized as a very useful tool in teaching and learning. T6 noted that he will definitely use quizzes online in his other modules. T7 mentioned that the language tutor suggested tools to use in lectures and he followed that and gave a different type of delivery which he considered as 'the development I experienced'. T9 also gave an example of making recordings of casual talk between lecturers and language tutors chatting about lecture content as pre-lecture materials for students to use before the lecture. However, for some subject teachers who do not go to the tutorials/seminars, there is no big chance to exchange pedagogy and promote innovative teaching.

These findings indicated that the language teacher acted as an articulator or facilitator to explain unclear content or asked the academic teacher to offer deeper explanation for some confusing content so that students can have better understanding. The language teacher can encourage students to talk in group discussions, which may be a difficulty for the academic teacher. Furthermore, all participating academic teachers perceived that the language teachers significantly benefit disciplinary teaching through the CLIL programme. The results suggest that the CLIL programme can provide significant help and support to the academic teacher in their content teaching. These findings meet the requirement of the CLIL programme, that is, to meet academic departments' needs and support academic teaching with language assistance (Jordan & Ford, 2016).

Research Question 2: **How Can CLIL Bridge the Gap for EAP and Disciplinary Teaching and Promote Deep Learning?**

As stated earlier, the CLIL programme in this EMI university was suggested by both the Language Centre and academic departments. General EAP provided in Year One and Year Two is inadequate to meet individual department's requirements. Since content is the starting point for a lesson plan and the EAP teachers are not familiar with the academic content and learning objectives, teachers were asked in the interview how they collaborated with EAP teachers to familiarize them with the content. The respondents provided details for this issue. For example, they had initial meeting at the beginning of the semester to share module specification, weekly curriculum and expected language assistance. EAP teachers can make a general semester plan. During teaching period, they conducted email exchange of ideas and lesson materials on a weekly basis for suggestions of both sides. After the lecture, they had post-lecture discussions and reflection on the teaching. They had discussions after the seminar to reflect good activities and suggest changes for the future. The most focused areas of EAP teachers are academic literacy skills as required by the specific modules, such as group discussions, presentation skills, writing essays and so forth in the academic community. Other areas include note taking and referencing. Some EAP teachers also give one-on-one consultations and are involved in assessment development and marking. Generally, the EAP teachers provide language assistance before, during and after the lecture. The modules where students have more contact hours with EAP teachers present more opportunities for students to benefit from the integration and develop their academic literacy.

One concern of the departments not adopting CLIL and EAP tutors who have newly joined the CLIL team is that without content background language tutors can fulfil their role of language support. After all, content knowledge is indispensable for deeper learning. Participants were asked about their perceptions in this regard. The majority of academic teachers stated that it is not a must for language tutors to have the content background. As T6 from the department of Architecture noted: 'No. Not necessary, specifically in the introductory classes. I don't want to put them in a position for which they are forced to enter a kind of uncomfortable space where they are forced to navigate an area which is not of their competence.' T6 also contended that the language teacher can help construct discourse, develop it, access the proper information to use the proper terminology and explain the kind of tools students can utilize. She addressed: 'The point is not being an expert in architecture, but teaching the students that there are ways to learn.'

Despite this, a few teachers claimed that it would be helpful if the language teacher is aware of some of the content, which can make the integration more efficient. They expressed their opinions: As T3 said: 'It will be good. We appreciate it. . . . It will definitely help. The perfect situation would be um, language tutors were there having the scientific background.' T4 also stated: 'It could help. She found the lectures and the content of the course very interesting, also as an opportunity to learn actually herself.' T5 compared the first year of collaboration and the most recent year and he recalled that in the first year of collaboration when the language tutors were new to this content area, the language support was constrained in grammar and glossary which students could learn on their own. He commented that it is 'totally fine without any background but now we are getting familiar with the knowledge so they step in more and it makes the cooperation more efficient. So why not?' T11 addressed this point: 'Content is essential. At least you should be keen on the content.'

However, two other participants expressed their concern if language tutors have the content background. One participant (T2) resisted that because it may 'encourage overstepping'. The other participant expressed his dislike of when the language tutor 'tries to snatch time in class and tries to interfere bring their own ideas without any consultations'.

Generally, the result suggested that although language teachers are not expected to learn the academic content themselves, it could be helpful if they are familiar with the content. It may also increase the language teacher's confidence to support students in their disciplinary learning.

In order to give EAP teachers more understanding of academic content, in the interview, academic teachers suggested that they can discuss with language teachers in advance, for example, before the new semester starts, to prepare materials and discuss class materials together so they can familiarize themselves with the subject. In this way, the EAP teacher can raise awareness of the disciplines. Moreover, they expect that the language teacher is at least interested in the discipline and is willing to focus on specific content and go into the particular module content that he or she is associated with.

These findings indicate that there is a great deal of communication between subject teachers and language teachers to promote collaboration. This meets the aim of facilitating greater communication between the subject teachers from departments and language teachers at the Language Centre (Jordan & Ford, 2016). However, Coyle (2005) pointed out that cognitively demanding materials are 'fundamental to learning' and developing cognitively demanding materials using accessible language remains a big challenge for language teachers. Due to the gap of content background, it might be difficult to expect EAP tutors to develop cognitive demanding materials to stimulate deeper learning. Language activities with a slight touch upon basic content might not be sufficient to motivate students and develop learners' higher order thinking skills.

Practical Implications and Relevance

According to the research findings, it is undoubtful that CLIL supplements disciplinary teaching and hence improves teaching and learning experiences for academic study in the university context. All interviewed subject teachers welcomed this collaboration and appreciated the language support. We would assume that language tutors' involvement will lead to improvement of learning experiences and assessment results. This study has provided detailed feedback and insights into both language tutors and academic staff in their teaching practices and communication. It can help EAP tutors and academic staff learn which specific activities and methodologies can efficiently improve students' performance so that these activities can be strengthened and shared across various contexts. For instance, EAP teachers without opportunities to collaborate with content lecturers can try to involve a bit of the disciplinary content when planning lessons. The writing style and vocabulary commonly practised in that community could also be considered when selecting materials and designing assessments. It has provided more evidence from subject teachers' perspectives of CLIL to echo Jordan and Ford's (2016) and Zappa-Hollman's (2018) studies that CLIL can enrich students' learning experience. The findings in this study have enriched the research in the CLIL field from subject teachers' positive attitudes towards the benefit of co-teaching in the CLIL programme, which supports Dalton-Puffer and Nikula's (2014) call for involvement from subject specialists to fill in this research gap. Meanwhile, the results in this study have found good a solution with co-teaching by EAP teachers and subject teachers for the problems addressed by Luo (2006) and Prasongporn (2009) regarding the lack of qualified CLIL teachers. Therefore, CLIL programmes with appropriate class activities and teaching methods or strategies by co-delivered teaching between EAP teachers and subject teachers can be adopted to enhance subject teaching and learning in various disciplines.

In the meantime, this research identified several issues about the CLIL programme. The most important issue is the level of integration of content and language, which is still not ideal. The research finding does not show a great degree of integrative assessment and lesson planning in most CLIL modules. Most of the interviewed subject teachers said that they seldom or never went to EAP teachers' seminars/tutorials nor went through materials created by EAP tutors. They explained that they trusted language tutors' expertise, and checking could be unnecessary extra workload. According to Sandholtz's model (2000), this level of collaboration is somewhat loose, where teachers share some responsibilities, with individual instruction. Only a few CLIL modules showed closer interaction where team planning and joint teaching took place. The other issues include some subject teachers sharing materials with the language tutors in the last minute and there is insufficient workload allocation from the EAP tutors' side. Two lecturers suggested that the language tutor's value could have been maximized if more workload were assigned. They think language tutors could contribute more; as one subject teacher noted, 'Ideally it could be a model of fifty and fifty that we could go in parallel, I as a biology teacher and language tutor as language support.' This implies that there is more to explore in the collaboration and that EAP tutors' contribution is recognized. Another issue was lack of continuity of EAP tutors and materials, and it was echoed by several subject teachers. The language tutors in CLIL modules were regularly rotated each academic year. This hindered collaboration. Lecturer 11 (Year 1 Film & Media) complained: 'They keep changing language tutors, it is a waste of my time.'

Thus, to solve these problems and improve the CLIL practices, subject teachers need to engage at a higher level by sharing materials in advance and getting involved more in language materials development and seminar activities. EAP tutors could also make efforts to maintain the continuity of materials and develop interest in the module content. Only in this way, true integration can be achieved. Furthermore, the findings of this research can be used as training resources for new personnel in the integrated learning team to promote effective and innovative teaching.

Conclusion

The primary rationale of practising CLIL in this EMI university is to help students with insufficient English proficiency comprehend the content courses and make them express themselves freely in academic learning. This study has found that CLIL is helpful for students' development in academic literacy and content comprehension from the academic teachers' perspective. However, the absence of interaction from subject lecturers' side in the seminars and language sessions may suggest that the involvement of EAP teaching in this CLIL programme is still perceived as very helpful but somewhat marginalized.

However, since these CLIL modules are compulsory for all students learning that subject, there is no way to compare the performance of CLIL learners and non-CLIL counterparts. Also, it is difficult to collect longitudinal evidence of assessment results to compare. Some teachers expressed the doubt of the reliability of comparison as students can make progress for various reasons. It is difficult to identify a correlation and attribute the performance improvement to CLIL. The other limitation is that learners' perceptions of CLIL are absent – for example, whether students fully take advantage of the linguistic support, whether CLIL has somewhat negative effects on subject learning and whether the language activities really promote their deeper learning process remain uncertain. Therefore, further research from CLIL learners' side is necessary to further justify the effectiveness of CLIL.

9

ESAP-in-EGAP

Implementing Sydney School Genre Pedagogy in Gulf Higher Education

Tony Myers, Jaime Buchanan, Jesse Balanyk and Timothy Nicoll

Introduction

Although government-funded tertiary education occurs exclusively in the medium of English, undergraduates in the United Arab Emirates habitually enter university unprepared in terms of language proficiency levels, genre familiarity and autonomous learning skills, further exacerbated by the absence of an entrenched academic reading culture. IELTS statistics from 2018 reveal that average scores in Gulf region states occupy the bottom five positions of the forty most frequent test-taking countries. The UAE holds the lowest overall scores for academic test takers, with an average of 4.97 (IELTS, n.d.). These issues pose significant challenges for teachers attempting to address them while still maintaining adherence to the curriculum. Finding a solution has become more pressing in recent times, as the tertiary sector has largely dismantled the foundation programmes which have been the traditional front line for acculturating nascent undergraduates to higher education cultural conventions. This chapter details one response to the changing educational landscape, examining how Sydney School genre pedagogy has been used for the first time in the region in higher education. It examines its use by in-sessional teachers to deliver a novel ESAP-in-EGAP model of EAP designed to equip students with the academic English and genre literacy aiming to enable fuller engagement with higher education discourse communities. It explores how teachers are employing a specific literacy pedagogy adopted from the Reading to Learn approach employed in the Australian school system, using it in higher education for the first time, and how they have embedded that in the teaching/learning cycle of deconstruction, joint reconstruction and independent construction. The chapter concludes with a review of both student and teacher impressions, and a discussion of the challenges that were encountered throughout the process, as well as how they might be overcome in the future.

Background Discussion

Gulf/UAE Context

Change in the Gulf region has been rapid and widespread. Since oil production began in earnest in the 1960s, the region has embarked on ambitious development across many facets of society, from infrastructure to health care to military (Kamal, 2018). In the UAE, an ambitious federal government strategy means that the education sector has followed a similarly accelerated growth since 1976 when the first higher education institution opened its doors in Al Ain, UAE (UAE University, 2020). Indeed, 'the country's adult literacy rate jumped from 32 percent among women and 57 percent among men in 1975 to above 90 percent for both in 2005' (UNESCO, as cited in Kamal, 2018). Cultural adaptations have struggled to keep pace with this rapid change. The Emirati population has had to make significant adaptations to ways of living, and this is particularly evident in higher education, with seventy-seven institutions (mostly international satellite locations of Western universities) operating in the UAE in 2020 (UAE MoE, 2020). However, while these foreign institutions bring increased educational opportunity to the UAE citizens and residents, they also impart the cultural and educational practices of their native contexts. Expectations of students include the assumption of self-directed learning and high levels of autonomy, independent and critical thinking, and an awareness (whether explicit or innate) of the writing conventions of academic study. When student performance failed to meet these tacit expectations, pre-sessional academic readiness sessions were inserted to bridge the academic literacies gap. These programmes were often skills-focused, and achievement-centred, with students required to meet external benchmark levels of proficiency in order to exit. Such programmes ran more or less successfully for twenty years, although their legitimacy and overall value for money were at times called into question by local government officials (Moussly, 2010; Salem & Swan, 2014).

Some challenges were well founded. Secondary school graduates have increasingly achieved higher proficiency rates on state-run standardized testing, with 23 per cent of students eligible for direct-entry in 2016, up from 10 per cent in 2010 (Kamal, 2018). However, as all three state-funded institutions teach in English, meeting requisite language proficiency standards and having knowledge of the discourse forms remain significant concerns for tertiary education in the UAE. Indeed, despite raising entry standards as a concomitant response to increases in quality in the secondary sector, the federal universities in the UAE still receive substantial applications of otherwise qualified individuals who fail to meet minimum language requirements of IELTS 5.5. In our own institution, some 45 per cent of new students gain admittance by enrolling on a conditional entry academic English course.

Institutional Context

Given the scale of the need to be addressed, but also tighter budget controls and a maximum allowable time frame of one semester for any programme to address them, a fifteen-week, semester-long EGAP course was favoured by the administration as the most efficient way of tackling the students' language deficit. This was not the approach favoured by most of the non-administrative stakeholders, specifically the teachers and students, both of whom disavowed the EGAP model as irrelevant to learners' real needs. Research supports the view that an ESAP model allows for greater flexibility, focuses student attention on discipline-specific language choices and does not conflate content with language teaching (Anderson, 2014; Halliday et al., 1964; Turner, 2004). As such, non-administrative stakeholders would have preferred a discipline-specific, parallel academic language and literacies support model, partly for reasons of time and partly for reasons of relevance.

They were not alone in questioning the value of the EGAP model. The literature has increasingly questioned the validity of a one-size-fits-all approach to academic English instruction. Hyland, for example, suggests there are 'serious problems with identifying a "common core" of language items' which can be used across all disciplines (2016, p. 20). Another challenge concerns genre relevance. Nesi and Gardner's (2013) pivotal curricular mapping indicated that there are a wide variety of genre families used in academia. EGAP curricula tend to favour essay writing, possibly because of its relevance to standardized testing systems such as IELTS, but the essay is not a highly valued genre for many disciplines, and expository writing does not adequately prepare higher education students even in the social sciences, whose arguments are expected to be supported by data. This is further exacerbated for students in scientific disciplines, whose generic demands are often far more expansive and more or less ignored by academic writing textbooks and course materials (Gardner, 2008; Gillett & Hammond, 2009; Seviour, 2015; Tribble, 2009). Another criticism comes from those who are concerned that EGAP programmes serve to reinforce the academic status quo, subsuming cultural and individual difference into the expected language conventions and that this has the effect of disenfranchizing students and perpetuating the existing power dynamics (Benesch, 2001; Chun, 2009; Lea & Street, 1998). Perhaps one of the most convincing charges comes from systemic functional linguists, who argue that since language is socially constructed and cannot be divorced from its context, a language syllabus that does not take this as its core is not only ineffective but absurd (Halliday et al., 1964; Martin, 1997; Monbec, 2020). Language as a resource for meaning-making necessarily derives from a particular rather than generic context, which precipitates the need for a means of specificity in its teaching.

All of these criticisms relate to the very real problem of transferability. After all, the G in EGAP stands for *general* rather than *generalizable*. This is a very real problem for an institution, such as ours, which specializes in the social sciences. While, as Bernstein points out, the sciences are vertical knowledge structures, which demonstrate 'underlying uniformities across an expanding range of apparently different phenomena' (2000, p. 162), the social sciences are horizontal knowledge structures which all introduce 'an apparently new problematic' (2000, p. 162) in each discipline. This makes general introductions more difficult to maintain relevance. For example, it is assumed that language lessons learned in one context can be applied in other, less similar contexts. Discussing this issue, Monbec notes that 'enabling transfer, however, remains a challenge' (2018, p. 88). Given the wide disparity in disciplinary discourses, it is perhaps unreasonable to expect novice university students to be able to make such connections and then apply them in new and unfamiliar contexts without equipping them with the appropriate metacognitive skills. This, then, is the context in which we had to create our course. While budgetary requirements necessitated a maximum length of one semester, and gatekeeping mandated an EGAP model, course design also had to serve the students' real needs to be apprenticed to an institution comprised of multiple discursive approaches to meaning-making. As Creme and Lea aver, a significant difficulty for university students involves knowing 'how to tackle the variety of different written assignments that [they] will be asked to complete throughout the course' (1997, p. 25). In other words, how could we deliver an ESAP-in-EGAP model of learning which would benefit all the stakeholders?

Application

Academic Language and Literacies Course Outline

Partly in preparation for designing the new course, the university's various majors' curricula were mapped according to the genre family classifications developed by Nesi and Gardner (2013). This involved identifying the genres students would be expected to master for each discipline, noting how they were specified in the rubrics, comparing model student answers, how they were sequenced and equally importantly, how they were concentrated. What we found was that students would be expected to tackle multiple different genres (in the College of Arts and Creative Enterprises, for example, they use twelve out of Nesi and Gardner's thirteen basic genres), and genre types, often within a single semester, and that there was no sense of sequencing in terms of moving from relatively simple to more complex genres. Equally, there were no genres, or genre types, which spanned all the majors. This lack of commonality made the delivery of a course that focused on individual genres or even genre types problematic. However, it did create a space, and evidenced the need, for creating a course that dealt with genre as a concept: focusing student attention on the various factors that influence how a text is structured and the style and tone of the language employed (Hyland & Bondi, 2012, pp. 17–18). In other words, it forced attention onto the fact of specialization itself. *This* is the generalized feature of all higher education, and to best help our students engage with this fact, we decided to equip them with the questions they could ask of any specialization, all of which boil down to one question: How do you legitimate knowledge in a particular discipline?

In other words, because students would have to face so many different genres, and very often in a short space of time, it was decided that the most efficacious approach for them would be to develop *genre literacy*. This involved a two-prong approach. Firstly, it entailed promoting a sense of genre awareness in students. Following Swales (1990), it was proposed that this would involve raising their consciousness of the variety of, and differences between, the genres they would be exposed to in academia. If this first part was essentially helping students to *notice* genre, the second part of the approach involved equipping them with the kinds of questions they could ask of any genre so that when faced with a new genre, students would be able to deal with it by themselves. These questions revolved around the purpose of the text, its audience, its organization and the writing choices needed to render it appropriately. One module, for example, asks the learner to consider whether a user manual has been written using language that a general reader would understand, while, on another, a focus question surrounding the executive summary asks, 'Does the text focus on informing and recommending a non-specialist reader?'

In terms of actualizing the first part of the approach, that of raising genre awareness, it was decided to select frequently occurring genres for some of the most popular majors. In order to maximize genre awareness, we picked genres with highly visible differences and deliberately omitted the essay. To that end, the genres picked were the recount (news story from the College of Communication and Media Sciences), the procedure (instruction manual from the College of Technical Innovation), the explanation (poster presentation from the College of Education), the summary (executive summary from the College of Business) the critique (art critique from the College of Art and Creative Enterprises) and the literature review (from the College of Natural and Health Sciences). A preliminary introduction to genre via emails was also included as it was determined that this was a text type familiar to most students, one all would be required to write and an area where faculty felt students needed to improve. It was also one where purpose, audience, organization and writing choices could be made very explicit. In keeping with Sydney School genre pedagogy, the genres were also sequenced in this order so that students would gradually become acculturated to more complex and sophisticated genres, which use increasingly more challenging writing choices. As such, an ideal sequence for the course was established, moving from the more common sense to the more uncommon sense (Martin, 1992, p. 545), which in terms of genre instantiations included moving from emails to the feature profile (a form of recount), to the explanation to the critique before finishing with the reflection (another high-value genre across disciplines).

Course design principles were informed by Sydney School genre pedagogy principles. As such, each module was built around the three key aspects of teacher/student roles, learning activities and learning modalities (Rose & Martin, 2012). Teacher/student roles refer to the social roles and status between actors in the learning context. Learning activities are those tasks that are undertaken within the context of a learning event. Learning modalities refer to the various media employed within the instructional setting. How course design for each of these aspects was developed will be explained in further detail.

Teacher/Student Roles

We adopted the Sydney School view of pedagogic relations, namely that the teacher functions in the role of expert knower and the student as learner. This model is based on research into first language acquisition, which occurs primarily through negotiated meaningful interactions with a more expert language user (Halliday, 1975; Painter, 1986). Second language learning can be accomplished using similar interactive patterns, with students guided in their academic literacy education by a teacher who takes the expert user position. This approach might be considered unprogressive, particularly within the context of communicative language teaching, where the majority consensus is that students learn best through the independent use of the language. However, following Bernstein (1996), the Sydney School contends that this approach only rewards successful students, while reinforcing negative feedback loops and demotivating others who do not intuitively or independently answer correctly the first time (Rose & Martin, 2012, p. 305). Instead, Sydney School posits it is the teacher's responsibility to ensure that each student has the scaffolding necessary to get the right answer, thereby creating a positive feedback loop and reinforcing a culture of success. Observations of student behaviours and interactions seemed to support this view, with greater participation of the whole student body and success even among the weaker students. This participation and attitudinal shift were in part related to the interpersonal relations that were established and also due to the careful scaffolding of class activities, discussed subsequently.

Learning Activities

Teaching was centred on the principles of explicit instruction via Rothery's Teaching and Learning Cycle of Field Building, Deconstruction, Joint Construction and Independent Construction (1994). The need to address the varied disciplines of the colleges provided several challenges. The first regarded content familiarity/exposure for both students and teachers, all of whom were non-specialists. In this regard, the field building aspect of the course required careful selection of materials that could ensure sufficient understanding of the topic to be able to then turn the focus to text organization and language choices that realize the generic expectations. Students struggle to analyse a text that they do not fully understand, so they therefore required preliminary activities that would adequately familiarize learners with the content and provide them with the vocabulary and knowledge to be able to then analyse and co-construct texts within the domain. In one sense, the model texts do not have to be accurate exemplars of the texts the students would face in the various colleges because the point of the course was to develop a generic genre literacy, not to establish an understanding of specific disciplinary discourses. We were therefore able to appropriate student examples and modify them to learners with both a low level of English and a barely nascent understanding of the specialized context from which the genres issued. However, at the same time, we wished to preserve an element of realism in order to at least honour students' wishes to engage with real text types as soon as possible, but also to acculturate students to the level and distinctiveness of the genres they would face. This meant that field building would be crucial to the success of the course.

One of the key ways in which we attempted to ensure the success of field building was by integrating the detailed reading sequence into teaching activities. This was done by applying the process within a higher education context. Rose and Martin (2012) explain in depth the intensive reading strategies employed to address literacy deficiencies in so-called remedial education in underserved sectors of Australian primary education. This is facilitated through careful pre-reading text preparation and scaffolding and contextualizing questions during the guided reading process that help model the cognitive processes that occur when an expert reader is decoding a text through five key stages of Prepare/Focus/Identify/Affirm/Elaborate. Outlined more comprehensively in Rose and Martin (2012), a brief explanation of the stages follows. *Prepare* contextualizes the text and points to the area of focus. *Focus* asks a direct question that is pitched at a sufficiently accessible level to be answered by all students who then *Identify* it. *Affirm* provides the opportunity for the student who answers to receive positive feedback about their performance, and *Elaborate* provides the opportunity for further explanation by the tutor, if necessary.

Our course implemented the detailed reading sequence into each module on two occasions. This was in order to ensure that high-value texts were understood at a more than surface level and also to develop critical literacy skills that are often a serious issue for our students. High-value texts were those that enabled students to have a sufficiently adequate understanding of the content area to be able to write meaningfully in it. As suggested by Rose and Martin (2012), we prepared teacher notes and a script that could be followed for the text in question, although we encouraged instructors to also undertake the process of identifying key language aspects for themselves. The process of preparing the scripts enabled us to identify pivotal linguistic features, for example, logical relators (where conjunctions are left implicit when using non-finite verb forms), that often prove problematic for students and which could then be further consolidated in note taking and summarizing activities, both of which are high-value academic writing skills that are often assumed as opposed to explicitly taught. For example, in the Executive Summary module, students are exposed to language that has been nominalized and are directed to consider it in an unpacked form that could then be repackaged for summarizing purposes. Recently, much systemic functional linguistic work has centred on *grammatical metaphor*, which is the term used to describe language that has been made incongruent through processes of nominalization and other language shifts. This language often causes significant challenges for students, and the ability to unpack this has been identified as a key determiner in successful academic writing. Systemic functional linguists have turned their attention to this area, investigating how it can contribute to successful text realization and be implemented in EAP teaching (Liardet, 2016a, 2016b, 2018; Liardet & Black, 2020; Yasuda, 2015). Walsh Marr (2019) outlines teaching activities that she undertook to similarly unpack and repack language in order to develop students' paraphrasing skills in another higher education context. In our course, these activities were then incorporated across a variety of modalities that we knew students would be encountering in their future and concurrent studies, thus providing important recycling and scaffolding of key academic skills.

Another key aspect of the pedagogic activities related to text production involved modifying the 3 × 3 toolkits outlined in Dreyfus et al. (2016) to a 1 × 9 feedback sheet. This adaptation was made in order to make the concepts more accessible, particularly for learners whose understanding of the concepts involved would necessarily be limited, but also for tutors, who demonstrated resistance to the new pedagogy (see *Discussion*). Key components of the assigned task were identified across the strata of ideational, interpersonal and textual meanings, and also addressed at the whole text, stage and clause levels, as outlined in Dreyfus et al. (2016). However, these key language features were listed in a table, which was used by students to self-assess their work across the various levels and meanings and by instructors, as well as peers, to provide feedback targeted at the different components. This enabled students to focus their attention on key instantiation differentiators across the teaching and learning cycle. Indeed, these were linked to genre taxonomy documents for each genre which helped to ensure that elements of genre in the abstract were periodically highlighted and learning was recycled. The 1 x 9 feedback sheet was also effective at focusing both tutor and peer feedback on key linguistic features of the genre in question, making sure that future outcomes were appropriate for purpose. As such, it represents a distinctive shift from grammar-based language teaching that promotes a surface-level focus to a more authentically genre-based approach. It also ensured that assessment expectations were understood before any evaluation of independent work occurred.

Learning Modalities

Final considerations included training students to understand and cope with content across the variety of modalities likely to be encountered in their tertiary studies. A key concern has been the uneven exposure to and understanding of different text and information sources that students arrive at university with. While some students begin studies with a high level of information, technology and academic literacy, others are unaware of basic concepts such as how a textbook is organized. To compensate, exposure to different media was embedded into the materials, both in the output genres and in the mode that provided content (for example, websites, textbooks or journal articles), with a so-called 'input genre' highlighted in each module. Lectures were also attended to in the explanation module that included a poster presentation, while interviews were spotlighted in the feature profile module. Teaching aimed to increase student understanding of some of the assumed understandings that were found to be absent in segments of our student population. Providing an explicit understanding of the structure and function of these components aimed to increase critical and information literacy that would then enable greater content uptake. While the multi-generic, non-discipline-specific approach articulated one aspect of the EGAP character of the course, the examination of the input genres spoke to another, which was the traditional teaching of academic skills such as source evaluation, note taking and presenting.

Professional Development

While the course was being developed, a series of professional development training sessions were also delivered in order to familiarize faculty with the principles and theories that formed the basis for the pedagogy. This was based on the belief that adapting to a different method of delivery would take time and that not all faculty would respond positively to change. A major tenet of Sydney School genre pedagogy, as outlined in Dreyfus et al. (2016), is that a shared nomenclature is necessary to enable discussion about language that results in learning. In keeping with the approach, professional development activities included introducing faculty to knowledge about language, the metalanguage used to describe language instantiations in genre pedagogy. The importance of addressing this has been argued by Monbec, among others, who notes that a 'lack of focus on a functional knowledge about language in some EAP curricula constitutes a form of knowledge-blindness which can have significant impact on learning outcomes' (2018, p. 92). On our course, two levels of metalanguage were used – metalanguage for teachers and a more limited range of metalanguage for students. This metalanguage was used because it enabled a different way of thinking of language – something that was key for both faculty, shifting from more grammar-based structural syllabi to a genre-based pedagogy, and students whose understanding of academic writing began and ended with the essay. However, where metalanguage was employed, it was unpacked into more congruent and specified language instances before being repacked to expedite the use of the metalinguistic resource (Hipkiss & Varga, 2018). Further details of the teacher training will be discussed in the following section.

Discussion

Challenges

The course faced a number of challenges due to both its novel design and the alterations forced on it due to institutional compliance requirements. Not the least of these challenges was the response of some of the teaching faculty. As Humphries and Burns note, 'When there is a strong clash between teachers' own beliefs and those underlying a curriculum innovation, teachers are likely to reject change' (2015, p. 240). This was very much the case with the move from a learner-centred stance to a teacher-centred one. For most teachers who began their EAP careers firmly ensconced in the communicative approach, this is a very different and difficult approach to accept. Maton argues that this is because there is a large degree of *clustering* in which a series of stances have become connected with learner-centred approaches in opposition to teacher-centred approaches. He identifies four areas in which this binary between the traditional, teacher-centred classroom is set against the modern, learner-centred classroom: abstract–concrete, objective–subjective, individual–collective, positivism–hermeneutics. The crucial point is that adherence to one part of the binary implies an adherence to all of it. This creates a large amount of resistance on the part of teachers to any approach which involves putting the teacher at the centre of the learning process. This proved the case at our institution where, despite teacher training provided via a blended learning approach across a semester, some faculty had difficulty committing to the course ethos in areas such as joint construction. As a result, instead of employing careful co-construction with the teacher in the role of 'expert knower', some faculty reverted to their communicative approach roots and put students into groups to co-construct with delayed teacher feedback rather than a true co-construction. Indeed, a number of faculty did not engage with the course objectives at all and instead adapted the course materials to their own long-standing teaching beliefs with a focus mainly on clause-level grammatical and lexical errors rather than seeking to address the text across multiple levels.

This reversion to traditional structural syllabus priorities was aided by institutional constraints imposed from without the university by an accreditation body. In this case, it meant that the course rubrics, which had been based on the 3 x 3 toolkits, outlined in Dreyfus et al. (2016), and based on assessing the writing across three levels (at the whole text, phase and sentence/clause levels), now needed two additional rows to match the five-level institutional rubric rule. The two additional levels were concerned with lexical and grammatical accuracy. The rationale behind that was that the course holds a gatekeeper position in the university. It therefore has to demonstrate that it matches the other accepted gatekeeper exams for the university, EmSAT, TOEFL and IELTS. The resulting compromise meant that the rubrics satisfied neither the new adherents of Sydney School genre pedagogy nor the proponents of traditional structural syllabuses. The washback was similarly affected, meaning that some students did not engage with the course aims as well as they might. Other areas in assessment also had to change in order to meet benchmarks. This included turning genre concept checks into summative rather than formative assessments. However, this actually seemed to help reinforce the achievement of learning outcomes rather than weaken them.

It is also worth noting that as part of the quarantine lockdown measures put in place following the Covid-19 outbreak, in its second semester, the course was affected after being forced online by the closure of all educational institutions in the UAE in early March 2020. Although the SLATE project (Dreyfus et al., 2016), which served as one of the inspirations for this course, was an online course, this was never designed to be. It made certain aspects of the course more difficult, in particular the Reading to Learn segments which, although teacher-led, rely on student interaction. It quickly became apparent that students were either unable or reluctant to talk online and preferred to write in text boxes instead. This slowed down interaction patterns considerably and often meant the focus was lost in the intervening time. Although this problem was most apparent in the Reading to Learn activities, other parts of the teaching/learning cycle were also hampered by a lack of visible paralinguistic signals which meant that issues had to be articulated by students with low-level language ability rather than being 'seen' by teachers. To counter these issues, teachers used more concept-check questions than usual, and an increased amount of formative review quizzes, as well as videos and screencasts of text modelling which students were able to refer to asynchronously. What was interesting was how the teacher-led nature of the pedagogy shifted from being classroom-focused to being extra-curricular, for example, in terms of teachers leading WhatsApp support groups where structured help could be offered outside of the online classroom. Indeed, online learning revealed how adopting a teacher-led stance does not necessarily mean adopting the other aspects of the constellation Maton notes as being identified with it. For example, teacher-led learning proved not to be inimically hierarchical in terms of a power dynamic but rather showed that teachers employed a deliberately inclusive tenor (as in the 'complex relations of power and solidarity that are played out in patterns of interpersonal meaning in discourse' (Hood, 2016, p. 194), such as the use of positive appraisal techniques (Coffin & Donohue, 2014, p. 239) to build an online community).

Overall Evaluation

By the course's first semester's end, it had become clear that there were both positives and negatives issuing from its operationalization. The first positive was that teachers reported that students produced high quality work. Despite early worries that the course might be too demanding for first semester undergraduates, it was felt that a majority of learners had met the learning outcomes. Indeed, some 85 per cent of students passed the course. Many teachers felt that adopting the teaching-learning cycle played a key role in the success of the students. Front-loading the teaching, and heavily scaffolding learners' engagement with the target structures, was seen as a very effective way to help them meet the learning outcomes. Despite initial misgivings, particularly with regard to the Reading to Learn activities, that students might feel 'talked at', the engagement with the teacher-led work was very clear. Conversations with students revealed that they felt relaxed and confident in the teacher's expertise and guidance, rather than worrying if they were in fact learning what they were supposed to be learning. It was also felt by many teachers that a key benefit of the course was the fact that the extensive scaffolding had a significant impact on cheating and plagiarism. By the time students came to submit their assignments, they felt confident enough to submit their own writing without undue external assistance. As one student noted in an end-of-semester reflection, 'as a next step, I will try to ask my instructor to give us a clear idea about my assignments such as, key points that I should include in my assignment to achieve the purpose of writing while I write different types of modules'. Students on the course were also highly engaged and appeared motivated by the fact that the course focused on real writing of a kind they would likely need to reproduce. As a result the course had high face validity for the students.

Conclusion

There is an argument, which we have drawn on here, that the educational context of the Gulf makes the putative learner-centred teaching promoted by progressivist educational philosophies a less appropriate form of approach than a teacher-centred one. Many Gulf students come from government-funded schools where teachers adopt a lecture-style for their lessons. When students get to university, it is therefore very difficult for them to adapt to the Western-style learner-centred teaching centred around practices of guided questioning that they often encounter in institutions staffed by expatriates where English is a medium of instruction. The lack of an extensive reading culture in the region means that students are at a disadvantage when trying to cope with higher education's expectations for independent learning. Sydney School genre pedagogy therefore seems well suited to use in the tertiary sector in this context. Another way to look at the Gulf context is in terms of the learner's developmental cline. Whenever a person undertakes the process of learning, models are needed to imitate and appropriate before this knowledge can be incorporated into their own. In the case of UAE students entering university from government schools, it is necessary to become cognizant of the many diverse genres they will face, as well as how to master them. For this to happen within the institutional time-to-graduation requirements, instruction needs to be front-loaded, efficient and therefore teacher-led. Paradoxically, then, as Christodoulou argues, 'teacher instruction is vitally necessary to become an independent learner' (2014, p. 36). Truly student-centred learning begins by recognizing a student's current place on the learning development cline and identifying how best they can be enabled to become self-directed. The ESAP-in-EGAP model outlined here is, in that sense, truly situated. It is an approach that meets student needs while still complying with institutional requirements. In so doing, it helps develop in learners an incipient sense of genre literacy which they can employ and refine as they move through academia and into their professional lives.

10

EAP Teachers Working in, with and through the Creative Arts

An Exploration

Clare Carr, Clare Maxwell, Anna Rolinska and Jennifer Sizer

In English for Specific Academic Purposes (ESAP), it is essential to understand context in order to best meet the needs of students and help them to understand the values and practices of their own academic discourse communities. These are already present within departments to be observed and do not need to be artificially recreated. As Maton (2014, p. 12) has observed:

> We . . . do not have to . . . attempt by ourselves to recreate what has taken, in the case of 'academic' knowledge, thousands of years and even more minds to develop.

Johns (1997, p. 71) advocated that in order to truly understand the values and practices of a discipline, it is necessary to become 'campus mediators and researchers', ethnographers who explore texts, contexts and roles. Therefore, building on the foundations of ethnographic work already undertaken in EAP by Swales (1998) and EAP in the creative arts by Riley-Jones (2012), this chapter aims to:

- explore the pedagogies of four EAP practitioners working in creative arts through themes emerging from reflections to gain a better understanding of the intertwining between EAP and creative pedagogies;
- consider the implications of our findings for practitioners working in similar contexts and roles and the broader implications for EAP practice.

Our shared understanding of creative arts/disciplines is inclusive of, but not limited to, creative and cultural industries conceptualized by O'Connor (2010) as 'core arts fields' such as visual and performing arts, 'cultural industries' such as gaming and music and 'creative industries and activities' such as design and architecture.

To analyse what makes teaching ESAP in the creative disciplines different, it is important to understand core values within that particular context. Arts education literature suggests that those include notions of ambiguity (e.g. Vaughan et al., 2008) and/or mystery (e.g. Elkins, 2006); the 'sticky curriculum' (e.g. Orr & Shreeve, 2018); curiosity and risk-taking; autonomy and making connections (e.g. Bennett & Burnard, 2016, cited in Burnard, 2016); active, problem- and enquiry-based learning, potentially leading to a more student-focused approach (Trigwell, 2002, cited in Orr & Shreeve, 2018) and also bridging the gap between theory and practice (e.g. QAA, 2019; Simones, 2017). Aspects of ambiguity, group work and identity work have been noted as particularly challenging for international students (Sovic & Blythman, 2006).

The multimodal and intertextual nature of the creative disciplines has been discussed (e.g. Kress, 2003, cited in Borg, 2012), as has the multidisciplinary nature of some aspects of the creative disciplines (e.g. Creative & Cultural Skills Development Plan, 2007, cited in Vaughan et al., 2008) and the experience gap between pre-university and Year 1. Many students may have little or no prior experience of academic study in the subject areas of History of Art, Architecture and/or Design (QAA, 2019), for example; however, in Music, for instance, the necessity for prior study in this or a related area is evident due to the entry requirement of a practical audition or a portfolio of prior work (UCAS, 2020). Although international students are also required to demonstrate spoken and writing skills in English (UCAS, 2020), there is some suggestion that where creative disciplines subjects in some institutions have a more academic and theoretical rather than practical focus, students with limited experience of the Western classical tradition in Music, for example, may find their own cultural capital to be very different to that of their department and/or institution (Moore, 2012).

Although these ideas are prevalent in higher education literature, because of the general positioning of EAP practitioners on 'the edge of academia' (Ding & Bruce, 2017), we often do not see the full picture. For those new to EAP in the creative disciplines, it can take time to identify what is important due to conflicting priorities. Teaching EAP within the creative disciplines can therefore be challenging and requires considerable resilience and determination; nevertheless, for those working with students and staff within the creative disciplines, it can be very rewarding. There is evidence of growing numbers of students, both international and non-international, studying subjects in, or related to, the creative arts (HESA, 2019), and for these reasons, we believe the varied lived practical experience and pedagogies of EAP practitioners working with and in the creative disciplines merit further and more detailed exploration.

Contexts and Methodology

Table 10.1 provides key information about the academic contexts and professional trajectories of the four authors of this chapter into teaching EAP in the creative disciplines.

The focus of our study involved exploring EAP pedagogies in relation to the pedagogical practices of the creative disciplines, another 'academic tribe' (Becher & Trowler, 2001). Earlier conversations and collaborations prior to this study had already raised our awareness of the extent to which our diverse contexts were shaping our practice (Carr et al., 2021), and we felt that an autoethnographic approach would allow us to study this in greater depth. Ellis et al. (2011, p. 1) define autoethnography as 'an approach ... that seeks to describe and systematically analyse personal experience in order to understand cultural experience'. Adopting an autoethnographic approach offered the opportunity to place ourselves, and our own experiences, at the centre of the research process in order to observe our situated practices, and we felt that the diversity of our accumulated experience and working contexts (see Table 10.1) could provide sufficiently rich data. We recognized that it would be in the collective pooling and interpretation of our narratives that we would be able to generate the data required to meet the aims of the study, hence our choice to engage in collaborative autoethnography (CAE). CAE would give us the added benefit of being able to 'analyse and interpret [our] data collectively in order to gain a meaningful

Table 10.1 Practitioner Contexts

Author (initials)	Location of Role within the Institution	Creative Discipline(s)	Level of Students
AR	Professional and Continuing Education department	Fine Art Design Architecture Simulation and Visualization	Foundation (UG) – in-sessional UG and PG – bespoke pre-sessional
CC	Centralized department for academic development	Music	UG (mainly Y1/Level 1), PGT, PGR In-sessional
CM	Seconded to School of Design from the Language Centre	Design	PGT in-sessional
JS	School of Languages and Applied Linguistics	Architecture, but role covers whole faculty	In-sessional mainly UG level 4/1st year, some PGT

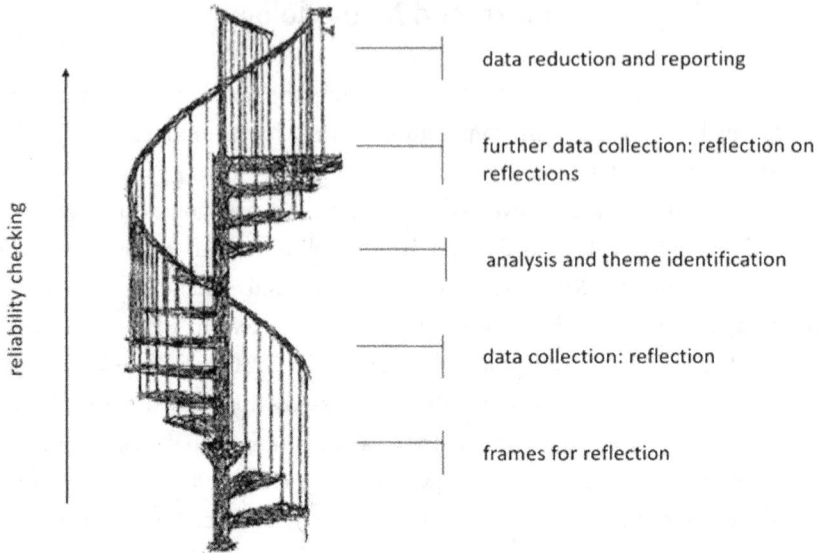

Figure 10.1 Our collaborative autoethnographic research process.

understanding of [the] sociocultural phenomena' (Chang et al., 2012, p. 24) of the academic communities of practice in which we work.

The autoethnographic process largely followed a variation on the iterative process of CAE elaborated by Chang et al. (2012), combined with stages of the process used by Adamson and Muller (2018). Figure 10.1 shows our own visual representation of the process, the spiral representing the element of repetition and review, and the staircase representing progress. Being based in four locations across the country, we agreed to generate our 'narratives' (Adamson & Muller, 2018) through written reflections that we would share using Google Drive. The process was enhanced via regular (generally weekly) video conferences, which created the space for 'conversational narrative' (Adamson & Muller, 2018) and through which we could explore our experiences, identify patterns, make links and comparisons and consider implications.

Stage 1: Identifying Frames for Reflection

We replicated the first stage of Adamson and Muller's (2018) process by identifying two fairly broad 'narrative frames' (Barkhuizen & Wette, 2008), which we felt could generate significant data and around which our reflections would be written. These were:

- Our experience of EAP in the creative arts, presented chronologically: how we came to teach in that context, what we noticed and learnt, and the impact on our practice
- A 'pivotal event' (Ellis et al., 2011, p. 276): something that changed us, our way of seeing or doing things, or was key in some way

Stage 2: Data Collection

The next stage was preliminary data collection (Chang et al., 2012), referred to by Adamson and Muller (2018) as 'joint narrativisation'. Individual reflections were written and shared in Google Docs, and the comments function used to create dialogue and deepen reflection via probing questions. In total this generated 13,842 words and upward of 304 comments in seven documents.

Stage 3: Data Analysis and Identifying Themes

Having already started to engage in 'preliminary meaning-making' (Chang et al., 2012) during our regular online meetings, at this stage we analysed the reflections and comments using a method called 'memoing' (Strauss & Corbin, 2008), which much resembles the coding method used in grounded theory (Northcott & Brown, 2006). From this we identified four key themes:

1. Spaces
2. Spoken communication
3. Written genres
4. Collaboration

We also became increasingly aware of the impact of creative pedagogies on our evolving teaching practices.

Stage 4: Further Reflection

We chose to reflect further, directly on the specific themes identified, creating 'reflections on the reflections'. This focused on synthesizing the various observations that had emerged from the reflections relating to the narrative themes and reflecting further on the implications from a personal perspective. An additional 11,091 words and thirty-seven comments were generated.

Stage 5: Data Reduction and Reporting

This stage involved a process of individual meaning-making (Chang et al., 2012), in which we each assumed responsibility for 'extracting the essence' (Adamson & Muller, 2018, p. 211) of one theme. We matched observations to our ongoing reading and understanding of the literature, creating a 'layered account' (Ellis et al., 2011) in order to gain a deeper understanding of our own contexts and the broader context of the creative arts. From here we were ready to start the group writing process for the final report.

Reliability Checking

The literature emphasizes the importance of reliability checking in collaborative autoethnography (Adamson & Muller, 2018; Ellis et al., 2011) in order to ensure that interpretations accurately represent the originally intended meaning. In this study, reliability checking was ongoing: the process of written comment and response in the Google Docs and our weekly online meetings allowed us to clarify, query and correct where necessary.

Findings and Discussion

Spaces

A persistent theme emerging from the reflections was space/s which is used by Low (2016) as an umbrella term to include context, environmental situation (Dudley-Evans & St John, 1998) and workplaces. There is significant variation in our spaces such as physical locations and workplaces (Table 10.1). CM, for example, is placed physically within the department providing opportunities to experience Graumann's (1983) identification process: identified within and able to identify with the workplace (cited in Hunziker et al., 2007) and move towards collaboration:

> *It was once I was seconded to the department... that I started to feel I was gaining real insight into the workings of those within it.... My physical presence in the*

School made me feel like I was part of it. As a result, I behaved differently which allowed me to approach other colleagues within the school differently. (CM)

In contrast, JS reflected on working in a separate building, a situation more common for EAP practitioners who find themselves in outsider positions, in a conceptual and sometimes physical third space (Ding & Bruce, 2017). JS observed that only entering the creative and cultural industries faculty for meetings and/or research indeed positions her as an 'outsider/visitor trying to fit in'. AR, similarly, reflected on the inverse situation of her art and design students early on being taught in 'her world' and their view of her sessions as somehow separate and less important.

Having the opportunity to work and/or teach within creative spaces can provide valuable insights into not only communicative practices but also learning and textual practices which shape these spaces (Bickford & Wright, 2006). Sustained engagement with the physical context over time (Geertz, 1973) encouraged thick descriptions similar to sensory ethnographic observations (Pink, 2015) in our reflections which evidenced the diverse nature and variety of the creative spaces within these contexts: seminar rooms, lecture theatres, labs, studios, workshops and practice rooms, resulting in diverse linguistic landscapes and learning soundscapes:

I'm in the 'seminar room' – a little cramped, with students hemmed in round one long cluster of tables, with an electronic whiteboard at one end, upright piano in the corner, and a portrait-shaped flipped whiteboard on wheels. (CC)

Walking along corridors and hearing students playing music, singing, acting etc., seeing the equipment used in textiles laboratories, with people stitching and sewing and selecting different coloured threads and fabrics. (CM)

Creative spaces are often designed for 'radical flexibility', often facilitated by the use of reconfigurable and movable furniture on casters (Lopez & Gee, 2006), which aims to de-centre the teacher and promote collaboration (Bickford & Wright, 2006). The decentralization is physical, as well as conceptual, resulting in authoritative spaces, such as areas surrounding a lectern and whiteboard, being replaced by shared interactional spaces (Lim et al., 2012). While these creative spaces sometimes host timetabled sessions for EAP practitioners, they are primarily for creative practice and may be found to house a 'stage and grand piano' (CC), or 'paint-smeared tables and students' own work' (AR). Some spaces may not even be immediately recognizable as learning spaces, as CM found in the 'Grass Studio': a space set up to resemble a garden, complete with shed and astroturf. These spaces host not only formal and informal learning but also independent study/practice, collaboration and even socializing, often outside timetabled hours (Brown, 2020).

At first glance, such creative spaces may appear less than ideal for EAP pedagogy, and our reflections document adjustment challenges. JS describes the noise permeating temporary partitions that physically divide students into 'mini-studios' and CC's reflection expresses the physical discomfort of the cramped space. CM recounted her initial unease in the 'Grass Studio', devoid of the traditional tools of our trade, such as whiteboard or tutor workstation, but has learnt to exploit opportunities afforded by the light and space, movable tables and partitions, and displayed artwork. Moving EAP teaching into these spaces allows us to reposition ourselves from 'sage on the stage' (whether a physical stage as encountered by CC or a metaphorical stage) towards more student-centred 'meddler in the middle' pedagogies (King, 2012; McWilliam, 2009). Therefore, developing a greater understanding of creative spaces and their affordances provides rich opportunities to draw on the environmental situation, contextual collaborations and artefacts in order to design more targeted and specific EAP provision.

Spoken Communication

Development of creative practice relies on sustained reflection mediated by speaking and writing (Turner & Hocking, 2004) and so communication features strongly in all four reflections. However, while CM and CC tend to focus more on writing, spoken communication is a recurrent theme in JS's and AR's reflections. This variability of focus results, among other things, from the student needs as perceived by the departments. Both JS and AR have been asked to support students in developing subject-specific interaction skills. Interestingly, each consistently refers to the studio, recognized not only as a 'space' but also as a signature creative pedagogy (Shreeve et al., 2010), which in certain contexts values modes of knowledge production other than writing, the more widely accepted 'guarantor' of academic acceptability (Doloughan, 2002). Orr and Shreeve (2018, p. 11) argue against the hegemony of written form and ascertain that studio-created artefacts can 'manifest high-quality academic approaches within the medium of choice'. This is not to say that language is redundant; on the contrary, it is necessary to 'mediate the understandings' constructed around the artefacts (Vaughan et al., 2008, p. 146) but it no longer plays the privileged role in discipline-specific communication. The studio interaction is truly multimodal, involving touchscreens, large sketchbook drawings, floorplans or models (JS) or artefacts at various stages of making (AR). Students are expected to be 'bilingual' in communicating visually and textually (Orr & Shreeve, 2018) or even multilingual when one considers the inter- and cross-disciplinary character of creative endeavours.

The studio space is messy and fluid and this shapes the interactions within it. JS, while observing a studio discussion, notices the use of anecdotes, banter and swearing. She summarizes her experience: 'The discussions I observed were much more informal, student-led and could cover a wide range of topics which could be difficult to participate in, understand and/or prepare for', and indeed the jokes from the observed discussion fell flat for the two international participants. AR senses that her students sometimes resist learning the language in a dedicated English class, which she tentatively attributes to her students often identifying themselves first and foremost as makers. What they may not realize, and AR is learning to realize, is that a broad range of social interactions across the domains, spilling over into the informal and private, allows students to 'forge a way to becoming a creative practitioner' (Orr & Shreeve, 2018, p. 7).

Other spoken genres unique to the studio environment include simulation assessments, e.g. mock interviews, exhibitions and, above all, critiques or reviews. A critique, or crit, is based on dialogue around the student's work. The artefact(s) and sketchbooks are put on display, subject to tutor's and peers' scrutiny. Shreeve et al. (2010, p. 131) frame the crit as a way of taking the work forward, describing it as 'quite generous and supportive in terms of the citing of references that the students are expected to make a note of and then go and research'. What this looks like in practice, however, seems fraught with uncertainty, especially for international students. First of all, as AR reports, the student work often draws on personal experience, including sexual and gender identity, faith or trauma. For this reason, the language needed 'is likely to be multi-layered and metaphorical, metaphysical and qualitative, rather than transparent and one-dimensional. It will not seek to exclude the personal and the affective from the cognitive and the social but to acknowledge changes which 'arise as a result of the interested actions of individuals' (Doloughan, 2002, p. 62), which eludes many of the standards generally found in EGAP materials. Secondly, crits observed by JS did not follow a typical presentation format with clear sections and transitions; instead, they seemed more reminiscent of a 'weather forecast'. JS reports that a student whose work is subject to critique 'can start anywhere on the map/design as long as it is logical, and image is used to guide audience'. She attributes the absence of verbal signposting to the presence of multimodal images on large computer screens. This shows how the verbal and the visual work together to create meaning, without either taking a dominant role. 'Another factor that seemed to heavily influence the structure was the audience (including tutors) who could (and did) interrupt and redirect review at any point' (JS). Through this process of Socratic questioning, the tutor may be 'elicit[ing] from the students themselves how they might best further and define the next step in the practice' (Turner & Hocking, 2004, p. 149). However, what often happens is that due to the language barrier and/or differences in academic culture, international students often fail to respond to the tutors' elicitations, forcing them to explicate what they were implying in their questions (Turner & Hocking, 2004).

Studio-specific communication patterns have serious implications for EAP teaching. Adaptation of EGAP materials to give them a creative slant is a start. For example, JS introduced creative note-taking techniques based on more subject-specific (design-based) TED talks, introducing visual mind maps which appeal to students' communicative styles and also allow them to practise associative thinking, which is of value in the studio (Orr & Shreeve, 2018). However, JS also reflected that this could be perceived as 'an obvious outsider trying to fit in'. More substantive interventions are therefore generally needed. To be meaningful game-changers, it is necessary to spend time observing the learning and teaching in the studio and even to shift the teaching focus. AR, despite a preference for teaching writing throughout her earlier career, decided to bring spoken interaction to the forefront of her teaching. In themed discussion classes, her students give presentations about artists and designers, which provide input for student-led interaction afterwards. While initially resisting teaching in a studio space, she now embraces its affordances for just-in-time teaching of interaction. On her pre-sessional course, the language teachers and studio tutors often share the teaching space, and while the latter drive the dialogue, AR intervenes to draw students' attention to implied meanings or links with the language class. Lastly, she experiments with other pedagogies typical of creative contexts, such as object-based learning, creating a safe space in which the students can engage in activities similar to those in the studio with a shift of focus from the artefacts to spoken communication.

Written Genres

The previous section highlighted the importance of language and verbalization in the creative arts and the almost unique role of spoken communication in the learning process (Orr & Shreeve, 2018) and in developing practice (Turner & Hocking,

2004). However, in spite of the moves to redress the balance between the perceived 'superiority' of writing over the created artefact (Borg, 2012; Orr & Shreeve, 2018), writing remains a central element of creative arts education and assessment.

Written communication and genres were a recurrent theme in our reflections and in which disciplinary differences became particularly apparent. In particular, it emerged that the common assessment paradigm of 'essay and oral presentation', encountered on many of the EGAP programmes we have taught on, apparently falls short of the needs of creative arts students. Although the word 'essay' is used, we noted that our students rarely write 'traditional' discursive or thematic essays. On analysis, what is presented as an 'essay' is often something quite different; CC's music students, for example, are required to produce 'various types of essay' that in reality take the form of book reviews, critical commentaries and literature reviews. Some of CM's design students do write essays but these are set by the Business School (which shares some of its modules) and thus not from a creative arts context. A particularly interesting example is that of the 'visual essay' required of AR's art and design students, a genre that was 'mysterious' to both her and her students, possibly encapsulating the ambiguity that can characterize the creative arts disciplines.

While our students do produce some of the 'traditional' academic genres (dissertations, literature reviews, research proposals), these generally exist alongside a range of other written genres, varying in style, language and format. CM's design students, for example, produce design portfolios, logbooks, reflective reports, business reports, advertising campaign proposals, case studies. Some of these reflect the 'increasing centrality of interdisciplinarity' (Orr & Shreeve, 2018, p. 5), leading to collaborative links across disciplines, which result in features from more 'recognizable' academic genres (such as those classified by Nesi & Gardner, 2012) being 'merged' with features from other text types to create a kind of 'hybrid' (Dovey, 2006). Features typical of a business report or reflective reports on design development are seen incorporated into final dissertations, for example (CM). CC's experience on the other hand highlights the fact that some genres are apparently completely unique to the discipline: seen in the programme notes, performance reviews and composition portfolios produced by her music students. In addition, while some genres have the same name (such as the 'portfolio', commonly used in art, design, music and architecture), in reality, they are often very different, even within a discipline or programme.

Borg (2012) asserts that 'writing in art and design education is different from writing in most other areas of university education' since they 'have their own forms of meaning-making, expressed through their creations' (p. 169), and we observed this to be the case across our disciplines. Borg (2012) highlights the innovative nature of writing in art and design education and the resultant innovative forms of assessment. The visual essay is an example of this: neither AR nor her students had a clear idea of what was required, due to the 'open-ness' (Vaughan et al., 2008) of the task brief and the lack of examples to help establish what was required. AR noted that 'often the subject lecturers don't know themselves or can't articulate [this]'. This 'open-ness' is a manifestation of the ambiguity central to the discipline (Orr & Shreeve, 2018; Vaughan et al., 2008) and 'the penchant for creativity and individualism' (Melles, 2007, p. 7), adopted as a way of settling students into a culture in which they 'feel comfortable with ambiguity' (Vaughan et al., 2008) and 'develop a tolerance of the unknown' (Orr & Shreeve, 2018). By default, then, EAP practitioners also need to work within this ambiguity, in this case assuming perhaps the role of 'guide on the side' (King, 1993) as we work with the students to explore and discover and potentially even innovate in order to understand.

In the midst of such variety and fluidity of written genres, our challenge as EAP practitioners is often deciding what to focus on, since there is no single formula for writing that can be used as a model across assignments. Melles (2007, p. 8) advocates the 'close analysis of texts with a view to informing students of the boundaries within which they write'. Where available student assignment samples have proved invaluable for helping to 'demystify' tasks: CM noted that her students often have access to such samples but receive little or no guidance on how to use them. She is thus able to 'fill the gap', using her expertise to guide the students through the recommended analysis. EAP practitioners can clearly play a part in 'support[ing] and scaffold[ing] the students in learning to cope with [ambiguity]' (Vaughan et al., 2008) by facilitating their understanding of the genres and the disciplinary conventions. To do so, however, requires understanding on our part or a willingness to 'work it out' (AR). Our reflections invariably noted that access to both samples of the required genres and the people who set the assignments has been key to our gaining understanding of the discipline. The creative and innovative nature of many of the genres we encounter means they are rarely found in available corpora such as the British Academic Written English corpus,[1] and in any case, the variation observed between

---

[1] The British Academic Written English (BAWE) corpus was developed at the universities of Warwick, Reading and Oxford Brookes under the directorship of Hilary Nesi and Sheena Gardner (formerly of the Centre for Applied Linguistics, Warwick), Paul Thompson (formerly of the Department of Applied Linguistics, Reading) and Paul Wickens (School of Education, Oxford Brookes), with funding from the ESRC (RES-000-23-0800). https://warwick.ac.uk/fac/soc/al/research/collections/bawe/

institutions, disciplines and programmes suggests that samples from outside of the specific context might not be appropriate. Access to these 'occluded genres' (Swales, 1996) requires a close, collaborative rapport with the departments, and it is through our close collaboration with subject academics that we have been able not only to access the samples but also to have the conversations that help gain an 'insider' understanding of the genres themselves.

Collaboration

Our reflections showed that collaborations with EAP departmental colleagues, EAP practitioners in other institutions, subject experts and students are central to our EAP practice in the creative arts, which provides multiple perspectives in our EAP course design (Tajino et al., 2005). Yet despite long advocation that EAP practitioners be embedded within departments and work closely with subject experts (Hyland, 2002; Wingate, 2015), the rotation of departmental staff between teaching roles and modules presents a constant challenge to keep pace with students, modules and assignments, subject specialists, module and programme leaders: each of us faces our own challenges in maintaining alignment with creative arts in our contexts, particularly given creative genres, ambiguity and the multimodal nature of these disciplines.

The first stage of collaboration with our creative arts departments was 'cooperation', in which we expressed willingness to help and gained reciprocation through direct access to spoken and written texts, staff and students, and wider practices. Whereas materials such as units of work had been shared by colleagues from within EAP, and other support had been given (e.g. information about happenings in the wider university, and contacts and connections to initiate and help to maintain relationships), we all felt this contextual information, unique to the academic community/ies of practice of each department and institution, is fundamental to understand and meet the diverse needs of creative arts students.

Gaining access to at least one 'critical counterpart' in a creative arts department, whose priorities or mission align with ours, seems to have been a pivotal moment for all of us, allowing us to gain access to contexts, people and texts. For CM and AR, embedded in the department, being able to observe lectures, studio tutorials and attend meetings has been a key means of keeping up-to-date with current assignments and happenings in the department. JS had the opportunity to shadow colleagues within the Architecture department, and thus observe crits and other practices. AR has co-marked assignments with a design tutor and a programme leader. For CC, two colleagues in the Music department with a specific remit to develop students' 'essay skills' (among other duties) quickly became critical contacts and collaborators on ESAP/ academic literacies/essay skills projects. It is interesting to note the accidental 'interdisciplinary triad' (Sandholtz, 2000, p. 49) in the latter example: albeit all of the subject specialists involved were experienced in their own fields, the triad helped to provide projects with a balanced variety of knowledge, experience, expertise and ideas which may not have been possible in a paired collaboration.

Northcott and Brown (2006, p. 374) suggest the need to 'adjust and accommodate ourselves to the other's frame of reference'. AR mentions having the opportunity to co-mark with a design tutor for three consecutive years and how this was an 'eye-opener' with regard to departmental expectations. As part of an *Enhancing the Student Learning Experience (ESLE)* project, CC had the opportunity to see marks and feedback given by module leaders on specially commissioned writing drafts and feedback. This provided valuable insight into the expectations module leaders have of music undergraduates across the 'pathways'. Both AR and CC found negotiating the line between specialist content, disciplinary values and writing input tricky, and it was reassuring to have the support of a departmental colleague to ensure that feedback was appropriately aligned. CM collaborates regularly and directly with a departmental colleague to align her own weekly EAP classes with what students are doing on their core modules. Since time is required to establish this kind of rapport, this can only happen if collaboration is close and long term.

Moving from cooperation towards building collaboration (Dudley-Evans & St John, 1998) with our respective creative arts departments has required strong personal interest in the subject area, and motivation and drive to grow our involvement. We all gained additional resource to develop our knowledge and pedagogy and facilitate collaboration through a variety of means: secondment (CM), new cross-institutional roles (AR), work shadowing and an interdisciplinary, internally funded EdD (JS) and applications for internal funding for a collaborative writing development project (CC). Willingness to go outside the EAP department and think creatively to access resources has been a key component in successful collaboration, and allowing time to do this and seek collaboration opportunities is one of the main ways in which departments and institutions foster and support important interdisciplinary and cross-institutional educational development.

Throughout our reflections, little mention was made of direct collaboration with students in the development of materials, which is becoming increasingly popular in the realm of learning developers (e.g. Levy & Polnariev, 2016). In some contexts, art and design students are expected to be co-constructors of the curriculum (Orr & Shreeve, 2018). In a pre-sessional context, and/or early stages of a taught in-sessional programme, students may be novices in their subject areas, particularly when beginning a conversion Master's as both AR and CM have found. We noted in our reflections that students, particularly international students, can find it difficult to articulate their needs or do not know what the options are at this stage. There is potential, given sufficient time, to involve a previous year's cohort, who might be able to articulate perceived needs, in preparation for the following year. For example, CC has learnt about disciplinary practices from PGR students working on composition portfolios in one-to-one writing consultations. Allowing space and time for students, EAP practitioners and subject experts to fully complete the reflective teaching and learning cycle could play a vital role in developing the knowledge, skills and experience required to be able to adopt such an emergent and flexible pedagogical approach that could increase the effectiveness of EAP in the creative arts context.

Conclusion: Implications for EAP Practice

This chapter set out to examine the nature of EAP in the creative arts through the lens of our own practice, across our varying disciplines and contexts, with a view to exploring the implications for those working in EAP in both the creative arts and beyond. While our reflections remain individual and potentially singular to our own contexts, they demonstrate many of the shared challenges and ways that we have adjusted to working within or alongside a different 'academic tribe' (Becher & Trowler, 2001).

One of the most striking observations about the 'Creative Arts' as a disciplinary area is the diversity that exists within it. We have observed differences not only between our respective disciplines but within them, be it at programme/module level or institutional. These differences shape the learning and teaching spaces which have in turn shaped our own ways of being and doing as EAP practitioners, in terms of both how we communicate with students and colleagues, and, most noticeably, how we have adapted our own teaching practices to align more closely with the practices within the departments in which we work. The differences in discourse practices and the constant evolution of new methods of assessment and oral and written communication driven by the creative and ambiguous nature of creative arts disciplines have required constant flexibility on our part that mirrors that required of the students themselves.

This evident diversity between and within creative arts disciplines, however, has equally served to highlight the commonalities, resulting in us adopting a similar pedagogical approach: an ethnographic approach that requires a willingness to leave the familiar spaces generally occupied by Language Teaching Units and occupy the creative arts spaces where we are able to observe the pedagogies and practices of our relative disciplines. For the EAP practitioner, working in collaboration with the creative arts departments is essential, since it affords access to these very diverse practices and to a lived experience of the challenges experienced by the students. An embedded role is ideal because it allows EAP practitioners the necessary time to research, to find out, to make contacts and to build working relationships. On the ground, it also allows time for the observation and shadowing of department colleagues, which in turn helps in aligning teaching with students' most pressing needs, which students may not be able to immediately identify for themselves.

We have seen that in the creative arts in particular EAP practitioners need to be resourceful and flexible and ready to work outside their comfort zone and inside a zone proximal to the discipline. Yet it is also important to acknowledge the mutual exchange of expertise that can occur through collaboration, with the EAP practitioner bringing both linguistic expertise and experience of teaching international students into the departments. This is not something that was focused on in any great measure in our reflections but would be an interesting area to explore: future research could benefit from an exploration of the perceptions of creative arts subject experts of their experiences of working with EAP practitioners and the effect on their pedagogies and practices.

11

Integrating a Signature Pedagogy into a Pre-sessional

Impact on Pedagogy in ESAP

Carole MacDiarmid, Anneli Williams, Kat Irwin and Brían Doonan

This chapter takes a case-study approach to consider the impact of integrating a signature medical school pedagogy (problem-based learning) into an English for Specific Academic Purposes (ESAP) pre-sessional bridging course for students going on to medical and life sciences at the University of Glasgow. It focuses on the perceived influence which this key element of the pre-sessional Biomed course, which was collaboratively created and is co-taught by medical faculty staff (medical lecturers and facilitators), has had on ESAP teaching and learning and how this has enhanced our understanding of not only academic discourse but also academic practices.

In this chapter, we outline the evolution of this pre-sessional ESAP course from one that initially employed a predominantly task-based pedagogy (Ellis, 2003) to one that is now immersed in the signature pedagogy (SP) (Shulman, 2005) of problem-based learning (PBL). We explore how an understanding of the facets of this SP have informed iterations of the ESAP component, its delivery and how, in uncovering also disciplinary practices, the ESAP lecturers (ESAPLs) have developed their own practice. We conclude by reflecting on how our professional knowledge and values as ESAPLs have developed through this collaboration and on implications for the wider field of EAP.

The Institutional Context

The institutional context of this study – the University of Glasgow (UofG) – defines itself as a broad-based research-led university operating in an international context. Like many UK higher education institutions of its type, over the last decade, the UofG has focused on its international ambitions and seen significant growth in its international student population. Between 2011–12 and 2018–19, international student numbers effectively doubled (from approximately 5,700 to 10,570) and now make up roughly one-third of the total student population. Approximately 20 per cent of international applicants require some form of English language tuition in order to meet conditions of entry to degree programmes. At the UofG, just over 40 per cent seek to meet this requirement via a foundation programme, with the remaining 60 per cent doing so via a pre-sessional English language programme. Not surprisingly, the growth trajectory of UofG pre-sessional student numbers has mirrored that in international student numbers, roughly doubling over the same period to a figure of 1101 in the summer of 2019 (despite the global pandemic, this number was not significantly different in 2020). It is also worth noting that as in many other Scottish universities, a large majority of international students who enrol on pre-sessional courses have applied for post-graduate taught (PGT) programmes of study.

Pre-sessional tuition is offered to students with English language proficiency at the lower end of B1 to the upper end of B2 Common European Framework of Reference for Languages (CEFR) (Council of Europe, 2001). The pre-sessional course runs in a series of four or five-week blocks for a total of thirty-six weeks from October to August, with the majority of students (80 per cent) joining for the last five or ten weeks only.

The kind of learning experience pre-sessional students have had at our institution over the last thirty years has changed considerably in response to alterations in the size and composition of the student cohort and evolving conceptualizations of what EAP instruction can and should aim to achieve. When student numbers were relatively small (<100), students were taught in multidisciplinary groups following an English for General Academic Purposes (EGAP) approach (Hyland, 2016). The syllabus was organized around weekly themes with carrier content selected on the basis of perceived general appeal and accessibility to the non-specialist. To meet the then professional BALEAP course accreditation requirement that each class be taught by at least two teachers, we chose to divide the teaching by skill with listening and speaking allocated to one instructor, reading and writing to another. Although not inevitable, this resulted in a tendency to treat the skills somewhat separately both in the classroom and in the design of the course material. Our approach to writing instruction in early iterations of pre-sessional courses also show traces of process approaches to writing instruction (Badger & White, 2000) and an interest in contrastive rhetoric (Kaplan, 1966). There was some albeit limited scope for students to engage with discipline-specific content in that they could choose the topic and source texts for an extended essay assignment as long as this fitted within a pre-determined rhetorical structure (situation-problem-solution-evaluation).

However, since 2005 we have developed a series of seven bridging courses which employ a broadly ESAP approach (Hyland, 2016) for the final five-week block of study. This approach entails a greater focus on the particular communicative practices and linguistic features associated with specific disciplines in the belief that it is competence in these areas that will underpin students' ability to study effectively at the next stage of their academic journey. The term ESAP, however, is used advisedly because in fact most of our individual bridging courses cater for students preparing for a variety of programmes within a relatively broad disciplinary area. The Biomedical Science Bridging course is one of these.

In 2019, eight-five students were enrolled on this course in preparation for academic study in twenty-five different PGT programmes, including Clinical Pharmacology, Advanced Nursing Science, Medical Genetics, Forensic Toxicology and Critical Care, as well as a clutch of others that are themselves interdisciplinary in nature: Food Security, Bioinformatics and Public Health. A further two students were enrolled on undergraduate programmes, one Pre-Veterinary Medicine, the other Pre-Clinical Medicine. The defining feature of this pre-sessional course is its incorporation of a PBL pedagogy, which is described in the following section.

Problem-Based Learning: A Signature Pedagogy

As many students are going on to professionally related degree programmes, at least *part* of their education will prepare them for professional practice. PBL is used on a number of programmes to this end.

PBL is a student-centred pedagogy common in medical education but also applied within other fields. Its origins can be traced to McMaster University in Canada, where concerns about the limitations of transmissive modes of education were accompanied by a growing understanding of the cognitive processes involved in learning (Barrows & Tamblyn, 1980). The challenge was to develop a pedagogy for medical education that would develop the skills and knowledge that practitioners would need in future professional life (Barrows,

1986). These skills included exploration, critical reasoning, problem-solving, collaborative practice and self-directed learning. PBL, which aims to develop all of these, is a signature pedagogy now employed in many medical education programmes.

In Shulman's (2005) discussion of education in preparation for professional practice, he defines SPs as approaches that reflect the 'three fundamental dimensions of professional work – to think, to perform, and to act with integrity' (p. 52). He describes how the characteristics of different professions are reflected in the practices of the academy and the ways in which professionals are educated; these SPs 'implicitly define *what counts as knowledge* in a field and *how things become known*. They define *how knowledge is analyzed, criticized, accepted, or discarded*' (italics added). In doing so, this education 'is preparation for 'good work' (p. 53). He also notes that SPs transcend individuals and institutions '*signature pedagogies are important precisely because they are pervasive*' (p. 53).

A SP has three levels:

> A *surface structure* . . . of concrete, operational acts of teaching and learning . . . a *deep structure*, a set of assumptions about how best to impart a certain body of knowledge and know-how . . . and an *implicit structure*, a moral dimension that comprises a set of beliefs about professional attitudes, values, and disposition. (p. 54)

SPs, with habits and routines which scaffold learning, also require active engagement of learners. This characterization of a pedagogy not only provides a useful framework for describing and understanding PBL but also provides a lens through which other pedagogical approaches in the academy can be explored. Potentially useful transferable skills might also be identified, which can then inform EGAP and ESAP practice more generally.

While there are many applications of PBL from a fully integrated approach to one where the PBL is an adjunct to a lecture-based-curriculum (see Wijnia et al., 2019), each model will include the PBL cycle. The cycle of instruction can be regarded as Shulman's surface structure. A cycle typically involves an initial stage which introduces the scenario and the problem and where participants brainstorm and share knowledge related to the case. The outcome of the first meeting is to identify learning objectives (LOs), for independent study, that will help solve or at least answer issues in the scenario. In the independent study period participants may research all, some or one LO and may meet in informal group settings out-of-class to share knowledge. All the group members then reconvene and the findings from this independent study will be applied to the scenario in order to reach some solution. This presentation and application stage offers a further opportunity to ask questions and for clarification, and for knowledge construction for the group and also at the individual level. There may also be a final stage to reflect on learning and the process. The role of the PBL facilitator (PBLF) is to scaffold learning by guiding the stages and to ensure students do not veer too far off track; they may also prompt and probe and on occasion check factual knowledge. Knowledge of how the cycle works provides ESAPLs with insights into observable surface-level practices but may not lead to or require an understanding of assumptions underpinning a pedagogy.

While there is no consensus that PBL as an approach is superior to a lecture-based curriculum, there is research to suggest that it leads to deeper engagement in learning (e.g. Dolmans et al., 2016). The pedagogical assumptions underpinning PBL (Shulman's deep structure) emphasize active engagement and the process of learning. Interaction and engagement with both the subject matter and the other participants are at its heart and it is very much a student-led endeavour. This dialogic and constructivist approach to learning (Schmidt et al., 2019) aims to develop the practical professional skills needed for future practice. The final reflection stage is intended to forge a stronger link between procedural and declarative knowledge (Barrows, 1986). In the context of medical/life science education, the implicit structure (the beliefs and values) can be exemplified in, for example, the role of counselling in medical genetics, in ethical issues and the disposition to enquiry. An interrogation of the beliefs and values and assumptions underpinning teaching and learning can provide an ESAPL with a more in-depth understanding of such pedagogies.

PBL is not without criticism. Colliver (2000) questions its overall effectiveness compared to more traditional forms of education; students and faculty may initially feel uncomfortable with the less prescribed curriculum content (Khoo, 2003); there are issues in how to assess, particularly if assessments are to be aligned with the learning process (Albanese, 2000); student expectations particularly for those students from educational backgrounds where active contributions are perhaps not the norm (Remedios et al., 2008), and the role of the PBLF and the extent to which they facilitate or obstruct contributions (Zhang et al., 2010), have also been researched. Notwithstanding these critiques, the approach is applied in many contexts and programmes within and beyond medical education (Savin-Baden & Major, 2004) and cited as a SP in many (Lock et al., 2018).

The principles which underpin the approach involve active and self-directed learning, themes also currently cited as important in many university settings, with a whole journal devoted to *Active Learning in Higher Education*. Affordances of PBL could also be said to provide opportunities to develop graduate attributes (Edwards, 2005), for example, helping students to become independent critical thinkers, reflective, investigative, resourceful and responsible learners (University of Glasgow, n.d.). The importance of dialogic interaction in the construction of knowledge is noted as a feature of socialization into academic discourse communities as well as being a part of the learning process itself (Duff, 2010).

The pedagogical assumptions underpinning PBL also sit well with principles of language learning that we draw on in our context (e.g. developing language and skills in academic contexts, Newton et al. (2018); opportunities for practice through genre-based pedagogies, Hyland (2003)). PBL has even been used as the basis of EAP courses themselves (e.g. Wood & Head, 2004).

As we shall see, an understanding of the assumptions and practices related to PBL is helpful in explaining how and why PBL is integrated into our ESAP course and its impact on the ESAP pedagogy that accompanies it. This is the focus of the next section.

The Development from EGAP to ESAP and the Integration of PBL

There were two primary drivers behind our move from an EGAP to a more ESAP-focused course. Within our EAP unit there was growing awareness of alternative, socially oriented ways of conceptualizing EAP, in particular genre-based pedagogy (Hyland 2003; Swales, 1990). Secondly, we began to receive overtures from academic departments seeking to better prepare international students for particular programmes of study, sometimes in response to recommendations from quality assurance processes, e.g. 'Periodic Subject Reviews'. These came initially from the Business School, the School of Law and a clutch of subjects within medicine and life sciences: Human Nutrition, Genetics and Sports Science. Interestingly, many of the concerns expressed by academic colleagues were not primarily focused on achievement (deficit model) but on the more socially oriented goals of enhancing international student engagement, integration and experience.

In response to these developments and enabled by significant growth in international student numbers (approximately 250), we chose to replace the final five-week component of our pre-sessional course with a suite of subject-specific courses. The shape and content of each course were largely determined by the scale and type of collaboration that could be achieved with the receiving academic departments. A strong commitment to collaboration resulted in courses that were effectively co-designed and functioned almost as foundation courses; weaker commitment resulted in courses that were very similar in structure and pedagogical approach to our previous generic model: in some cases, it was simply a question of substituting pre-existing reading and listening texts with discipline-specific material while maintaining many of the same tasks. There, we employed a task-based pedagogy (Ellis, 2003) but with an increasing commitment to the analysis of written genres (Swales, 1990).

The Biomed Bridging course sat roughly midway between these two poles, mainly because of the decision to incorporate three PBL cycles within the pre-existing syllabus structure. Because PBL requires learners to discuss, research and present information relating to the core problem, a greater integration of skills was required. An examination of our course material archive shows that in early versions of this course there were attempts to link the content of reading, speaking and in some cases listening lessons around the core PBL themes; however, the design of tasks still bore the hallmarks of our previous segregated study skills approach. Reading lessons, for example, were designed around relatively short texts and made extensive use of comprehension questions to ensure that students understood the content. Tasks which focused on specific reading skills, e.g. identifying the salient points within a series of paragraphs, tended to treat the exercise in a self-contained manner. In other words, there was little explicit reference to the purpose for which that exercise served in preparation for the PBL. Speaking lessons required students to speak about texts relevant to the week's PBL theme but directed learners to use set phrases typical of more formal seminar style presentations:

The topic of my presentation . . .
If you have any questions, I would be happy to answer those at the end of the presentation.

Later iterations of the course show that in response to feedback from students and academic partners, tasks were modified in a way that show an evolving understanding of the assumptions underlying what PBL actually requires students to do – how they need to engage with texts and with each other. Learning via PBL is a very cognitively demanding endeavour with the skills of reading, writing, listening and speaking interacting in complex ways.

The course has been taught each year since 2007. In its most recent incarnation, the course is tightly structured around two main components: PBL scenarios and an independent written project (essay). The PBL scenarios cover three themes – Food additives (week 1), Medical genetics and Ethics (week 2), and Cancer (weeks 3 and 4) – and become progressively more challenging. The cycle of work on our ESAP course reflects a typical PBL cycle outlined earlier but with additional ESAP-specific augmentations to further scaffold and support learning and engagement. The PBL topic is introduced to the whole cohort at the start of the week in a session delivered by one of the medical lecturers (MLs). Following this initial lecture, students form smaller workshop groups (around 12–14) and, under the guidance of a PBLF, now typically PhD student graduate teaching assistants with subject knowledge, the scenario is discussed and topics for further research are identified and delegated. These sessions provide authentic opportunities for pushed output (Gass & Mackey, 2007) and provide an opportunity for ESAPLs to observe and note aspects of interaction and language for feedback in a later ESAP session. A list of recommended source materials is also provided by the MLs to guide the independent study.

Extracts from the recommended reading materials form the basis of the reading lessons each week (typically two to three 90-minute sessions). During these sessions, students learn about the PBL topic and develop the reading skills which are relevant both to PBL and to the extended subject-specific essay that students research and write over the five-week course. Whereas in earlier iterations of the course, reading lessons tended to focus more on content via comprehension questions, reading tasks in the current course materials require students to navigate longer texts via tasks that aim to develop familiarity with the rhetorical structure of the genre (typically research papers), information search skills and critical evaluation in both the selection and reading of texts:

a) *What sort of a text is this? Who do you think is its intended audience?*
b) *Do you think this is a reliable and valid source of medical information? Give reasons for your answer.*

If you do not have time to read a research paper in detail but want a general idea of its content, which sections would you read and in what order?

These are the skills that enable the reader to be more in control of the reading process and purposeful in how they approach the text – important for fulfilling the research task required for the second stage of the PBL cycle. A key task for the teacher is to help students acquire the relevant language and awareness of rhetorical structure within the text without losing sight of their primary purpose for reading: to search for and critically evaluate information relevant to the problem at hand.

Reading tasks frequently segue into tasks that require students to give concise oral summaries of information and indicate how their contribution has been informed by their reading. The ESAPL's role here is to involve students in the task of evaluating speaking performance and effectively coach one another:

> *While listening to the other members of your group, help them to improve the clarity of their speech by asking them to repeat or rephrase the information if it is unclear to you.*
>
> *When you have all shared your information, decide what conclusions you can draw. Prepare a short summary of your conclusions (2-4 sentences) and elect one of your members to present it to the class.*
>
> *When all of the groups have spoken, discuss the relative strengths and weaknesses of your contributions. Which group produced the most articulate, concise and valid conclusion of the evidence?*

These tasks prepare students for the second PBL workshop later in the week when they report back to their PBL group the results of their investigation and, in further discussion, develop their understanding. Again, the ESAPL takes the role of silent observer, noting aspects of the students' performance that may require further attention.

Listening lessons (one per week) and speaking lessons (usually two per week) with the ESAPLs also prepare students for the discussion element of PBLs. Lecture-focused listening lessons have been supplemented with material based on a panel discussion among experts and tasks require students to exercise critical judgement:

> *The two main speakers are called Dr. Mary McNaughton-Collins and Dr. Philip Kantoff. What are their credentials?*

and to notice how the discussion unfolds and knowledge is co-constructed:

> *Listen to this section once for an overview of the main points. For each cancer trial:*
> - *What does the first speaker do?*
> - *How does the second speaker respond?*

Speaking lessons which in earlier versions of the course tended to emphasize individual presentation skills were modified to include more of the informal interactive language required to engage effectively in a working PBL group. For example:

> You notice that a quiet student is trying to speak, but other students keep speaking first. You can help the quiet student to get the attention of the group:
>
>> I think Carla is trying to make a point.
>> Nikki, did you want to make a point?

An emphasis on active listening and highlighting to students a range of different ways to get involved in a discussion (e.g. commenting, seeking clarification) became more prominent. The shift in emphasis towards interactive skills was further consolidated when the end-of-course oral presentation was replaced with an assessed group discussion task outlined in the following.

In the final stage of our PBL cycle, learning is consolidated via a timed writing session when each student is asked to write a brief synopsis of the topic (or an aspect of it), for which they receive feedback the following week. This exercise serves a dual purpose: firstly, to reinforce the students' ability to communicate in a way that is clear and concise (a requirement of Biomed programmes), and secondly to provide the ESAP lecture with sufficient examples of the students' written output to enable formative feedback and evaluation (a requirement of the pre-sessional EAP course). Like the formative feedback on 'pushed' oral output after the PBL sessions, the writing feedback is responsive to learner needs. In the overall design, then, we can see the PBL as embedded in the ESAP course, in a similar fashion to the approach advocated for in-sessional courses (e.g. Sloan & Porter, 2010).

Extended writing skills are mainly addressed via the subject-specific essay input, which forms a separate strand of the course. Students are asked to produce a short essay (1,500 words) on an aspect of medicine or science relevant to their context, i.e. their country and/or area of interest. Each year, with guidance from the MLs, broad essay topics are suggested with a list of starter references. Students select a topic of interest and formulate their own extended essay title which must be approved by their ESAPL, usually to ensure that there will be an element of evaluation and argumentation involved. Most recently, topics such as managing emerging infectious diseases, dietary supplements and stem cell research have been included, deliberately broad enough to appeal to the diverse cohort. In the process of producing their individual text, students develop a variety of reading and writing skills; however, the main aim is learning to recognize and make appropriate use of valid scientific literature. Sessions on various aspects of assignment writing are timetabled each week, as well as a session where students can present and/or discuss their work in progress.

This closer integration of elements of the course is also reflected in the evolution of the approach to assessment. In earlier iterations of the course, along with the extended essay coursework, students were assessed via discrete item tests of reading and listening, and an individual oral presentation related to an aspect of their essay. The need to ensure a degree of parity of assessment across the seven bridging courses has exerted a somewhat conservative influence on the design of the end-of-course assessments. However, the most recent developments ensure more constructive alignment (Biggs & Tang, 2011) of the course aims and content, the approach to delivery (i.e. the pedagogy) and the assessed work. Discrete item tests of reading and listening remain, as does the extended essay – albeit with modifications: texts deemed irrelevant have been removed or replaced. More significantly, the final speaking assessment requires students to integrate reading, listening and speaking skills via a seminar discussion for which each student reads a different text on the same theme. Students then present a summary to the group followed by a discussion, which requires participants to share knowledge and negotiate a collaborative response to a number of questions (Givan, 2019). The assessed PBL is carried out in smaller groups of three to four students to maximize speaking opportunities and facilitate individual assessment. This change not only foregrounds the importance of dialogic interaction in the process of learning (Basturkmen, 2016) but also ensures higher engagement and motivation in the ESAP lesson. The assessment, then, in essence encapsulates the PBL SP approach that is threaded through the course and assesses both directly and indirectly in line with the course's intended learning outcomes.

The Evolving ESAP Lecturer Role

Since the mode of delivery of Biomed course offers the learners a more 'immersive' experience, this requires the teaching team to have a clear understanding of roles within the collaboration. MLs deliver lectures introducing the PBL themes and supply suggestions for extended essay themes. PBLFs provide implicit exposure to epistemology and approaches to knowledge construction, albeit in rehearsal mode, rather than with specific subject knowledge or areas to develop in mind. Here, the central role of the PBL cycle also ensures a differentiated role for the ESAPL from that of our other courses. While the PBLF scaffolds content knowledge (Hmelo-Silver & Barrows, 2008), the EAP lecturers' role is to scaffold and facilitate entry to these practices both before and in response to participation. For example, in addition to specific lessons facilitating access and thereby engagement, the ESAPL role in the PBL component is that of observer, monitor of progress and provider of formative feedback on participation and academic language and skills. While giving feedback in itself is not unusual (Lyster et al., 2013), the EAP lecturer's role in the PBL is *only* to observe, not prompting for participation as might normally occur in an EAP lesson. This observer role along with closer contact with the MLs and PBLFs offers the ESAPLs a unique opportunity to observe not only learner interactions but that of the facilitators and as such *academic practice* and values in action. This is, in our context at least, rarely available to ESAP tutors on pre-sessionals, and since it moves the focus beyond the study of academic texts and discourse to academic practices, arguably provides a more rounded understanding of the broader disciplinary area and approach at hand.

While the integration and observation of the various elements of PBL make the disciplinary culture and epistemology of the Biomed field much more visible to the ESAPL, the collaboration also has the potential to make the culture and epistemology of ESAP more visible to our collaborators in the medical and life sciences schools. The EAP unit's ownership of the course and gatekeeping role means that ESAPLs had ultimate responsibility for and visibility in ensuring that the content and approach to teaching in the course fit together. It was because the ESAPLs were able to reflect on the links through their own observations and the way students engaged (or disengaged when they did not perceive the assessment to be linked to PBL classes) that changes to assessment came about.

While the course is convened and taught by a permanent member of the EAP staff team and a core of returning teachers with specific interests in these disciplines, each year new lecturers join the team. To support these ESAPLs, there is a need to articulate the culture and epistemology of ESAP, as we understand it, drawing on our interdisciplinary knowledge base from education to applied linguistics. Shulman's (1986) conception of teacher knowledge is a useful framework in this regard. It includes knowledge of how to teach, pedagogical content knowledge (PCK), subject content, curricular knowledge and the 'ability to relate the content of a given course or lesson to topics or issues being discussed simultaneously in other classes' (p. 7). In the Biomed pre-sessional course context, this means the ability to relate what is occurring in the PBL sections to the ESAP components, being able to utilize appropriate methods for language/EAP teaching in a disciplinary-specific context (PCK), and as part of this, content knowledge in relation to features of academic discourse and genres, and approaches to linguistic analysis. Here Ferguson's (1997) conception of specialized knowledge (for language for specific purposes instructors) is useful. He maintains that specialized knowledge also requires a knowledge of 'disciplinary cultures and values ... the epistemological bases of different disciplines ... [and] of genre and discourse' (p. 85). The focus on more typical skills and texts certainly requires teachers to analyse and negotiate genre and discourse of the area in order to help learners 'unpack' specialist texts and to engage with the practices, in this case PBL. However, the opportunity to observe PBLs also enables the ESAPLs to gain greater insights into the disciplinary cultures and epistemological practices and values that Ferguson identifies as key aspects of specialized teacher knowledge noted earlier. Central to PBL is the role and value of critical reasoning, constructing knowledge through collaboration and also the notion of a non-finite body of knowledge. This knowledge of values and epistemology is also reflected in the understanding through observation of how all the elements interact and the development of a more integrated and constructively aligned course.

The approach to teacher induction has thus also evolved. Earlier induction programmes included a strong focus on assessment and an introduction to general lesson planning or the specific course. More recent programmes include more of a focus on developing and expanding the EAP/ESAP teacher knowledge base, including a number of sessions involving the discussion of relevant research articles (e.g. disciplinary-specific lexis; genre families). Although these still primarily focus on developing content knowledge of specialized genres and discourse (Ferguson, 1997), there is some focus on how the PBL sessions are congruently embedded with the overall course of instruction and the course assessments.

In summary, the gradual move in our Biomed pre-sessional from an EGAP to an ESAP instantiated one with embedded PBL saw a pedagogical shift from a predominantly task-based (Ellis, 2003) to a more genre-based approach (Hyland 2003; Swales, 1990). This has altered the way in which the four skills are handled in the classroom and how they are assessed. The pedagogical focus also foregrounds the place of dialogic interaction in the learning process (Basturkmen, 2016) and how this is facilitated in skills lessons. Another shift pertains to the more constructively aligned course aims, content and approach to delivery and assessment (Biggs & Tang, 2011).

Future Directions and Implications for the Wider Context

The Biomed course is one that continues to evolve alongside our own knowledge and expertise. While there have been considerable developments in the course design which have impacted on the pedagogy (e.g. approaches to dealing with reading texts, the observational role of the ESAPLs in PBLs), there are still areas that prove challenging or which can be explored in more detail.

One of the most obvious is that with the increase in student numbers and the wider range of subject backgrounds, students can feel disadvantaged when not focusing explicitly on their own specific subjects. This challenge of working with mixed-disciplinary groups is not unusual on pre-sessional courses (Flowerdew, 2019; Hyland, 2016) but does require the ESAPLs to foreground the academic skills and literacies that the students are developing and also to help identify appropriate essay topics and readings. At present, the extended writing task is an essay. The contributing medical lectures are content with the broad approach and topics. This, however, may or may not be the most common genre that the majority of students in this college will need to master, particularly as we see a more diversified group (see Gardner & Nesi, 2013, for a discussion on genre families in the disciplines).

The current approach to focusing on language is primarily responsive to learners' written and interactive spoken outputs, but exploration of prominent lexicogrammatical patterns found in written and spoken texts may inform aspects of language and discourse that can be focused on in the classroom. This could be augmented by a more prominent focus on functional knowledge about language and by providing tools which learners can apply when working in their future, possibly different subject areas (Monbec, 2018). This in turn will require a strong teacher knowledge base (Ding & Bruce, 2017) not only of features, along with a further exploration of effective ways to apply this in the ESAP context (i.e. more scholarship into specific pedagogical approaches). Even closer collaboration could include discussions of formative and summative assessments of student work, providing insights for ESAPLs, MLs and PBLFs, an approach advocated, for example, by Caulton et al. (2019), as could explorations of the extent to which skills and knowledge transfer occur and are relevant to future study (Monbec, 2018).

Although this ESAP course is clearly very context-specific and benefits from close collaboration from a dedicated set of MLs and facilitators, there are a number of implications that are potentially of value to the wider EAP teaching community.

Examining disciplinary practices from an SP perspective has helped us to look beyond the surface features of disciplinary practices and discourse and engage with the core beliefs and values that underpin them. Grappling with what it means to be a 'good' practitioner or scholar within a discipline has enabled us to develop a course that is more coherent than our previous efforts and deliver instruction that is more purposeful and dynamic. It has allowed us to go well beyond training students to 'mimic' aspects of academic performance and experience what it means to be a member of a scholarly group that is alive to its core purpose. This approach offers an additional lens through which the ESAP practitioner more generally can develop.

In spite of the difficulty of some of the content, the course is popular among EAPLs for its energizing effect. As responsibility for assessment lies with the EAP unit, we retain ownership of the course, which helps to ensure a balance of power and parity of esteem among the partners in the collaboration. The course is designed to serve the interests of both parties: EAPLs have access to content that incentivizes learning and communication among students, therefore easing the task of developing and assessing students' language proficiency. MLs benefit from a better prepared student cohort and advance knowledge of what the cohort is like in terms of their communicative competence within the specific PBL setting. This more collaborative approach moves us beyond cooperation and the service provider stance that has been discussed in other programmes (e.g. Barron, 2003).

Considering our own practice from an SP perspective helps to keep us in touch with the core beliefs and values that, in our view, underpin our field, including an ethical commitment to developing our understanding of the academy through scholarly investigation and collaborative practice.

Conclusion

In this chapter, we have shown how the pedagogical focus of an ESAP pre-sessional course has been informed and developed by a collaboration with subject specialists not only in the design of components but also in the delivery. In reflecting on the development of the approaches to teaching, Shulman's (2005) framework for describing SPs and both Shulman (1986) and Ferguson's (1997) taxonomies of teacher knowledge have been informative. These enabled us to show how the collaboratively delivered course also offers an approach to developing the ESAP practitioner's knowledge base, one that moves beyond a knowledge of genres and discourse to the underlying assumptions and principles within disciplines.

Acknowledgement

We would like to express our gratitude to Graeme Givan, one of our EAS colleagues at the University of Glasgow, for his contributions to our chapter and to the overall development of the Biomed course.

Afterword

The events of 2020 upended the world of higher education. In many contexts globally, quarantines and travel restrictions brought on changes in course delivery, and resulting questions around access brought into focus the very fundamentals of the goals of education: what are we preparing students for, and are we accomplishing this in the most effective way?

The contributions to this volume have shown us the importance of geographical, sociopolitical, linguistic, institutional and educational contexts in determining how EAP pedagogies are instantiated worldwide. As EAP is influenced by the overlapping worlds of higher education and English language teaching and the variety of influential sociocultural and political factors at play therein, 2020 also brought about a sea change in EAP pedagogies, from mode of delivery to the nature of the academic language and literacy practices needed for success in an online higher education environment. Indeed, this is a rich and promising line of inquiry for future EAP scholarship: the nature of EAP practitioners' Technological Pedagogical Content Knowledge, or TPACK (Mishra & Koehler, 2006).

Prior to 2020, fully online EAP provision was rare. The initial transition in early 2020 to online delivery of EAP (and in language education more widely) in many contexts worldwide was sometimes a rushed, crisis-prompted response, rather than a properly planned and designed online language education experience (Gacs et al., 2020). What was and will be the effect on EAP curriculum and instruction of both this initial, crisis-prompted response and the subsequent transition to a more sustainable model of fully online language education? How do the affordances of online language education – flexibility, autonomy, opportunity for individualization, authentic materials, communicative tasks – interplay and influence pedagogies of EAP (Gacs et al., 2020)?

Similarly, the nature of higher education has changed through 2020 and some of these changes may become permanent. Teaching, research and service in the academy have moved online in many contexts, and international student mobility activity has also diminished. Therefore, with regard to the 'A' in EAP, the nature of what EAP is preparing people for is changing. Pre-recorded, subtitled lectures instead of live ones or digital collaboration with co-researchers instead of being in the lab together, for instance, require a different set of language and literacy practices. If in some contexts EAP provision has traditionally supported future student mobility – students enrolling as degree-seeking students abroad or participating in exchanges to English-medium institutions – and these activities are declining while internationalization at home activities rise, then the nature and role of EAP provision and pedagogies will change. Indeed, given the astounding growth of EMI in recent years (Macaro et al., 2018), exploration of, and research into, EAP pedagogies in such contexts, currently lacking, is essential. Without it, a more in-depth understanding of the role EAP can play in facilitating EMI will keep EAP on the margins.

In certain chapters of this volume, although they were written up before spring 2020, we read about the influence of technologies such as learning management systems, plagiarism detection platforms, web-based technologies and tools, and multimedia resources. We could also imagine how the practice of EAP in the contexts laid out in these chapters is changing now in light of the rise in online teaching and learning and the changing nature of the activities of the academy. Does online course delivery and digital scholarship affect doctoral student identities? Do different technologies facilitate the teaching of SFL concepts and metalanguage or facilitate collaboration with colleagues and collaborators in specific disciplines? Does it change our pedagogies around writing for publication or students' willingness to engage in language brokerage practices? Is the nature of the linguistic preparation required of teacher trainees now different if online instruction may play a more important role in their future teaching contexts? Have the signature pedagogies of medical education and in the creative arts changed, necessitating an adjustment in how EAP is taught and learned and what an EAP teacher therefore needs to know?

Indeed, the contributions in the volume have highlighted a range of aspects relevant to the teacher knowledge base with obvious implications for EAP teacher education. Not surprisingly, knowledge of particularly written genres continues to play a key role in the EAP classroom. How writing can be facilitated, for example, through genre-based pedagogies applied in context-sensitive ways, leveraging SFL or developmental thinking, demonstrates the interface between our content knowledge and pedagogical content knowledge. The importance of understanding situated academic practices and how this may then be practically realized is illustrated in pedagogical approaches to tackling literacy brokering and integrating a signature pedagogy. Similarly, an understanding of the specific disciplines students are, or will be, studying along with the backgrounds they come from, be it professional or educational, has clear implications for pedagogy. What do students need to be able to do and how best do we support them on that journey? The potential for collaboration with colleagues in specific subject areas outwith EAP units provides rich potential not only to inform our practices but also for our scholarship. Research is clearly informing practice; we now need to carry out more research into the efficacy of practices in different contexts.

The insights from these chapters also show that for EAP teacher education and development we need not only to go beyond exploration of texts and discourse; we also need to delve deeper into understanding academic disciplines and practices and consider how context-sensitive and context-specific approaches may be designed and applied. It is perhaps telling that we have only one chapter dedicated specifically to aspects of EAP teacher education. This too is an area ripe for scholarship and discovery. What and how we facilitate new and experienced practitioners is under-reported. EAP teacher educators also then need to explore the most effective ways that teacher education itself can be carried out. There is still much to explore in this exciting and even expanding field.

Finally, in the chapters of this volume, we have seen how influential and important contextual factors are in determining how EAP practice is carried out in different countries and institutions. With the now added factors of remote delivery, increased prevalence of video and communications technologies, shifting role of the instructor in online education and changing student mobility patterns, we expect the spectrum of EAP practice to grow wider and EAP teacher development and training to expand to add the technological to the pedagogical content knowledge. With that will come increasing numbers of pedagogies to research and explore and teach in this rich and vibrant field.

References

Adamson, J., & Muller, T. (2018). Joint autoethnography of teacher experience in the academy: Exploring methods for collaborative enquiry. *International Journal of Research Method in Education, 41*(2), 207–19. https://doi.org/10.1080/1743727X.2017.1279139

Adiche, C. (2009, July). *Chimamanda Ngozi Adichie: The danger of a single story* [Video]. TED Conferences. https://www.ted.com/talks/chimamanda_adichie_the_danger_of_a_single_story

Aidarova, L. (1982). *Child development and education.* Progress Publishers.

Airey, J. (2016). EAP, EMI or CLIL? In K. Hyland & P. Shaw (Eds.), *The Routledge handbook of English for academic purposes* (pp. 71–83). Routledge.

Aitchison, C., Kamler, B., & Lee, A. (2010). Introduction: Why publishing pedagogies? In C. Aitchison, B., Kamler, & A. Lee (Eds.), *Publishing pedagogies for the doctorate and beyond* (pp. 1–11). Routledge.

Albanese, M. (2000). Problem-based learning: Why curricula are likely to show little effect on knowledge and clinical skills. *Medical Education, 34*(9), 729–38. https://doi:10.1046/j.1365-2923.2000.00753.x

Alexander, O. (Ed.). (2007). New approaches to materials development for language learning. *Proceedings of the 2005 joint BALEAP/SATEFL conference.* Peter Lang.

Alexander, O. (2019). The contribution of Halliday to EAP writing instruction: A personal journey. *Journal of English for Academic Purposes, 41*, 100769.

Alexander, O., Argent, S., & Spencer, J. (2008). *EAP essentials: A teacher's guide to principles and practice.* Garnet Education.

Alptekin, C. (2002). Towards intercultural communicative competence in ELT. *ELT Journal, 56*(1), 57–64. https://doi.org/10.1093/elt/56.1.57

Anderson, J. R. (1993). Problem solving and learning. *American Psychologist, 48*, 35–44.

Anderson, R. (2014). A parallel approach to ESAP teaching. *Procedia – Social and Behavioral Sciences, 136*, 194–202.

Anderson, T. (2020). The socialization of L2 doctoral students through written feedback. *Journal of Language, Identity & Education.* https://doi.org/10.1080/15348458.2020.1726758

Andres, L., Bengtsen, S., Gallego Castaño, L., Crossouard, B., Keefer, J., & Pyhältö, K. (2015). Drivers and interpretations of doctoral education today: National comparisons. *Frontline Learning Research, 3*, 5–22.

Angelova, M., & Riazantseva, A. (1999). 'If you don't tell me, how can I know?': A case study of four international students learning to write the U.S. way. *Written Communication, 16*(4), 491–525.

Apple, M. W. (2004). Race and the politics of educational reform. In M. Ossen (Ed.), *Culture and learning: Access and opportunity in the classroom* (pp. 299–314). Information Age Publication Inc.

Atkinson, D. (1999). *Scientific discourse in sociohistorical context: The philosophical transactions of the Royal Society of London (1675–1975)*. Lawrence Earlbaum.

Badenhorst, C., & Guerin, C. (2016). Post/graduate research literacies and writing pedagogies. In C. Badenhorst & C. Guerin (Eds.), *Research literacies and writing pedagogies for masters and doctoral writers* (pp. 1–24). Brill.

Badger, R., & White, G. (2000). A process genre approach to teaching writing. *ELT Journal, 54*(2), 153–60. https://doi:10.1093/elt/54.2.153

Baker, S., Bangeni, B., Burke, R., & Hunma, A. (2019). The invisibility of academic reading as social practice and its implications for equity in higher education: A scoping study. *Higher Education Research & Development, 38*(1), 142–56.

Bakhtin, M. (2002). *Questões de literatura e estética: A teoria do romance* (5th ed.). Hucitec.

BALEAP. (2008). Competency framework for teachers of English for academic purposes. www.baleap.org.uk/media/uploads/pdfs/teap-competency-framework.pdf

Barkhuizen, G., & Wette, R. (2008). Narrative frames for investigating the experience of language teachers. *System, 36*, 372–87. https://doi.org/10.1016/j.system.2008.02.002

Barnacle, R. (2005). Research education ontologies: Exploring doctoral becoming. *Higher Education Research & Development, 24*(2), 179–88.

Barnacle, R., & Mewburn, I. (2010). Learning networks and the journey of 'becoming doctor'. *Studies in Higher Education, 35*(4), 433–44.

Barron, C. (2003). Problem-solving and EAP: Themes and issues in a collaborative teaching venture. *English for Specific Purposes, 22*(3), 297–314. https://doi:10.1016/s0889-4906(02)00016-9

Barrows, H. S. (1986). A taxonomy of problem-based learning methods. *Medical Education, 20*(6), 481–6. https://doi:10.1111/j.1365-2923.1986.tb01386.x

Barrows, H. S., & Tamblyn, R. M. (1980). *Problem-based learning: An approach to medical education*. Springer Publishing.

Barton, D., & Hamilton, M. (2000). Literacy practices. In D. Barton, R. Hamilton, & R. Ivanič (Eds.), *Situated literacies: Reading and writing in context* (pp. 7–14). Routledge.

Basturkmen, H. (2016). Dialogic interaction. In K. Hyland & P. Shaw (Eds.), *The Routledge handbook of English for academic purposes* (pp. 15–164). Routledge.

Basturkmen, H. (2019). ESP teacher education needs. *Language Teaching, 52*(3), 318–30.

Bazerman, C. (1988). *Shaping written knowledge: The genre and activity of the experimental article in science*. Colorado State University.

Bazerman, C., & Prior, P. (Eds.). (2004). *What writing does and how it does it: An introduction to analyzing texts and textual practices*. Lawrence Erlbaum Associates.

Beaumont, J., Lang, T., Leather, S., & Mucklow, C. (1995). *Report from the policy subgroup to the nutrition task force low income project team of the department of health.* Radlett, Institute of Grocery Distribution.

Becher, T., & Trowler, P. R. (2001). *Academic tribes and territories* (2nd ed.). Open University Press.

Benesch, S. (1999). Thinking critically, thinking dialogically. *TESOL Quarterly, 33*(3), 573–80. https://doi.org/10.2307/3587682

Benesch, S. (2001). *Critical English for academic purposes: Theory, politics, and practice.* Lawrence Erlbaum. https://doi.org/10.1016/j.jeap.2008.09.002

Benesch, S. (2009). Theorizing and practicing critical English for academic purposes. *Journal of English for Academic Purposes, 8*(2), 81–5.

Bennett, K. (2007). Epistemicide!: The tale of a predatory discourse. *The Translator, 13*(2), 151–69. doi:10.1080/13556509.2007.10799236

Bennett, S., Harper, B., & Hedberg, J. (2002). Designing real-life cases to support authentic design activities. *Australian Journal of Educational Technology, 18*(1), 1–12 doi: 10.14742/ajet.1743.

Bernstein, B. (1996). *Pedagogy, symbolic control and identity.* Taylor and Francis.

Bernstein, B. (1999). Vertical and horizontal discourse: An essay. *British Journal of Sociology of Education, 20*(2), 157–73. http://dx.doi.org/10.1080/01425699995380

Bernstein, B. (2000). *Pedagogy, symbolic control and identity: Theory, research, critique.* Rowman & Littlefield.

Beyond Brown. (2004). Summary of Lau v Nichols, 1974. https://www-tc.pbs.org/beyondbrown/brownpdfs/launichols.pdf

Biber, D. (2006). *University language: A corpus-study of spoken and written registers.* John Benjamins.

Bickford, D. J., & Wright, D. (2006). Community: The hidden context for learning. In D. G. Oblinger (Ed.), *Learning spaces* (pp. 4.1–4.22). Educause. https://www.educause.edu/research-and-publications/books/learning-spaces/chapter-4-community-hidden-context-learning

Biggs, J. B., & Tang, C. S. (2011). *Teaching for quality learning at university: What the student does* (4th ed.). Open University Press.

Bissoondath, N. (2002). *Selling illusions: The cult of multiculturalism in Canada.* Penguin Group.

Blaj-Ward, L. (2014). *Researching contexts, practices and pedagogies in English for academic purposes.* Palgrave Macmillan.

Blue, G. (1988). Individualising academic writing tuition. In P. C. Robinson (Ed.), *Academic writing: Process and product* (pp. 95–9). Modern English Publications.

Bond, B. (2020). *Making language visible in the university: English for academic purposes and internationalisation.* Multilingual Matters.

Borg, E. (2012). Writing differently in art and design: Innovative approaches to writing tasks. In L. Clughen & C. Hardy (Eds.), *Writing in the disciplines: Building supportive cultures for student writing in UK higher education* (pp. 169–86). Emerald Group Publishing Limited.

Borg, S. (2010). Language teacher research engagement. *Language Teaching, 43*(4), 391–429. doi:10.1017/S0261444810000170

Boud, D., & Lee, A. (Eds.). (2009). *Changing practices of doctoral education*. Routledge.

Boughey, C., & McKenna, S. (2016). Academic literacy and the decontextualised learner. *Critical Studies in Teaching and Learning, 4*(2), 1–9.

Bowen, G. A. (2009). Document analysis as a qualitative research method. *Qualitative Research Journal, 9*(2), 27–39. https://doi.org/10.3316/QRJ0902027

Breshears, S. (2019). The precarious work of English language teaching in Canada. *TESL Canada Journal, 36*(2), 26–47. https://doi.org/10.18806/tesl.v36i2.1312

Brinton, D., Snow, M. A., & Wesche, M. B. (1989). *Content-based second language instruction*. Heinle and Heinle.

Brown, J. B. (2020, May 11). From denial to acceptance: A turning point for design studio in architecture education. Distance Design Education. https://distancedesigneducation.com/2020/05/11/from-denial-to-acceptance-a-turning-point-for-design-studio-in-architecture-education/

Browne, K. (2008). Culture and identity. In K. Browne (Ed.), *Sociology AS & AQA* (3rd ed., pp. 1–15). Polity Press.

Bruce, I. (2011). *Theory and concepts of English for academic purposes*. Palgrave Macmillan.

Bunting, I. (2006). The higher education landscape under apartheid. In N. Cloete, P. Maassen, R. Fehnel, T. Moja, T. Gibbon, & H. Perold (Eds.), *Transformation in higher education* (pp. 35–52). Springer.

Burnard, P. (2016). Considering creative teaching in creative learning. In E. Haddon & P. Burnard (Eds.), *Creative teaching for creative learning in higher music education* (Ch. 4). Routledge Education. https://doi.org/10.4324/9781315574714

Burns, A. (2005). Action research: An evolving paradigm? *Language Teaching, 38*(2), 57–74. https://doi.org/10.1017/S0261444805002661

Burns, A. (2010). *Doing action research in English language teaching: A guide for practitioners*. Routledge.

Butt, D., Fahey, R., Feez, S., Spinks, S., & Yallop, C. (2000). *Using functional grammar: An explorer's guide* (2nd ed.). National Centre for English Language Teaching and Research, Macquarie University.

Byram, M. (1997). *Teaching and assessing intercultural communicative competence*. Multilingual Matters.

Byram, M., Gribkova, B., & Starkey, H. (2002). *Developing the intercultural dimension in language teaching: A practical introduction for teachers*. Council of Europe.

Cadman, K. (2005). *Trans/forming 'King's English' in global research education: A teacher's tale*. Doctoral dissertation, University of Adelaide. https://digital.library.adelaide.edu.au/dspace/bitstream/2440/22336/8/02whole.pdf

Campion, G. C. (2016). 'The learning never ends': Exploring teachers' views on the transition from General English to EAP. *Journal of English for Academic Purposes, 23*(1), 59–70. https://doi.org/10.1016/j.jeap.2016.06.003

Canadian Bureau of International Education. (2020, February 21). International students in Canada continue to grow in 2019. https://cbie.ca/international-students-in-canada-continue-to-grow-in-2019/

Canagarajah, A. S. (2002). *A geopolitics of academic writing*. University of Pittsburgh Press.

Caplan, N. A. (2019). Asking the right questions: Demystifying writing assignments across the disciplines. *Journal of English for Academic Purposes, 41*, 100776. https://doi.org/10.1016/j.jeap.2019.100776

Carr, C., Maxwell, C., Rolinska, A. & Sizer, J. (2021). EAP teachers working in, with and through the creative arts: Reflections on a conference workshop aimed at exploring current practices. In M. Evans, B. Bond, & A. Ding (Eds.), *Proceedings of the 2019 BALEAP conference: Innovation, exploration and transformation*. Garnet.

Castelló, M., Inesta, A., & Corcelles, M. (2013). Learning to write a research article: Ph.D. students' transitions toward disciplinary writing regulation. *Research in the Teaching of English, 47*(4), 442–77.

Caulton, D., Northcott, J., & Gillies, P. (2019). EAP and subject specialist academic writing feedback collaboration. In M. Gillway (Ed.), *Proceedings of the 2017 BALEAP conference: Addressing the state of the union: Working together = learning together* (pp. 157–64). Garnet Education.

Chaiklin, S. (2002). A developmental teaching approach to schooling. In G. Wells & G. Glaxton (Eds.), *Learning for life in the 21st century* (pp. 167–80). Blackwell.

Chang, H., Ngunjiri, F. W., & Hernandez, K. C. (2012). *Collaborative autoethnography*. Left Coast Press.

Charles, M., & Pecocari, D. (2016). *Introducing English for academic purposes*. Routledge.

Cherryholmes, C. (1988). *Power and criticism: Poststructural investigations in education*. Teachers College Press.

Christodoulou, D. (2014). *Seven myths about education*. Routledge.

Chun, C. (2009). Contesting neoliberal discourses in EAP: Critical praxis in an IEP classroom. *Journal of English for Academic Purposes, 8*(2), 111–20. https://doi.org/10.1016/j.jeap.2008.09.005

Coffin, S. and Donohue, J. (2014). *A language as social semiotic based approach to teaching and learning in higher education*. John Wiley & Sons Inc.

Coll, S. D. (2015). *Enhancing students' learning experiences outside school (LEOS) using digital technologies*. Doctoral dissertation, Curtin University.

Colliver, J. A. (2000). Effectiveness of problem-based learning curricula: Research and theory. *Academic Medicine. Journal of the Association of American Medical Colleges, 75*(3), 259–66. https://doi:10.1097/00001888-200003000-00017

Conrad, N. L. (2019). Revisiting proofreading in higher education: Toward an institutional response to Editors Canada's guidelines for ethical editing of student texts. *TESL Canada Journal, 36*(1), 172–83. https://doi.org/10.18806/tesl.v36i1.1309

Conrad, N. L. (2020). Proofreading revisited: Interrogating assumptions about postsecondary student users of proofreading. *Journal of English for Academic Purposes, 46*, Article 100871. https://doi.org/10.1016/j.jeap.2020.100871

Corcoran, J., Gagné, A., & McIntosh, M. (2018). A conversation about 'editing' plurilingual scholars' thesis writing. *Canadian Journal for Studies in Discourse and Writing/Rédactologie, 28*, 1–25. https://doi.org/10.31468/cjsdwr.589

Council of Europe. (2001). *Common European Framework of reference for languages: Learning, teaching, assessment*. Language Policy Unit. www.coe.int/t/dg4/linguistic/source/framework_en.pdf

Coxhead, A. (2000). A new academic word list. *TESOL Quarterly, 34*(2), 213–34. https://doi.org/10.2307/3587951

Coyle, D. (2005). *CLIL-Planning tools for teachers*. University of Nottingham.

Coyle, D. (2018). The place of CLIL in (Bilingual) education. *Theory into Practice, 57*(3), 166–76. https://doi.org/10.1080/00405841.2018.1459096

Coyle, D., Hood. P., & Marsh, D. (2010). *CLIL: Content and language integrated learning*. Cambridge University Press.

Creme, P., & Lea, M. (1997). *Writing at university: A guide for students*. Open University Press.

Cummins, J., & Early, M. (2010). *Identity texts: The collaborative creation of power in multilingual schools*. Trentham Books Ltd.

Curtain, H. A., & Pesola, C. A. (1994). *Languages and children: Making the match* (2nd ed.). Longman.

Dafouz, E., & Smit, U. (2020). *Road-mapping English medium education in the internationalised university*. Palgrave Macmillan.

Dalton-Puffer, C. (2013). A construct of cognitive discourse functions for conceptualising content-language integration in CLIL and multilingual education. *European Journal of Applied Linguistics, 1*(2), 216–53. https://doi.org/10.1515/eujal-2013-0011

Dalton-Puffer, C., & Nikula, T. (2014). Content and language integrated learning. *The Language Learning Journal, 42*(2), 117–22. https://10.1017/S0267190511000092

Davydov, V. V. (1984). Substantial generalization and the dialectical-materialistic theory of thinking. In M. Hedegaard, P. Hakkarainen, & Y. Engstrom (Eds.), *Learning and teaching on a scientific basis* (pp. 11–32). Aarhus Universitet Press.

Davydov, V. V. (1988a). The concept of theoretical generalization and problems of educational psychology. *Studies in Soviet Thought, 36*(2), 169–202.

Davydov, V. V. (1988b). Problems of developmental teaching: The experience of theoretical and experimental psychology research. *Soviet Education, 30*(8), 6–97.

Davydov, V. V. (1988c). Problems of developmental teaching: The experience of theoretical and experimental psychological research. *Soviet Education, 30*(9), 3–83.

Davydov, V. V. (1988d). Problems of developmental teaching: The experience of theoretical and experimental psychological research. *Soviet Education, 30*(10), 3–77.

Davydov, V. V. (1990). *Types of generalization in instruction: Logical and psychological problems in the structuring of school curricula*. National Council of Teachers of Mathematics.

Davydov, V. V. (1999). The content and unsolved problems of activity theory. In Y. Engstrom, R. Miettinen, & R.-L. Punamaki (Eds.), *Perspectives on activity theory* (pp. 39–52). Cambridge University Press.

Dearden, J. (2014). *English as a medium of instruction – a growing global phenomenon*. British Council. https://www.britishcouncil.es/sites/default/files/british_council_english_as_a_medium_of_instruction.pdf

Dearden, J., & Macaro, E. (2016). Higher education teachers' attitudes towards English medium instruction: A three-country comparison. *Studies in Second Language Learning and Teaching, 6*(3), 455–86. doi: 10.14746/ssllt.2016.6.3.5

DeChazal, E. (2012). The general-specific debate in EAP: Which case is the most convincing for most contexts? *Journal of Second Language Teaching and Research, 2*(1), 135–48.

Dei, G. J. (1999). The denial of difference: Refraining anti-racist praxis. *Race Ethnicity and Education, 2*(1), 17–38. https://doi.org/10.1080/1361332990020103

Denman, J., Tanner. R., & Graaff, R. (2013). CLIL in junior vocational secondary education: Challenges and opportunities for teaching and learning. *International Journal of Bilingual Education and Bilingualism, 16*(3), 285–300. https://doi.org/10.1080/13670050.2013.777386

Department of Education. (1997). White Paper 3. Retrieved from https://www.justice.gov.za/commissions/FeesHET/docs/1997-WhitePaper-HE-Tranformation.pdf

Department of Higher Education and Training. (2015). Minimum requirements for teacher education qualifications. http://www.dhet.gov.za/Teacher%20Education/National%20Qualifications%20Framework%20Act%2067_2008%20Revised%20Policy%20for%20Teacher%20Education%20Quilifications.pdf

Derewianka, B. (2011). *A new grammar companion for teachers*. Primary English Teaching Association Australia.

Devitt, A. (2009). Teaching critical genre awareness. In C. Bazerman, A. Bonini, & D. Figueiredo (Eds.), *Genre in a changing world* (pp. 337–51). Parlor Press.

Dhawan, S. (2020). Online learning: A panacea in the time of COVID-19 crisis. *Journal of Educational Technology Systems, 49*(1), 5–22. https://doi.org/10.1177/0047239520934018

Ding, A., & Bruce, I. (2017). *The English for academic purposes practitioner: Operating on the edge of academia*. Palgrave Macmillan. https://doi.org/10.1007/978-3-319-59737-9

Dolmans, D. H. J. M., Loyens, S. M. M., Marcq, H., & Gijbels, D. (2016). Deep and surface learning in problem-based learning: A review of the literature. *Advances in*

Health Sciences Education: Theory and Practice, 21(5), 1087–112. https://doi:10.1007/s10459-015-9645-6

Doloughan, F. J. (2002). The language of reflective practice in art and design. *Design Issues, 18*(2), 57–64. https://doi.org/10.1162/074793602317355783

Douglas, S. R. (2013). The lexical breadth of undergraduate novice level writing competency. *Canadian Journal of Applied Linguistics, 16*(1), 152–70. http://journals.hil.unb.ca/index.php/CJAL/article/view/21176

Dovey, T. (2006). What purposes, specifically? Re-thinking purposes and specificity in the context of the 'new vocationalism'. *English for Specific Purposes, 25*, 387–402. https://doi.org/10.1016/j.esp.2005.10.002

Draper, M. J., Ibezim, V., & Newton, P. M. (2017). Are essay mills committing fraud? An analysis of their behaviours vs the 2006 Fraud Act (UK). *International Journal for Educational Integrity, 13*(1), Article 3. https://doi.org/10.1007/s40979-017-0014-5

Draper, M. J., & Newton, P. M. (2017). A legal approach to tackling contract cheating? *International Journal for Educational Integrity, 13*(1), Article 11. https://doi.org/10.1007/s40979-017-0022-5

Dreyfus, S., Humphrey, S., Mahboob, A., & Martin, J. (2016). *Genre pedagogy in higher education: The SLATE project*. Palgrave Macmillan.

Dudley-Evans, T., & St John, M. J. (1998). *Developments in ESP: A multi-disciplinary approach*. Cambridge University Press.

Duff, P. A. (2010). Language socialization into academic discourse communities. *Annual Review of Applied Linguistics, 30*, 169–92. https://doi:10.1017/S0267190510000048

Dukhan, S., Cameron, A., & Brenner, E. (2016). Impact of mother tongue on construction of notes and first-year academic performance. *South African Journal of Science, 112*(11–12), 1–6. https://doi.org/10.17159/sajs.2016/20160037

Durnin-Vermette, F., Kapoor, T., Maxwell, S., & Fograscher, M. (2016). Dietary dependence on foreign crops. The University of British Columbia Open Case Studies. https://cases.open.ubc.ca/dietary-dependence-on-foreign-crops/

Edwards, S. (2005). Higher education in the twenty-first century: Examining the interface between graduate attributes, online and problem-based learning at Monash university. *Technology, Pedagogy and Education, 14*(3), 329–52. https://doi:10.1080/14759390500200210

Egbo, B. (2009). *Teaching for diversity in Canadian schools*. Pearson Education Canada.

Eggins, S. (2004). *An introduction to systemic functional linguistics* (2nd ed.). Continuum.

Elkins, J. (2006). Afterword: On beyond research and new knowledge. In K. Macleod & L. Holdridge (Eds.), *Thinking through art. Reflections on art as research* (pp. 241–48). Routledge.

Ellis, C., Adams, T. E., & Bochner, A. P. (2011). Autoethnography: An overview. *Forum: Qualitative Research, 12*(1), Article 10. http://www.qualitative-research.net/index.php/fqs/article/view/1589

Ellis, R. (2003). *Task-based language learning and teaching*. Oxford University Press.

Ellis, R. (2010). Second language acquisition, teacher education and language pedagogy. *Language Teaching, 43*(2), 182–201. doi:10.1017/S0261444809990139

Emmons, K. K. (2009). Uptake and the biomedical subject. In A. Bonini, D. de Carvalho Figuereido, & C. Bazerman (Eds.), *Genre in a changing world* (pp. 134–57). WAC Clearinghouse and Parlor Press.

Engeström, Y. (2015). *Learning by expanding* (2nd ed.). Cambridge University Press.

European Commission. (2020). Bologna process and the European higher education area. https://ec.europa.eu/education/policies/higher-education/bologna-process-and-european-higher-education-area_en

Ferguson, G. (1997). Teacher education and LSP: The role of specialised knowledge. In R. Howard & G. Brown (Eds.), *Teacher education for LSP* (pp. 80–9). Multilingual Matters.

Fernandez-Llimos, F. (2016). Bradford's law, the long tail principle, and transparency in journal impact factor calculations. *Pharmacy Practice, 14*(3), 842. doi:10.18549/PharmPract.2014.03.842

Ferreira, A. A., & Zappa-Hollman, S. (2019). Disciplinary registers in a first-year program: A view from the context of curriculum. *Language, Context and Text, 1*(1), 148–93. https://doi.org/10.1075/langct.00007.fer

Ferreira, M. M. (2005). A concept-based approach to writing instruction: From the abstract concept to the concrete performance. Doctoral dissertation, The Penn State University. Electronic theses and dissertations for Graduate School.

Ferreira, M. M. (2015). A promoção do letramento acadêmico em inglês por meio do ensino desenvolvimental: Contribuições da teoria histórico-cultural. Tese de Livre-Docência, Universidade de São Paulo. Repositório USP.

Ferreira, M. M., & Lantolf, J. P. (2008). A concept-based approach to teaching: Writing through genre analysis. In J. P. Lantolf & M. P. Poehner (Eds.), *Sociocultural theory and the teaching of second languages* (pp. 285–320). Equinox.

Ferreira, M. M., & MacDiarmid, C. (2019). Resources for English for academic purposes teacher education. https://www.britishcouncil.org.br/sites/default/files/uk_collaboration_call_-_ebook_-_ferreiramacdiarmid.pdf

Ferreira, M. M., & Stella, V. C. R. (2018). *Redação Acadêmica: múltiplos olhares para o ensino da escrita acadêmica em português e línguas estrangeiras*. Humanitas.

Flowerdew, J. (2016). English for specific academic purposes (ESAP) writing: Making the case. *Writing & Pedagogy, 8*(1), 5–32. doi: 10.1558/wap.v8i1.30051

Flowerdew, J. (2019). Power in English for academic purposes. In K. Hyland & L. C. Wong, *Specialised English: New directions in ESP and EAP research and practice* (pp. 50–62). Routledge.

Flowerdew, J., & Peacock, M. (2012). The EAP curriculum issues, methods and challenges. In J. Flowerdew & M. Peacock (Eds.), *Research perspectives on EAP* (pp. 177–94). Cambridge University Press.

Freire, P. (1970). *Pedagogy of the oppressed*. Seabury.

Freire, P. (2002). *Pedagogia do oprimido* (32nd ed.). Paz e Terra.

Gacs, A., Goertler, S., & Spasova, S. (2020). Planned online language education versus crisis-prompted online language teaching: Lessons for the future. *Foreign Language Annals, 53*(2), 380–92. https://doi.org/10.1111/flan.12460

Galloway, N., Numajiri, T., & Rees, N. (2020). The 'internationalisation', or 'Englishisation', of higher education in East Asia. *Higher Education, 80*(3), 395–414. doi:10.1007/s10734-019-00486-1

Gao, G. Z., & Cao, J. X. (2015). Effects of CLIL on EAP learners: Based on sample analysis of doctoral students of science. *International Journal of Applied Linguistics & English Literature, 4*(5), 113–23.

Gardner, S. (2008, July). Integrating ethnographic, multidimensional, corpus linguistic and systemic functional approaches to genre description: An illustration through university history and engineering assignments. In E. Steiner & S. Neumann (Eds.), *Data and interpretation in linguistic analysis: 19th European systemic functional linguistics conference and workshop 23rd-25th July 2007* (pp. 1–34). Universitaat des Saarlandes.

Gardner, S. (2016). A genre-instantiation approach to teaching English for specific academic purposes: Student writing in business, economics and engineering. *Writing & Pedagogy, 8*(1), 150–71.

Gardner, S., & Donohue, J. (Eds.). (2020). Halliday's influence on EAP Practice [Special Issue]. *Journal of English for Academic Purposes*, 44.

Gardner, S., & Nesi, H. (2013). A classification of genre families in university student writing. *Applied Linguistics, 34*(1), 25–52. http://doi.org/10.1093/applin/ams024

Gass, S. M., & Mackey, A. (2007). Input, interaction, and output in second language acquisition. In B. VanPatten & J. Williams (Eds.), *Theories in second language acquisition: An introduction* (pp. 175–99). Lawrence Erlbaum.

Geertz, C. (1973). *The interpretation of cultures: Selected essays*. Basic Books.

Gérin-Lajoie, D. (2008). The issue of diversity in the Canadian educational context. In D. Gérin-Lajoie (Ed.), *Educators' discourses on student diversity in Canada: Context, policy, and practice* (pp. 9–28). Canadian Scholars' Press Inc.

Gibbs, W. W. (1995). Lost science in the third world. *Scientific American*, August, 92–9.

Gillett, A. (2011). *Speaking. Using English for academic purposes: A guide for students in higher education*. http://www.uefap.com/

Gillett, A., & Hammond, A. (2009). Mapping the maze of assessment: An investigation into practice. *Active Learning in Higher Education, 10*, 120–37. https://doi.org/10.1177/1469787409104786

Giroux, H. A. (1977). The politics of the hidden curriculum. *Independent School, 37*(1), 42–3.

Giroux, H. A. (1992). Literacy, pedagogy, and the politics of difference. *College Literature, 19*(1), 1–11.

Giroux, H. A. (2010). Rethinking education as the practice of freedom: Paulo Freire and the promise of critical pedagogy. *Policy Futures in Education, 8*(6), 715–21,

Givan, G. (2019, October 23). *Integrating reading into writing and speaking assessment on an EAP bridging course* (paper presentation). University of St Andrews learning and teaching conference: Innovative assessment in higher education, St Andrews, Scotland.

Glynn, C., & Spenader, A. (2020). Critical content based instruction for the transformation of world language classrooms. *L2 Journal, 12*(2), 72–93. https://doi.org/10.5070/L212246307

Go, A. (2005). Moving beyond tokenism. *Canadian Issues*, 40–2.

Grandinetti, M., Langellotti, M., & Ting, Y. L. (2013). How CLIL can provide a pragmatic means to renovate science education – even in a sub-optimally bilingual context. *International Journal of Bilingual Education and Bilingualism, 16*(3), 354–74. https://doi.org/10.1080/13670050.2013.777390

Grant, C. A., & Sleeter, C. E. (2010). Race, class, gender and disability in the classroom. In & C. A. M. Banks (Eds.), *Multicultural education: Issues and perspectives* (7th ed., pp. 59–80). John Wiley & Sons.

Graumann, C. F. (1983). On multiple Identities. *International Social Science Journal, 35*, 309–21.

Grimm, N. M. (2009). New conceptual frameworks for writing center work. *The Writing Center Journal, 29*(2), 11–27.

Guo, S., & Jamal, Z. (2007). Nurturing cultural diversity in higher education: A critical review of selected models. *Canadian Journal of Higher Education, 37*(3), 27–49. https://files.eric.ed.gov/fulltext/EJ799706.pdf

Halliday, M. A. K. (1975). *Learning how to mean: Explorations in the development of language*. Edward Arnold.

Halliday, M. A. K., & Matthiessen, C. M. I. M. (2013). *Halliday's introduction to functional grammar* (4th ed.). Routledge.

Halliday, M. A. K., McIntosh, A., & Strevens, P. (1964). *Linguistic sciences and language teaching*. Longman.

Hamp-Lyons, L. (2011). English for academic purposes. In E. Hinkel (Ed.), *Handbook for research in second language teaching and learning* (pp. 89–103). Routledge.

Hanks, J. (2017). *Exploratory practice in language teaching: Puzzling about principles and practices*. Palgrave Macmillan.

Hanks, J. (2019). From research-as-practice to exploratory practice-as-research in language teaching and beyond. *Language Teaching, 52*(2), 143–87. https://doi.org/10.1017/S0261444819000016

Haque, E. (2007). Critical pedagogy in English for academic purposes and the possibility for 'tactics' of resistance. *Pedagogy, Culture & Society, 15*(1), 83–106. https://doi.org/10.1080/14681360601162311

Harwood, N. (2018). What do proofreaders of student writing do to a master's essay? Differing interventions, worrying findings. *Written Communication, 35*(4), 474–530. https://doi.org/10.1177/0741088318786236

Harwood, N. (2019). 'I have to hold myself back from getting into all that': Investigating ethical issues associated with the proofreading of student writing. *Journal of Academic Ethics, 17*, 17–49. https://doi.org/10.1007/s10805-018-9322-5

Harwood, N., Austin, L., & Macaulay, R. (2010). Ethics and integrity in proofreading: Findings from an interview-based study. *English for Specific Purposes, 29*(1), 54–67. https://doi.org/10.1016/j.esp.2009.08.004

Harwood, N., Austin, L., & Macaulay, R. (2012). Cleaner, helper, teacher? The role of proofreaders of student writing. *Studies in Higher Education, 37*(5), 569–84. https://doi.org/10.1080/03075079.2010.531462

Hayot, E. (2014). *The elements of academic style: Writing for the humanities*. Columbia University Press.

Hedegaard, M. (2002). *Learning and child development: A cultural-historical study*. Aarhus University Press.

Heng Hartse, J. (2019, November 15). *'We have a customized writing service team with all Caucasians': Advertising 'writing services' to second language writers*. Symposium on Second Language Writing, Arizona State University.

Higher Education Statistics Agency. (2019). What do HE students study? Retrieved 29 June 2020, from https://www.hesa.ac.uk/data-and-analysis/students/what-study

Hipkiss, A. M., & Varga, P. A. (2018). Spotlighting pedagogic metalanguage in reading to learn – How teachers build legitimate knowledge during tutorial sessions. *Linguistics and Education, 47*, 93–104. https://doi.org/10.1016/j.linged.2018.08.002

Hmelo-Silver, C. E., & Barrows, H. S. (2008). Facilitating collaborative knowledge building. *Cognition and Instruction, 26*(1), 48–94. https://doi:10.1080/07370000701798495

Hood, S. (2016). Systemic functional linguistics and EAP. In K. Hyland & P. Shaw (Eds.), *The Routledge handbook of English for academic purposes* (pp. 193–205). Routledge.

Humphries, S., and Burns, A. (2015). 'In reality it's almost impossible': CLT-oriented curriculum change. *ELT Journal, 69*(3), 239–48. https://doi.org/10.1093/elt/ccu081

Humphrey, S., Love, K., & Droga, L. (2011). *Working grammar: An introduction for secondary English teachers*. Pearson Australia.

Hunziker, M., Buchecker, M., & Hartig, T. (2007). Space and place – Two aspects of the human-landscape relationship. In F. Kienast, O. Wildi, & S. Ghosh (Eds.), *A changing world: Challenges for landscape research* (pp. 47–62). Springer. https://doi.org/10.1007/978-1-4020-4436-6_5

Hurst, E. (2016). Navigating language: Strategies, transitions, and the 'colonial wound' in South African education. *Language and Education, 30*(3), 219–34. https://doi.org/10.1080/09500782.2015.1102274

Hurst, E., & Mona, M. (2017). 'Translanguaging' as a socially just pedagogy. *Education as Change, 21*(2), 126–48. https://doi.org/10.17159/1947-9417/2017/2015

Hyland, K. (2002). Specificity revisited: How far should we go now? *English for Specific Purposes, 21*(4), 385–95. https://doi.org/10.1016/S0889-4906(01)00028-X

Hyland, K. (2003). Genre-based pedagogies: A social response to process. *Journal of Second Language Writing, 12*, 17–29. https://doi:10.1016/s1060-3743(02)00124-8

Hyland, K. (2004). Disciplinary interactions: Metadiscourse in L2 postgraduate writing. *Journal of Second Language Writing, 13*(2), 133–51. https://doi.org/10.1016/j.jslw.2004.02.001

Hyland, K. (2006). *English for academic purposes: An advanced resource book*. Routledge.

Hyland, K. (2007). Genre pedagogy: Language, literacy and L2 writing instruction. *Journal of Second Language Writing, 16*(3), 148–64. doi:10.1016/j.jslw.2007.07.005

Hyland, K. (2008). As can be seen: Lexical bundles and disciplinary variation. *English for Specific Purposes, 27*(1), 4–21. https://doi.org/10.1016/j.esp.2007.06.001

Hyland, K. (2011). Discipline and divergence: Evidence of specificity in EAP. In S. Etherington (Ed.), *Proceedings of the 2009 BALEAP conference: English for specific academic purposes* (pp. 13–22). Garnet Education.

Hyland, K. (2016). General and specific EAP. In K. Hyland & P. Shaw (Eds.), *The Routledge handbook of English for academic purposes* (pp. 17–29). Routledge.

Hyland, K., & Bondi, M. (Eds.). (2006). *Academic discourse across the disciplines*. Peter Lang AG.

Hyland, K., & Hamp-Lyons, L. (2002). EAP: Issues and directions. *Journal of English for Academic Purposes, 1*(1), 1–12. https://doi.org/10.1016/S1475-1585(02)00002-4

Hyland, K., & Hyland, F. (2006). Feedback on second language students' writing. *Language Teaching, 39*(2), 83–101. https://doi.org/10.1017/S0261444806003399

Hyland, K., & Shaw, P. (2016). *The Routledge handbook of English for academic purposes*. Routledge.

Hyland, K., & Wong, L. L. (Eds.). (2019). *Specialised English: New directions in ESP and EAP research and practice*. Routledge.

IELTS. (n.d.). *Demographic data 2018*. https://www.ielts.org/teaching-and-research/demographic-data

Ilorah, R. (2006). The dilemma of the HBUs in South Africa. *South African Journal of Higher Education, 20*(3), 79–96.

Irwin, D., & Liu, N. (2019). Encoding, decoding, packing and unpacking via agnation: Reformulating general knowledge into disciplinary concepts for teaching English academic writing. *Journal of English for Academic Purposes, 42*, 100782. https://doi.org/10.1016/j.jeap.2019.100782

Jacobs, C. (2007). Towards a critical understanding of the teaching of discipline-specific academic literacies: Making the tacit explicit. *Journal of Education, 41*(1), 59–81.

Jappinen, A. (2005). Thinking and content learning of mathematics and science as cognitional development in content and language integrated learning (CLIL): Teaching through a foreign language in Finland. *Language and Education, 19*(2), 147–68. https://doi.org/10.1080/09500780508668671

Jiménez Catalán, M. R., & Ruiz de Zarobe, Y. (2009). The receptive vocabulary of EFL learners in two instructional contexts: CLIL versus non-CLIL instruction. In M. R. Jimenez Catalan & Y. Ruiz de Zarobe (Eds.), *Content and language integrated learning: Evidence from research in Europe* (pp. 81–92). Multilingual Matters.

Johns, A. (1997). *Text, role and context*. Cambridge University Press.

Johnson, B. (1982). Editor's preface. *Yale French Studies, 63*, Iii–Vii. doi:10.2307/2929827

Jordan, E., & Ford, J. (2016). *Report on modules jointly delivered by the Language Centre and academic departments*. Unpublished internal report at the Language Centre, XJTLU, China.

Jordan, R. (1997). *English for academic purposes: A guide and resource book for teachers*. Cambridge University Press.

Kamal, K. (2018, December 18). *Education in the United Arab Emirates*. https://wenr.wes.org/2018/08/education-in-the-united-arab-emirates

Kamler, B. (2008). Rethinking doctoral publication practices: Writing from and beyond the thesis. *Studies in Higher Education, 33*(3), 283–94. https://doi.org/10.1080/03075070802049236

Kamler, B., & Thomson, P. (2014). *Helping doctoral students write: Pedagogies for supervision* (2nd ed.). Routledge.

Kaplan, R. B. (1966). Cultural thought patterns in intercultural education. *Language Learning, 16*(1–2), 1–20.

Kazemian, B., Behnam, B., & Ghafoori, N. (2013). Ideational grammatical metaphor in scientific texts: A Hallidayan perspective. *International Journal of Linguistics, 5*(4), 1–23.

Kemmis, S., McTaggart, R., & Nixon, R. (2014). *The action research planner*. Springer.

Kettle, M. (2017). *International student engagement in higher education: Transforming practices, pedagogies and participation*. Multilingual Matters,

Khoo, H. E. (2003). Implementation of problem-based learning in Asian medical schools and students' perceptions of their experience. *Medical Education, 37*(5), 401–9. https://doi:10.1046/j.1365-2923.2003.01489.x

Kim, J., Park, Y., Song, J., & Jo, I. (2014). Predicting students' learning performance by using online behavior patterns in blended learning environments: Comparison of two cases on linear and non-linear model. *Proceedings of the 7th International Conference on Educational Data Mining* (pp. 407–8). London.

King, A. (1993). From sage on the stage to guide on the side. *College Teaching, 41*(1), 30–5. https://doi.org/10.1080/87567555.1993.9926781

King, J. (2012, August 2). *How to become a usefully ignorant EAP teacher?* [Blog post]. Teaching EAP. https://teachingeap.wordpress.com/2012/08/02/how-to-become-a-usefully-ignorant-eap-teacher/

Kinginger, C. (2002). Defining the zone of proximal development in US foreign language education. *Applied Linguistics, 23*(2), 240–61. https://doi.org/10.1093/applin/23.2.240

Kirk, S. (2017). Waves of reflection: Seeing knowledges in academic writing. In J. Kemp (Ed.), *Proceedings of the 2015 BALEAP conference – EAP in a rapidly changing landscape: Issues, challenges and solutions* (pp. 109–18). Garnet.

Klapwijk, N., & Van der Walt, C. (2016). English-plus multilingualism as the new linguistic capital? Implications of university students' attitudes towards languages of instruction in a multilingual environment. *Journal of Language, Identity & Education*, 15(2), 67–82. https://doi.org/10.13140/RG.2.1.1493.6806

Kreber, C. (2001). Learning experientially through case studies? A conceptual analysis. *Teaching in Higher Education*, 6(2), 217–28. https://doi.org/10.1080/13562510120045203

Krumsvik, R. J. (2016). *En doktorgradsutdanning i endring: Et fokus på den artikkelbaserte ph.d.-avhandlingen. Doctoral education in transition: A focus on the article-based PhD thesis*. Fagbokforlaget.

Kubota, R. (2015). Race and language learning in multicultural Canada: Towards critical antiracism. *Journal of Multilingual and Multicultural Development*, 36(1), 3–12, https://doi.org/10.1080/01434632.2014.892497

Kwan, B. S. C. (2010). An investigation of instruction in research publishing offered in doctoral programs: The Hong Kong case. *Higher Education*, 59, 55–68.

Lasagabaster, D. (2011). English achievement and student motivation in CLIL and EFL settings. *Innovation in Language Learning and Teaching*, 5(1), 3–18. https://doi.org/10.1080/17501229.2010.519030

Lasagabaster, D. (2018). Fostering team teaching: Mapping out a research agenda for English-medium instruction at university level. *Language Teaching*, 51(3), 400–16. https://doi.org/10.1017/S0261444818000113

Lassig, C. J., Dillon, L. H., & Diezmann, C. M. (2013). Student or scholar? Transforming identities through a research writing group. *Studies in Continuing Education*, 35(3), 299–314. https://doi.org/10.1080/0158037X.2012.746226

Lea, M. R., & Street, B. V. (1998). Student writing in higher education: An academic literacies approach. *Studies in Higher Education*, 23(2), 157–72. https://doi.org/10.1080/03075079812331380364

Lee, A. (2010). When the article is the dissertation: Pedagogies for a PhD by publication. In C. Aitchison, B. Kamler, & A. Lee (Eds.), *Publishing pedagogies for the doctorate and beyond* (pp. 12–29). Routledge.

Lee, A. (2011). Professional practice and doctoral education: Becoming a researcher. In L. Scanlon (Ed.), *'Becoming' a professional* (pp. 153–69). Springer.

Lee, A., & Kamler, B. (2008). Bringing pedagogy to doctoral publishing. *Teaching in Higher Education*, 3(5), 511–23. https://doi.org/10.1080/13562510802334723

Lee, K. (2007). Online collaborative case study learning. *Journal of College Reading and Learning*, 37(2), 82–100. https://doi.org/10.1080/10790195.2007.10850199

Lei, J., & Hu, G. (2019). Doctoral candidates' dual role as student and expert scholarly writer: An activity theory perspective. *English for Specific Purposes*, 54, 62–74. https://doi.org/10.1016/j.esp.2018.12.003

Levy, M. A., & Polnariev, B. A. (2016). *Academic and student affairs in collaboration: Creating a culture of student success*. Routledge. https://doi.org/10.1080/2194587X.2017.1371043

Liardet, C. (2016a). Nominalization and grammatical metaphor: Elaborating the theory. *English for Specific Purposes, 44*, 16–29. https://doi.org/10.1016/j.esp.2016.04.004

Liardet, C. L. (2016b). Grammatical metaphor: Distinguishing success. *Journal of English for Academic Purposes, 22*, 109–18. https://doi.org/10.1016/j.jeap.2016.01.009

Liardet, C. L. (2018). 'As we all know': Examining Chinese EFL learners' use of interpersonal grammatical metaphor in academic writing. *English for Specific Purposes, 50*, 64–80. https://doi.org/10.1016/j.esp.2017.11.005

Liardet, C. L., & Black, S. (2020). Trump vs. Trudeau: Exploring the power of grammatical metaphor for academic communication. *Journal of English for Academic Purposes, 45*, 100843. https://doi.org/10.1016/j.jeap.2020.100843

Lillis, T., & Curry, M. J. (2010). *Academic writing in a global context: The politics and practices of publishing in English*. Routledge.

Lillis, T., Harrington, K., Lea, M., & Mitchell, S. (Eds.). (2016). *Working with academic literacies: Case studies towards transformative practice*. The WAC Clearinghouse/ Parlor Press. httsp://doi.org/10.37514/PER-B.2015.0674

Lillis, T., & Scott, M. (2007). Defining academic literacies research: Issues of epistemology, ideology and strategy. *Journal of Applied Linguistics, 4*(1), 5–32. https://doi.org/10.1558/japl.v4i1.5

Lim, F. V., O'Halloran, K. L., & Podlasov, A. (2012). Spatial pedagogy: Mapping meanings in the use of classroom space. *Cambridge Journal of Education, 42*(2), 235–51. https://doi.org/10.1080/0305764X.2012.676629

Llinares, A., Morton, T., & Whittaker, R. (2012). *The roles of language in CLIL*. Cambridge University Press.

Lock, J., Kim, B., Koh, K., & Wilcox, G. (2018). Navigating the tensions of innovative assessment and pedagogy in higher education. *The Canadian Journal for the Scholarship of Teaching and Learning, 9*(1), 1–18. https://doi:10.5206/cjsotl-rcacea.2018.1.8

Lompscher, J. (1984). Problems and results of experimental research on the formation of theoretical thinking through instruction. In M. Hedegaard, P. Hakkarainen, & Y. Engstrom (Eds.), *Learning and teaching on a scientific basis* (pp. 293–357). Aarhus Universitet Press.

Lompscher, J. (1999). Learning activity and its formation. In M. Hedegaard & J. Lompscher (Eds.), *Learning activity and development* (pp. 139–66). Aarhus University Press.

Lonn, S., & Teasley, S. D. (2009). Saving time or innovating practice: Investigating perceptions and uses of learning management systems. *Computer & Education, 53*(3), 686–94. https://doi.org/10.1016/j.compedu.2009.04.008

Lopez, H., & Gee, L. (2006). Estrella Mountain Community College: The learning studios project. In D. Oblinger (Ed.), *Learning spaces* (pp. 19.1–19.7). Educause.

https://www.educause.edu/research-and-publications/books/learning-spaces/chapter-19-estrella-mountain-community-college-learning-studios-project

Low, S. (2016). *Spatializing culture: The ethnography of space and place*. Routledge.

Luke, A. (2004). Two takes on the critical. In B. Norton (Ed.), *Critical pedagogies and language learning* (pp. 21–9). Cambridge University Press.

Luo, Q. L. (2006). CLIL and its implication for China EFL's teaching. *Journal of Beijing University of Aeronautics and Astronauts, 19*(3), 70–2.

Lyster, R., Saito, K., & Sato, M. (2013). Oral corrective feedback in second language classrooms. *Language Teaching, 46*(1), 1–40. https://doi:10.1017/S0261444812000365

Macaro, E. (2018). *English medium instruction: Content and language in policy and practice*. Oxford University Press.

Macaro, E., Akincioglu, M., & Dearden, J. (2016). English medium instruction in universities: A collaborative experiment in Turkey. *Studies in English Language Teaching, 4*(1), 51–76. https://doi.org/10.22158/selt.v4n1p51

Macaro, E., Curle, S., Pun, J., An, J., & Dearden, J. (2018). A systematic review of English medium instruction in higher education. *Language Teaching, 51*(1), 36–76. doi:10.1017/S0261444817000350.

MacDonald, J. (2017). The margins as third space: EAP teacher professionalism in Canadian universities. *TESL Canada Journal, 34*(1), 106–16. https://doi.org/10.18806/tesl.v34i1.1258

Malone, K. (2018, January 27). The long road to reconciliation. *CBC News*. https://www.cbc.ca/news2/interactives/road-to-reconciliation-kenora/

Marche, S. (2016, November 1). Canadian exceptionalism. https://www.opencanada.org/features/canadian-exceptionalism-0

Markova, A. K. (1979). *The teaching and mastery of language*. M. E. Sharpe Inc.

Marsh, C. J., & Willis, G. (2007). *Curriculum: Alternative approaches, ongoing issues*. Merrill.

Martin, J. R. (1992). *English text: System and structure*. John Benjamins.

Martin, J. R. (1997). Analysing genre: Functional parameters. In F. Christie & J. R. Martin (Eds.), *Genres and institutions: Social processes in the workplace and school* (pp. 3–39). Continuum.

Martin, J. R., Matthiessen, C. M. I., & Painter, C. (2010). *Deploying functional grammar*. The Commercial Press.

Martin, J. R., & Rose, D. (2005). Designing literacy pedagogy: Scaffolding asymmetries. In J. Webster, C. Matthiessen, & R. Hasan (Eds.), *Continuing discourse on language* (pp. 251–80). Continuum.

Matarese, V. (2016). *Editing research: The author editing approach to providing effective support to writers of research papers*. Information Today.

Maton, K. (2011). Theories and things: The semantics of disciplinarity. In F. Christi & K. Maton (Eds.), *Disciplinarity: Functional linguistics and sociological perspectives* (pp. 62–86). Bloomsbury,

Maton, K. (2014). *Knowledge and knowers: Toward a realist sociology of education*. Routledge Education.

Maton, K. (2016). Legitimation Code Theory: Building knowledge about knowledge building. In K. Maton, S. Hood, & S. Shay (Eds.), *Knowledge-building: Educational studies in Legitimation Code Theory* (pp. 1–23). Routledge.

Maton, K., & Chen, R. (2020). Specialisation codes: Knowledge, knowers and student success. In J. R. Martin, K. Maton, & Y. J. Doran (Eds.), *Accessing academic discourse: Systemic functional linguistics and Legitimation Code Theory* (pp. 35–58). Routledge.

May, M. S. (2012). Diversity dynamics operating between students, lecturers and management in a historically Black university: The lecturers' perspective. *SA Journal of Industrial Psychology*, *38*(2), 138–46.

May, S. (1999). Critical multiculturalism and cultural difference: Avoiding essentialism. In S. May (Ed.), *Rethinking multicultural & antiracist education* (pp. 11–41). Falmer Press.

McCarty, W., Crow, S. R., Mims, G. A., Potthoff, D. E., & Harvey, J. S. (2016). Renewing teaching practices: Differentiated instruction in the college classroom. *Journal of Curriculum, Teaching, Learning, and Leadership in Education*, *1*(1), 35–44.

McLaren, P. (2007). *Life in schools: An introduction to critical pedagogy in the foundations of education*. Pearson Education.

McWilliam, E. (2009). Teaching for creativity: From sage to guide to meddler. *Asia Pacific Journal of Education*, *29*(3), 281–93. https://doi.org/10.1080/02188790903092787

Melles, G. (2007). Genre-based pedagogy for design-oriented theses in postgraduate design education. *visual: design: scholarship*, *3*(2), 5–16.

Meneghini, R., & Packer, A. L. (2007). Is there a science beyond English? *Embo Reports*, *8*(2), 112–16. https://doi.org/10.1038/sj.embor.7400906

Mishra, P., & Koehler, M. J. (2006). Technological pedagogical content knowledge: A framework for teacher knowledge, *Teachers College Record*, *108*(6), 1017–54.

Monastersky, R., & Sousanis, N. (2015). The fragile framework: Can nations unite to save earth's climate? *Nature*, *527*, 7579.

Monbec, L. (2018). Designing an EAP curriculum for transfer: A focus on knowledge. *Journal of Academic Language and Learning*, *12*(2), A88–A101. https://journal.aall.org.au/index.php/jall/article/view/509

Monbec, L. (2020). Systemic functional linguistics for the EGAP module: Revisiting the common core. *Journal of English for Academic Purposes*, *43*, 100794. https://doi.org/10.1016/j.jeap.2019.100794

Moore, G. (2012). Tristan chords and random scores: Exploring undergraduate students' experiences of music in higher education through the lens of Bourdieu. *Music Education Research*, *14*(1), 63–78. https://doi.org/10.1080/14613808.2012.657164

Moore, T. (2007). The 'processes' of learning: On the use of Halliday's transitivity in academic skills advising. *Arts and Humanities in Higher Education*, 6(1), 50–73. https://doi.org/10.1177/1474022207072199

Mott-Smith, J. A., Tomaš, Z., & Kostka, I. (2017). *Teaching effective source use: Classroom approaches that work*. University of Michigan.

Moussly, R. (2010, September 26). Foundation programmes to be eliminated. *Gulf News*. https://gulfnews.com/uae/education/foundation-programmes-to-be-eliminated-1.687288

Moustafa, K. (2015). The disaster of the impact factor. *Science and engineering ethics*, 21(1), 139–42.

Murphy, P. (2008). Defining pedagogy. In K. Hall, P. Murphy, & J. Soler (Eds.), *Pedagogy and practice: Culture and identities* (pp. 28–39). SAGE publications.

Murray, R. (2010). Becoming rhetorical. In C. Aitchison, B. Kamler, & A. Lee (Eds.), *Publishing pedagogies for the doctorate and beyond* (pp. 101–16). Routledge.

Namakula, H., & Prozesky, M. (2019). In-between access and transformation: Analysing a university writing centre's academic support programme for education students as third space. *Stellenbosch Papers in Linguistics Plus (SPiL Plus)*, 57, 39–56.

Nance, E., Vadnais, A., Hicks, C., & Lawson, T. (2017). Insistence on cosmetically perfect fruits and vegetables. *UBC Case Studies*. http://cases.open.ubc.ca/insistence-on-cosmetically-perfect-fruits-vegetables/

Nesi, H., & Gardner, S. (2012). *Genres across the disciplines: Student writing in higher education*. Cambridge University Press.

Nesi, H., & Gardner, S. (2013). A classification of genre families. *Applied Linguistics*, 34(1), 25–52. https://doi.org/10.1093/applin/ams024

Newman, F., & Holzman, L. (1993). *Lev Vygotsky: Revolutionary scientist*. Routledge.

Newton, J. M., Ferris, D. R., Goh, C. C. M., Grabe, W., Stoller, F. L., & Vandergrift, L. (2018). *Teaching English to second language learners in academic contexts: Reading, writing, listening, and speaking*. Routledge.

Newton, P. (2016). Academic integrity: A quantitative study of confidence and understanding in students at the start of their higher education. *Assessment & Evaluation in Higher Education*, 41(3), 482–97. https://doi.org/10.1080/02602938.2015.1024199

Newton, P. M. (2018). How common is commercial contract cheating in higher education and is it increasing? A systematic review. *Frontiers in Education*, 3, 1–18. https://doi.org/10.3389/feduc.2018.00067

Newton, P. M., & Lang, C. (2016). Custom essay writers, freelancers, and other paid third parties. In T. Bretag (Ed.), *Handbook of Academic Integrity* (pp. 249–71). Springer. https://doi.org/10.1007/978-981-287-098-8_38

Nieto, S., & Bode, P. (2011). *Affirming diversity: The sociopolitical context of multicultural education* (6th ed.). Pearson Publication.

Nieuwenhuis, J. (2020). Qualitative research designs and data gathering techniques. In K. Maree (Ed.), *First steps in research* (3rd ed., pp. 79–116). Van Schaik.

Northcott, J., & Brown, G. (2006). Legal translator training: Partnership between teachers of English for legal purposes and legal specialists. *English for Specific Purposes, 25*(3), 358–75. https://doi.org/10.1016/j.esp.2005.08.003

Nygaard, L. P., & Solli, K. (2021). *Strategies for writing a thesis by publication in the social sciences and humanities*. Routledge.

O'Connor, J. (2010). *The cultural and creative industries: A literature review* (2nd ed.). Creativity, Culture and Education. https://www.creativitycultureeducation.org/publication/the-cultural-and-creative-industries-a-literature-review/

Okuda, T., & Anderson, T. (2018). Second language graduate students' experiences at the writing center: A language socialization perspective. *TESOL Quarterly, 52*(2), 391–413. https://doi.org/10.1002/tesq.406

Ontario Ministry of Education. (2008). Supporting English language learners: Practical guide for Ontario educators: Grades 1 to 8. Queen's Printer for Ontario. http://www.edu.gov.on.ca/eng/document/esleldprograms/guide.pdf

Ornstein, A. C., & Hunkins, F. P. (2018). *Curriculum: Foundations, principles and issues* (7th ed.). Pearson.

Orr, S., & Shreeve, A. (2018). *Art and design pedagogy in higher education: Knowledge, values and ambiguity in the creative curriculum*. Routledge Education.

Ozer, O. (2020). English medium instruction at tertiary level in Turkey: A study of academic needs and perceptions. *Journal of Higher Education and Science, 10*(1), 88–95. https://doi.org/10.5961/jhes.2020.370

Painter, C. (1986). The role of interaction in learning to speak and learning to write. In C. Painter & J. R. Martin (Eds.), *Writing to mean: Teaching genres across the curriculum*. Applied Linguistics Association of Australia (Occasional Papers 9), 62–97.

Paltridge, B., & Starfield, S. (2020). Change and continuity in thesis and dissertation writing: The evolution of an academic genre. *Journal of English for Academic Purposes, 48*, 100910. doi:https://doi.org/10.1016/j.jeap.2020.100910

Paré, A. (2010). Slow the presses: Concerns about premature publication. In C. Aitchison, B. Kamler, & A. Lee (Eds.), *Publishing pedagogies for the doctorate and beyond* (pp. 31–46). Routledge.

Paré, A. (2017). Re-thinking the dissertation and doctoral supervision/Reflexiones sobre la tesis doctoral y su supervisión. *Journal for the Study of Education and Development, 40*(3), 407–28. https://doi.org/10.1080/02103702.2017.1341102

Pessoa, S., Mitchell, T., & Miller, R. (2017). Emergent arguments: A functional approach to analyzing student challenges with the argument genre. *Journal of Second Language Writing, 38*, 42–55. https://doi.org/10.1016/j.jslw.2017.10.013

Pinar, W. F., Reynolds, W. M., Slattery, P., & Taubman, P. M. (1995). *Understanding curriculum: An introduction to the study of historical and contemporary curriculum discourses*. Peter Lang.

Pink, S. (2015). *Doing sensory ethnography* (2nd ed.). SAGE Publications Ltd.

Prasongporn, P. (2009, June). *CLIL in Thailand: Challenges and possibilities*. [Conference Paper]. Access English EBE Symposium, Jakarta, Indonesia.

Prøitz, T. S., & Wittek, L. (2019). New directions in doctoral programmes: Bridging tensions between theory and practice? *Teaching in Higher Education, 25*(5), 60–578. https://doi.org/10.1080/13562517.2019.1577813

Quality Assurance Agency for UK Higher Education. (2019). *Subject benchmark statements.* https://www.qaa.ac.uk/quality-code/subject-benchmark-statements

Queensland Government, Department of Education and Arts. (n.d). Literacy – the key to learning. http://education.qld.gov.au/publication/production/ reports/pdfs/literacy-framework-06.pdf

Raimes, A. (1991). Instructional balance: From theories to practices in the teaching of writing. In J. Alatis (Ed.), *Georgetown University roundtable on language and linguistic.* Georgetown University Press.

Remedios, L., Clarke, D., & Hawthorne, L. (2008). Framing collaborative behaviors: Listening and speaking in problem-based learning. *Interdisciplinary Journal of Problem-Based Learning, 2*(1). https://doi:10.7771/1541-5015.1050

Riazi, A. M., Ghanbar, H., & Fazel, I. (2020). The contexts, theoretical and methodological orientation of EAP research: Evidence from empirical articles published in the *Journal of English for Academic Purposes. Journal of English for Academic Purposes*, 48. doi:10.1016/j.jeap.2020.100925

Richards, J. C., & Rodgers, T. S. (2001). *Approaches and methods in language teaching* (2nd ed.). Cambridge University Press.

Riley-Jones, G. (2012). Critical thinking as an embodied criticality: The lived experiences of international art students. *Journal of Writing in Creative Practice, 5*(3), 401–21. https://doi.org/10.1386/jwcp.5.3.401_1

Rose, D., & Martin, J. (2012). *Learning to write, reading to learn: Genre, knowledge and pedagogy in the Sydney School.* Equinox.

Rothery, J. (1994). Exploring literacy in school English: Write it right resources for literacy and learning. Metropolitan East Disadvantaged Schools Program.

Rothery, J., & Stenglin, M. (1994). Write it right resources for literacy and learning: Exploring literacy in school English. Disadvantaged Schools Program. Metropolitan East Region, NSW Department of Education.

Rubin, B., Fernandes, R., Avgerinou, M. D., & Moore, J. (2010). The effect of learning management systems on student and faculty outcomes. *The Internet and Higher Education, 13*(1), 82–3.

Ruiz de Zarobe, Y. (2013). CLIL implementation: From policy-makers to individual initiative. *International Journal of Bilingual Education and Bilingualism 16*(3), 231–43. https://doi.org/10.1080/13670050.2013.777383

Sala-Bubaré, A., & Castelló, M. (2017). Exploring the relationship between doctoral students' experiences and research community positioning. *Studies in Continuing Education, 39*(1), 16–34. https://doi.org/10.1080/0158037X.2016.1216832

Salem, O., & Swan, M. (2014, February 4). Foundation year at UAE state universities to be scrapped in 2018. *The National.* https://www.thenational.ae/uae/education/foundation-year-at-uae-state-universities-to-be-scrapped-in-2018-1.466783

Sandholtz, J. H. (2000). Interdisciplinary team teaching as a form of professional development. *Teacher Education Quarterly*, *27*(3), 39–54.
Saunders, D. (2009, June 26). Canada's mistaken identity. *Globe and Mail*. https://www.theglobeandmail.com/news/world/canadas-mistaken-identity/article787370/
Savin-Baden, M., & Major, C. H. (2004). *Foundations of problem-based learning*. Open University Press.
Scarcella, R. (2003). *Academic English: A conceptual framework*. University of California Linguistic Minority Research Institute.
Schmidt, H. G., Rotgans, J. I., & Yew, E. H. J. (2019). Cognitive constructivist foundations of problem-based learning. In M. H. Moallem, W. Hung, & N. Dabbagh (Eds.), *The Wiley handbook of problem-based learning* (pp. 25–49). Wiley Blackwell.
Schmidt, R. W. (1990). The role of consciousness in second language learning. *Applied Linguistics*, *11*, 129–58.
Schmidt-Unterberger, B. (2018). The English-medium paradigm: A conceptualisation of English-medium teaching in higher education. *International Journal of Bilingual Education and Bilingualism*, *21*(5), 527–39.
Scott, M., & Turner, J. (2008). Problematising proofreading. *Journal Writing*, *3*, 1–5. Zeitschrift-schreiben.eu
Seburn, T. (2015). *Academic reading circles*. The Round: CreateSpace Publishing.
Selvi, A. F. (2014). The medium of instruction debate in Turkey: Oscillating between national ideas and bilingual ideals. *Current Issues in Language Planning*, *15*(2), 133–52.
Sennett, J., Finchilescu, G., Gibson, K., & Strauss, R. (2003). Adjustment of black students at a historically white South African university. *Educational Psychology*, *23*(1), 107–16.
Seviour, M. (2015). Assessing academic writing on a pre-sessional EAP course: Designing assessment which supports learning. *Journal of English for Academic Purposes*, *18*, 84–9. https://doi.org/10.1016/j.jeap.2015.03.007
Sharmini, S., & Spronken-Smith, R. (2020). The PhD – is it out of alignment? *Higher Education Research & Development*, *39*(4), 821–33. https://doi.org/10.1080/07294360.2019.1693514
Shor, I. (1999). What is critical literacy? *Journal of Pedagogy, Pluralism, and Practice*, *1*(4), Article 2.
Shreeve, A., Sims, E., & Trowler, P. (2010). 'A kind of exchange': Learning from art and design teaching. *Higher Education Research & Development*, *29*(2), 125–38. https://doi.org/10.1080/07294360903384269
Shulman, L. S. (1986). Those who understand: Knowledge growth in teaching. *Educational Researcher*, *15*(2), 4–14. https://doi:10.1177/002205741319300302
Shulman, L. S. (2005). Signature pedagogies in the professions. *Daedalus*, *134*(3), 52–9. https://doi:10.1162/0011526054622015
Simones, L. L. (2017). Beyond expectations in music performance modules in higher education: Rethinking instrumental and vocal music pedagogy for the twenty-first century. *Music Education Research*, *19*(3), 252–62. https://doi.org/10.1080/14613808.2015.1122750

Sloan, D., & Porter, E. (2010). Changing international student and business staff perceptions of in-sessional EAP: Using the CEM model. *Journal of English for Academic Purposes, 9*(3), 198–210. https://doi:10.1016/j.jeap.2010.03.001

Song, H. (2013a). Deconstruction of cultural dominance in Korean EFL textbooks. *Intercultural Education, 24*(4), 382–90. https://doi.org/10.1080/14675986.2013.809248

Song, H. (2013b). How international is EIL? A critical discourse analysis of cultural representations in a Korean EFL education television program. *Critical Intersections in Education, 1*(2), 97–110. https://jps.library.utoronto.ca/index.php/cie/article/view/17120

Song, H. (2019). Action research as a praxis for transformative teaching practice in ELT classrooms. *TESL Ontario Contact Magazine, 45*(3), 7–15. http://contact.teslontario.org/action-research-as-a-praxis-for-transformative-teaching-practice-in-elt-classrooms/

Soudien, C. (2008). The intersection of race and class in the South African university: Student experiences. *South African Journal of Higher Education, 22*(3), 662–78.

Sovic, S., & Blythman, M. (2006). The international students' experience project at UAL: Issues of engagement for international students in art and design. http://adm-hea.brighton.ac.uk/resources/features/the-international-students2019-experience-project-at-ual-issues-of-engagement-for-international-students-in-art-and-design/index.html

Starfield, S. (2016). Quotidian ethics in the neoliberal university: Research and practice collide. In P. I. De Costa (Ed.), *Ethics in applied linguistics research: Language researcher narratives* (pp. 53–65). Routledge. https://doi.org/10.4324/9781315816937

Stockman, F., & Mureithi, C. (2019, September 7). Cheating, Inc.: How writing papers for American college students has become a lucrative profession overseas. *New York Times*. https://www.nytimes.com/2019/09/07/us/college-cheating-papers.html

Stoller, F., & Grabe, W. (1997). A six-T's approach to content-based instruction. In M. A. Snow & D. M. Brinton (Eds.), *The content-based classroom: Perspectives on integrating language and content* (pp. 77–94). Addison Wesley Longman Publishing Company.

Storch, N., Morton, J., & Thompson, C. (2016). EAP pedagogy in undergraduate contexts. In K. Hyland & P. Shaw (Eds.), *The Routledge handbook of English for academic purposes* (pp. 501–12). Routledge.

Strauss, A. L., & Corbin, J. K. (2008). *Basics of qualitative research: Techniques and procedures for developing grounded theory*. Sage.

Swain, M. (2006). Languaging, agency and collaboration in advanced second language proficiency. In H. Byrnes (Ed.), *Advanced language learning: The contribution of Halliday and Vygotsky* (pp. 95–108). Continuum.

Swales, J. M. (1990a). *Genre analysis: English in academic and research settings*. Cambridge University Press.

Swales, J. M. (1990b). Shaping written knowledge: The genre and activity of the experimental research article in science: Charles Bazerman. Madison, WI: University of Wisconsin Press, 1988, pp. 356.. *English for Specific Purposes*, 9(1), 98–101. https://doi.org/10.1016/0889-4906(90)90032-8

Swales, J. M. (1996). Occluded genres in the academy: The case of the submission letter. In E. Ventola & A. Mauranan (Eds.), *Academic writing: Intercultural and textual issues* (pp. 45–58). John Benjamins Publishing Co.

Swales, J. M. (1998). Textography: Toward a contextualization of written academic discourse. *Research on Language and Social Interaction*, 1(31), 109–21. https://doi.org/10.1207/s15327973rlsi3101_7

Swales, J. M. (2017). Standardisation and its discontents. In M. Cargill & S. Burgess (Eds.), *Publishing research in English as an additional language: Practices, pathways and potentials* (pp. 239–53). University of Adelaide Press.

Swales, J. M., & Feak, C. B. (1994). *Academic writing for graduate students: A course for non-native speakers*. University of Michigan Press.

Swales, J. M., & Feak, C. B. (2000). *English in today's research world*. Michigan University Press.

Swales, J. M., & Feak, C. B. (2004). *Academic writing for graduate students*. The University of Michigan Press.

Swales, J. M., & Feak, C. B. (2012). *Academic writing for graduate students: Essential skills and tasks*. The University of Michigan Press.

Sword, H. (2012). *Stylish academic writing*. Harvard University Press.

Tajino, A., James, R., & Kijima, K. (2005). Beyond needs analysis: Soft systems methodology for meaningful collaboration in EAP course. *Journal of English for Academic Purposes*, 4(1), 27–42. https://doi.org/10.1016/j.jeap.2004.01.001

Tardy, C. (2019). *Genre-based writing: What every ESL teacher needs to know*. University of Michigan.

Thompson, G. (1996). *Introducing functional grammar*, Arnold.

Thomson, P., & Kamler, B. (2013). *Writing for peer reviewed journals: Strategies for getting published*. Routledge.

Thomson, P., & Walker, M. (2010). Doctoral education in context: The changing nature of the doctorate and doctoral students. In P. Thomson & M. Walker (Eds.), *The Routledge doctoral student's companion: Getting to grips with research in Education and the Social Sciences* (pp. 9–26). Routledge.

Tomlinson, C. A. (2017). *How to differentiate instruction in academically diverse classrooms* (3rd ed.). ASCD Publishing.

Tribble, C. (2009). Writing academic English – A survey review of current published resources. *ELT Journal*, 63(4), 400–17. https://doi.org/10.1093/elt/ccp073

Truth and Reconciliation Commission of Canada. (2015). *Honouring the truth, reconciling for the future: Summary of the final report of the Truth and Reconciliation Commission of Canada*. http://www.trc.ca/assets/pdf/Honouring_the_Truth_Reconciling_for_the_Future_July_23_2015.pdf

Tulbure, C. (2013). The effects of differentiated approach in higher education: An experimental investigation. *Procedia – Social and Behavioral Sciences, 76*, 832–6.

Turhan, B., & Kırkgöz, Y. (2018). Motivation of engineering students and lecturers toward English medium instruction in Turkey. *Journal of Language and Linguistic Studies, 14*(1), 261–77.

Turner, J. (2004). Language as academic purpose. *Journal of English for Academic Purposes, 3*(2), 95–109. https://doi.org/10.1016/S1475-1585(03)00054-7

Turner, J. (2011). Rewriting writing in higher education: The contested spaces of proofreading. *Studies in Higher Education, 36*(4), 427–40. https://doi.org/10.1080/03075071003671786

Turner, J. (2012). Academic literacies: Providing a space for the socio-political dynamics of EAP. *Journal of English for Academic Purposes, 11*(1), 17–25. https://doi.org/10.1016/j.jeap.2011.11.007

Turner, J., & Hocking, D. (2004). Synergy in art and language: Positioning the language specialist in contemporary fine art study. *Art Design and Communication in Higher Education, 3*(3), 149–62.

Turner, W. D., Solis, O. J., & Kincade, D. H. (2017). Differentiating instruction for large classes in higher education. *International Journal of Teaching and Learning in Higher Education, 29*(3), 490–500.

UAE Ministry of Education. (2020). List of licensed institutions. https://www.moe.gov.ae/En/MediaCenter/News/Pages/licensedInstitutions.aspx

UAE University. (2017). About UAEU. https://www.uaeu.ac.ae/en/about/

Universities and Colleges Admissions Service. (2020). Music subject guide: Where can I study music? Retrieved 29 June 2020, from https://www.ucas.com/explore/subjects/music

University of British Columbia: The Centre for Sustainable Food Systems Teaching & Learning Team. (2018). Urban agriculture. The University of British Columbia Open Case Studies. https://cases.open.ubc.ca/urban-agriculture/

University of Glasgow. (n.d.). University of Glasgow graduate attributes. https://www.gla.ac.uk/media/Media_183776_smxx.pdf

Usher, R. (2002). A diversity of doctorates: Fitness for the knowledge economy? *Higher Education Research & Development, 21*(2), 143–53. https://doi.org/10.1080/07294360220144060

Van Viegan, S., Wernicke, M., & Zappa-Hollman, S. (2019). Language and higher education [Special issue]. *TESL Canada, 36*(1). https://teslcanadajournal.ca/index.php/tesl/issue/view/159

Vaughan, S., Austerlitz, N., Blythman, M., Grove-White, A., Jones, B. A., Jones, C. A., Morgan, S., Orr, S., & Shreeve, A. (2008). Mind the gap: Expectations, ambiguity and pedagogy within art and design higher education. In L. Drew (Ed.), *The student experience in art and design higher education: Drivers for change* (pp. 125–48). Jill Rodgers Associates.

Viceland. (2017, February 17). *Indigenous peoples in the Canadian residential schools: RISE* [Video]. YouTube. https://www.youtube.com/watch?v=9QMZaOVOin8&feature=youtu.be

Vygotsky, L. S. (1978). *Mind in society*. Harvard University Press.

Walsh Marr, J. (2019). Making the mechanics of paraphrasing more explicit through grammatical metaphor. *Journal of English for Academic Purposes, 42*, 1–7. https://doi.org/10.1016/j.jeap.2019.100783

Walsh Marr, J., Lynch, S., & Tervit, T. (2021). Defining with purpose: Connecting lexicogrammatical features to textual purpose in authentic undergraduate texts. *TESOL Quarterly, 55*(4), 1092–1101.

Wang, T., & Li, L. Y. (2008). Understanding international postgraduate research students' challenges and pedagogical needs in thesis writing. *International Journal of Pedagogies and Learning, 4*(3), 88–96. https://doi.org/10.5172/ijpl.4.3.88

Werther, C., Denver, L., Jensen, C., & Mees, I. M. (2014). Using English as a medium of instruction at university level in Denmark: The lecturer's perspective. *Journal of Multilingual and Multicultural Development, 35*(5), 443–62. https://doi.org/10.1080/01434632.2013.868901

Wijnia, L., Loyens, S. M. M., & Rikers, M. J. P. (2019). The problem-based learning process: An overview of different models. In M. H. Moallem, W. Hung, & N. Dabbagh (Eds.), *The Wiley handbook of problem-based learning* (pp. 273–95). Wiley Blackwell.

Wilkinson, R. (2013). English-medium instruction at a Dutch university: Challenges and pitfalls. In A. Doiz, D. Lasagabaster, & J. M. Sierra (Eds.), *English-medium instruction at universities: Global challenges* (pp. 3–24). Multilingual Matters.

Wingate, U. (2015). *Academic literacy and student diversity: The case for inclusive practice*. Multilingual Matters. https://doi.org/10.1111/ijal.12119

Wingate, U. (2015, December 14–15). *Academic literacy across the curriculum: Towards a collaborative instructional approach* [Conference Paper]. International Conference on English Across the Curriculum, The Hong Kong Polytechnic University, Hong Kong.

Wingate, U. (2018). Academic literacy across the curriculum: Towards a collaborative instructional approach. *Language Teaching, 51*, 349–64. https://doi.org/10.1017/S0261444816000264

Wingate, U., & Tribble, C. (2012). The best of both worlds? Towards an English for academic purposes/academic literacies writing pedagogy. *Studies in Higher Education, 37*(4), 481–95. https://doi.org/10.1080/03075079.2010.525630

Winter, E. (2015). A Canadian anomaly? The social construction of multicultural national identity. In S. Guo & L. Wong (Eds.), *Revisiting multiculturalism in Canada* (pp. 51–68). Sense Publishers.

Wisker, G. (2016). Agency and articulation in doctoral writing: Building the messy research journey into a well-constructed thesis. In C. Badenhorst & C. Guerin (Eds.), *Research literacies and writing pedagogies for masters and doctoral writers* (pp. 184–201). Brill.

Wolpe, H. (1995). The debate on university transformation in South Africa: The case of the University of the Western Cape. *Comparative Education, 31*(2), 275–92.

Wood, A., & Head, M. (2004). 'Just what the doctor ordered': The application of problem-based learning to EAP. *English for Specific Purposes, 23*(1), 3–17. https://doi:10.1016/S0889-4906(03)00031-0

Yang, W. (2014). Content and language integrated learning next in Asia: Evidence of learners' achievement in CLIL education from a Taiwan tertiary degree programme. *International Journal of Bilingual Education and Bilingualism, 18*(4), 361–82. https://doi.org/10.1080/13670050.2014.904840

Yasuda, S. (2015). Exploring changes in FL writers' meaning-making choices in summary writing: A systemic functional approach. *Journal of Second Language Writing, 27*, 105–21. https://doi.org/10.1016/j.jslw.2014.09.008

Yerushalmi, Y. H. (1991). *Freud's Moses: Judaism terminable and interminable*. Yale University Press.

Yin, R. K. (2009). *Case study research: Design and methods*. Sage Publications.

YOK. (2020). YOK lisans atlası. Yükseköğretim Kurulu. https://yokatlas.yok.gov.tr/lisans-anasayfa.php

Yu, S. (2020). Giving genre-based peer feedback in academic writing: Sources of knowledge and skills, difficulties and challenges. *Assessment & Evaluation in Higher Education*, 1–18. https://doi.org/10.1080/02602938.2020.1742872

Zappa-Hollman, S. (2018). Collaborations between language and content university instructors: Factors and indicators of positive partnerships. *International Journal of Bilingual Education & Bilingualism, 21*(5–6), 591–606. https://doi.org/10.1080/13670050.2018.1491946

Zhang, M., Lundeberg, M., McConnell, T. J., Koehler, M. J., & Eberhardt, J. (2010). Using questioning to facilitate discussion of science teaching problems in teacher professional development. *Interdisciplinary Journal of Problem-Based Learning, 4*(1). https://doi:10.7771/1541-5015.1097

Index

academic brokers 28
academic disciplines 108
academic/discipline-specific
    discourse 98
Academic English Program (AEP) 43
academic literacy/literacies 8
academic texts
    analysis/argumentation 52–4
    literacy brokering in 29–31
    nominalization 44–7
    Rheme in 49–52
    theme patterns in 48–52
academic writing course (AWC) 60–1, 64–8, 75–90
    aims 78–9
    application 87–90
    context 78–9
    critical EAP 76–7
    developmental teaching 76
        application 77, 87–90
        background 76–8
        and critical EAP 76, 78–87
        implementation 78–87
        outcome 86–7
    implementation 78–87
    lesson plans 80
    pedagogical implementation, contributions of 90
    research articles (example) 82–6
    summary writing (example) 80–2
    visual representations/models 79–80
action research in education 13–14
    Canadian culture and identity project 14–15
    Canadian multiculturalism 15–24
Adamson, J. 156–7
addressivity 62
Aksit, Necmi 8
Aksit, Tijen 8
Alexander, O. 94–5, 103, 105
arts education literature 154
Atkinson, D. 84
Australia 2, 33, 137, 144

autoethnography 155–68

Balanyk, Jesse 8
Bazerman, C. 84
BEd programmes 95–6
Benesch, S. 112
Bernstein, B. 140, 143
Biomed course 169, 181–2
Bond, B. 5
Borg, E. 163–4
Boughey, C. 95, 102–3
Brazil 4, 8, 75–90
Brazilian higher education, EAP in
    75–90; *see also* academic writing course (AWC)
British Academic Written English
    (BAWE) corpus 164 n.1
Brown, G. 166
Buchanan, Jaime 8
Bunting, I. 93
Burns, A. 13, 147
Byram, M. 12, 22

Canada 7, 11–24, 43, 171
Canadian culture and identity
    project 14–15
Canadian multiculturalism 13, 15–24
    EAP in unit on equity and
        diversity 18–22
        comparing discourses 20–1
        institutional discourse 19–20
        reality analysis 21–2
    intensive academic reading
        method 17
    requisite course texts 16–17
    research project overview 16
    students' critical understanding
        17–18
Canagarajah, A. S. 8, 77
Cao, J. X. 126
Caplan, N. A. 58
Carr, Clare 8
Chang, H. 156

China 17
  CLIL in 8, 124–5
  EAP in 4
  students 23–4
  university 6
Chinese Canadians 17
Chinese Exclusion Act 17–18
Chinese Head Tax 17–18
Christodoulou, D. 150
claim 55
collaborations 3, 5–8, 32, 43, 125–9, 132–5, 158–160, 165–7
collaborative autoethnography (CAE) 155–6
communication 160–2
Conrad, Nina 7
content and language integrated learning (CLIL) 13, 123–35
  in China 124–5
    benefits 127–8
    co-teaching with language tutors in 129–31
    deep learning 127, 131–3
    for disciplinary teaching 131–3
    for EAP 127–33
    in EMI university, China 124–5
    programmes 8, 124–6
    provision 3
    relevance 133–5
    research context 124–6
    in university context 123–4
  principle 123
content-based instruction (CBI) 8, 111
contract cheating 29–30
copy editing 30
Coyle, D. 92–3, 126–7, 133
Creating a Research Space (CARS) model 66
creative arts, EAP in 153–68
  autoethnography 155–6
  collaborations 165–7
  contexts 155–6
  creative spaces 158–60
  data analysis 157
  data collection 157
  data reduction and reporting 158
  frames for reflection, identification of 156–7
  implications 167–8
  methodology 155–6

reflection 157–8
reliability checking 158
spaces 158–60
spoken communication 160–2
themes identification 157
written genres 162–5
Creme, P. 140
critical EAP 76–87
  in academic writing course in english 75–87
  in equity/diversity 18–22
critical literacy 110–13, 122, 144, 146
critical pedagogy 76–87, 110–13, 122
cultures 12
Curry, M. J. 28

Dalton-Puffer, C. 125, 128, 134
Davydov's developmental teaching; *see* developmental teaching, EAP
deep learning 127, 131–3
Department of Higher Education and Training, South Africa 94
Derewianka, B. 44
developmental teaching, EAP 76
  aims 78–9
  application 77, 87–90
  background 76–8
  context 78–9
  and critical EAP 76–87
  implementation 78–87
  learning actions 76–7
  lesson plans 80
  outcome 86–7
  research articles (example) 82–6
  summary writing (example) 80–2
  visual representations/models 79–80
Devitt, A. 35
differentiated instruction (DI) 111–12
diversity 18–22
doctoral writing pedagogies 59–74
  academic writing course 64–8
  in doctoral education 61–2
  initiatives for doctoral students in professional fields 68–73
    fostering 72–3
    LCT (*see* Legitimation Code Theory (LCT))
  possibilities 73–4
  student experiences 62–4

Doonan, Brían 8
Dreyfus, S. 145–6, 148

educational technology 8
e-learning platforms 111
Ellis, C. 155
empirical thinking 76
Engeström, Y. 79
English as an Additional Language (EAL) 2, 28
English for academic purposes (EAP) 1–10, 123–4, 185–7
  in academic writing course in English 75–90
  in Brazilian university 75–90
  CLIL programmes for 127–33
  contexts for 3–4
  creative arts in 153–68
  development 2–3
  ESAP-in-EGAP model of 137–51
  importance 9–10
  literacy brokering in classroom 7, 27–42
  pedagogies in 4–5, 8, 59–74
  practice 9
  practitioner case studies 5–7
  programme in Canada 7, 11–26
  research 5–7, 11–26, 28–32, 57–74
  systemic functional linguistics 8, 43–58
  tasks in 123
  in teacher education 91–106
  in Turkey 107–22
English for general academic purposes (EGAP) 1, 3, 7–8, 95
  with CBI in EMI context 108–22
    course guidelines 113–14
    course themes 114
    implementation 114–18
    philosophical foundations 109–10
  discussion 118–21
  four-quadrant pedagogical model of 122
  PAS, pedagogical foundations of 110–13
    content-based instruction 111
    content knowledge 110–11
    critical literacy 112
    differentiated instruction 111–12
    preparation/implementation 112–13
  in Turkey 107–22

English for Specific Academic Purposes (ESAP) 1, 3, 7–9, 95, 108, 121, 153
  development 174–9
  in EGAP model of learning 137–51
  implications 181–3
  lecturer role 179–81
  pedagogy 169–83
    institutional context 169–71
    lecturer role 179–81
    pre-sessional course 169–71
    problem-based learning 171–9
English-medium instruction (EMI)
  EAP programme in 107–22
  in Hong Kong 124
  implementation 107
  in South African universities 2, 8, 103–6
  in Turkey 107–22
equity 18–22
essentialism 109

Feak, C. B. 80–1
feedback 30–1
Ferguson, G. 4, 180–1, 183
Ferreira, Marília Mendes 8, 75
first-year writing course 31–2
Ford, J. 134
form-focused teaching 44
Freire, Paulo 77, 112

Gao, G. Z. 126
Gardner, S. 139, 141
genre literacy 141–2; *see also* Sydney School genre pedagogy
ghostwriting 34–7
Gillett, A. 103
Go, A. 17–18
grammatical metaphor 45, 145; *see also* nominalization
Grandinetti, M. 126
Graumann, C. F. 158

Hanks, J. 6
historically Black universities (HBUs) 93, 96–7
historically white universities (HWUs) 93, 97–9
Hortons, Tim 14
Humphries, S. 147

Hurst, E. 94
Hyland, K. 6, 139

intercultural communicative competence (ICC) 12, 22
Irwin, Kat 8

Jacobs, C. 126
Jappinen, A. 126
Johns, A. 153
Johnson, Barbara 73
joint narrativisation 157
Jordan, E. 134

Kamler, B. 60, 65–6
Kemmis, S. 13
knowledge
 pedagogical 4
 teachers 4
Koehler, M. J. 110–11

Laboratory of Academic Literacy (LLAC), São Paulo 75
Langellotti, M. 126
language brokers 28
language of learning and teaching (LoLT) 91
Lau v. *Nicholas* case 21
Lea, M. R. 103, 140
learning management systems (LMS) 111
Lee, A. 62
Legitimation Code Theory (LCT) 69–70
lexicogrammatical errors 30–1
Liardet, C. 45
Lillis, T. 28
literacy brokering in classroom, EAP 7, 27–42
 academic brokers 28
 definition 27–8
 discussion 40–1
 exploration of 33–6
 ghostwriting 34–7
 language brokers 28
 lesson, context for 31–6
 literacy brokers 38
 literature review 28–31
 vs. peer review 38–9
 scenarios and reflection 41–2

students' responses 36–40
 direct *vs.* indirect interventions 38
 to ghostwriting 36–7
 peer review 38–9
 to unacceptable practice 39–40
 using their own words 37
 types in academic contexts 29–31
Llinares, A. 128
Low, S. 158
Lu, Xiucai 8
Luo, Q. L. 134

Macaro, E. 104–5
MacDiarmid, Carole 8
McGaughey, John 7
McKenna, S. 95, 102–3
Malone, K. 17–18
Maphalala, Mncedisi C. 8
Marche, S. 16, 18
Marr, Jennifer Walsh 8, 145
Martin, J. R. 58, 141, 144
Maton, K. 153
Max, Clare 8
memoing 157
Mishra, P. 110–11
Mona, M. 94
Monbec, L. 5, 140, 147
Moodle, learning management system 113, 116
Mott-Smith, J. A. 31
Mpofu, Nhlanhla 8
Muir, Tom 8
Muller, T. 156–7
multicultural education, EAP programme 7, 11–26
 action research 13–14
 Canadian culture and identity project 14–15
 Canadian multiculturalism, critical approach to 15–24
 pedagogical implications 24–5
 students 13
 teaching and research context 12–14
 theoretical foundations 12
multiculturalism 11
Mureithi, C. 37
Murray, R. 62
Myers, Tony 8

Nesi, H.   139, 141
Nicoll, Timothy   8
Nikula, T.   128, 134
nominalization   44–7
non-deceitful behaviour   31
North America   2, 33, 77, 111
Northcott, J.   166
Norway   59, 62

O'Connor, J.   153
Orr, S.   160
Oslo Metropolitan University   64–8

Paltridge, B.   61
Paré, Anthony   61–2, 70
pedagogical content knowledge (PCK)   4, 110–11
pedagogy   4–5
  critical   76–87
  critical literacy   112
  for doctoral students in professional fields   59–74
  of EAP teachers   8
  in ESAP   169–83
  signature   9, 169–83
  Sydney School genre   8, 137–51
peer review   38–9
perennialism   109
PhD programmes; *see* doctoral writing pedagogies
plagiarism   31, 40
Prasongporn, P.   134
pre-service secondary school teachers, training of   8
pre-sessional course/tuition   3, 8–9, 162, 167, 169–183
problem-based learning (PBL)   171–9
Productive Academic Skills (PAS) course   107–8, 110–13
  content-based instruction   111
  content knowledge   110–11
  critical literacy   112
  differentiated instruction   111–12
  discussion on   118–21
  guidelines   113–14
  implementation   114–18
  phases of   114–18
  preparation   112–13
  themes   114
proofreading   30

Reading to Learn approach   137–8, 148–9
relational processes   55–7
research articles (example)   82–6
Rheme   49–52
Rhodes Must Fall movement   94
Richards, J. C.   111
Riley-Jones, G.   153
Rodgers, T. S.   111
Rolinska, Anna   8
Rose, D.   58, 141, 144
Rothery, J.   58, 143
Routledge Handbook of English for Academic Purposes (Hyland & Shaw)   6

Sandholtz, J. H.   134
sciences   140
Seburn, T.   17
Shreeve, A.   160
Shulman, L. S.   110–11, 172, 180, 183
signature pedagogy (SP)   9, 169–83
Six-T's Approach   111
Sizer, Jennifer   8
SLATE project   148
Solli, Kristin   8
Song, Heejin   7
South Africa   8, 91–106
South African Sign Language (SASL)   92
South African universities, teaching EAP in   91–106
  background   92–6
  course aim/content   96–102
  cross-case study analysis   102–6
  education system   93–4
  EMI approach   92–3, 103–6
  general academic purposes   102–3
  historically Black universities   93, 96–7
  historically white universities (HWUs)   93, 97–9
  instruction at universities   94–6
  official languages   92
  practical implications and relevance   106
  stand-alone model   95
spoken communication   160–2
stand-alone model   95
Starfield, S.   61
Stenglin, M.   58

Stockman, F.   37
Street, B. V.   103
Student Code of Conduct   34
study skills model   103
summary writing (example)   80–2
Swain, M.   124, 127
Swales, J. M.   80–1, 141, 153
Sydney School genre pedagogy   8, 137–51
   academic language   141–2
   challenges   147–9
   in Gulf/UAE context   138–9
   in institutional context   139–40
   learning activities   143–6
   learning modalities   146
   literacies course outline   141–2
   overall evaluation   149–50
   professional development training   146–7
   teacher/student roles   143
systemic functional linguistics (SFL)   8, 43–58
   analysis/argumentation   52–4
   grammatical metaphor   45
   nominalization   44–7
   relational processes   55–7
   Rheme   49–52
   text flows   47–52
   themes   48–52

teachers
   CLIL, perceptions of   123–35
   creative arts, working in, with and through   153–68
      autoethnography   155–68
      collaborations   165–7
      contexts   155–6
      data analysis   157
      data collection   157
      data reduction and reporting   158
      frames for reflection, identification of   156–7
      implications   167–8
      methodology   155–6
      reflection   157–8
      reliability checking   158
      spaces   158–60
      spoken communication   160–2
      themes identification   157
      written genres   162–5

education   91–106
   background   92–6
   course aim/content   96–102
   cross-case study analysis   102–6
   EMI approach   92–3, 103–6
   general academic purposes   102–3
   instruction at universities   94–6
   practical implications and relevance   106
   in South African education system   93–4
   stand-alone model   95
   knowledge   4
   pedagogy of   8
Teaching English as a Second Language (TESL)   11
technological pedagogical content knowledge (TPAK)   111
Test of Academic Literacy Levels (TALL)   97
text flows   47–52
themes   48–52
theoretical thinking   75–6, 78–9
third-party intervention, students' academic texts; *see* literacy brokering in classroom, EAP
Thomson, P.   60, 65–6
Ting, Y. L.   126
Tiny Text   65–6
Tomlinson, C. A.   111
Tulbure, C.   112
Turkey   8, 107–8, 118
Turnitin   116, 120

UAE   138–9, 148, 150
United Kingdom (UK)   2–4, 6, 8, 30, 170
United States   6–7, 16, 33

verbs   52–3
visual essay   164
visual representations/models   79–80

Werther, C.   103
Wilkinson, R.   103–4
Williams, Anneli   8
Wingate, U.   92, 103
Winter, E.   16, 18
Wolpe, H.   93–4

Wong, L. L. 6
written genres 162–5

Yin, R. K. 95

Zappa-Hollman, S. 126, 134
zone of proximal development
    (ZDP) 76, 76 n.1, 90
Zou, Bin 8

www.ingramcontent.com/pod-product-compliance
Lightning Source LLC
Chambersburg PA
CBHW062216300426
44115CB00012BA/2083